Merleau-Ponty and Nancy on Sense and Being

New Perspectives in Ontology
Series Editors: Peter Gratton, Southeastern Louisiana University, and Sean J. McGrath, Memorial University of Newfoundland, Canada

Publishes the best new work on the question of being and the history of metaphysics

After the linguistic and structuralist turn of the twentieth century, a renaissance in metaphysics and ontology is occurring. Following in the wake of speculative realism and new materialism, this series aims to build on this renewed interest in perennial metaphysical questions, while opening up avenues of investigation long assumed to be closed. Working within the Continental tradition without being confined by it, the books in this series will move beyond the linguistic turn and rethink the oldest questions in a contemporary context. They will challenge old prejudices while drawing upon the speculative turn in post-Heideggerian ontology, the philosophy of nature and the philosophy of religion.

Editorial Advisory Board
Maurizio Farraris, Paul Franks, Iain Hamilton Grant, Garth Green, Adrian Johnston, Catherine Malabou, Jeff Malpas, Marie-Eve Morin, Jeffrey Reid, Susan Ruddick, Michael Schulz, Hasana Sharp, Alison Stone, Peter Trawny, Uwe Voigt, Jason Wirth, Günter Zöller

Books available
The Political Theology of Schelling, Saitya Brata Das
Continental Realism and Its Discontents, edited by Marie-Eve Morin
The Contingency of Necessity: Reason and God as Matters of Fact, Tyler Tritten
The Problem of Nature in Hegel's Final System, Wes Furlotte
Schelling's Naturalism: Motion, Space and the Volition of Thought, Ben Woodard
Thinking Nature: An Essay in Negative Ecology, Sean J. McGrath
Heidegger's Ontology of Events, James Bahoh
The Political Theology of Kierkegaard, Saitya Brata Das
The Schelling–Eschenmayer Controversy, 1801: Nature and Identity, Benjamin Berger and Daniel Whistler
Hölderlin's Philosophy of Nature, edited by Rochelle Tobias
Affect and Attention after Deleuze and Whitehead: Ecological Attunement, Russell J. Duvernoy
The Philosophical Foundations of the Late Schelling: The Turn to the Positive, Sean J. McGrath
Schelling's Ontology of Powers, Charlotte Alderwick
Collected Essays in Speculative Philosophy, by James Bradley and edited by Sean J. McGrath
Merleau-Ponty and Nancy on Sense and Being: At the Limits of Phenomenology, by Marie-Eve Morin

www.edinburghuniversitypress.com/series/epnpio

Merleau-Ponty and Nancy on Sense and Being

At the Limits of Phenomenology

MARIE-EVE MORIN

EDINBURGH
University Press

Edinburgh University Press is one of the leading university presses in the UK. We publish academic books and journals in our selected subject areas across the humanities and social sciences, combining cutting-edge scholarship with high editorial and production values to produce academic works of lasting importance. For more information visit our website: edinburghuniversitypress.com

© Marie-Eve Morin, 2022, 2023

Edinburgh University Press Ltd
The Tun – Holyrood Road
12(2f) Jackson's Entry
Edinburgh EH8 8PJ

First published in hardback by Edinburgh University Press 2022

Typeset in 11/13 Adobe Garamond
by Cheshire Typesetting Ltd, Cuddington, Cheshire

A CIP record for this book is available from the British Library

ISBN 978 1 4744 9242 3 (hardback)
ISBN 978 1 4744 9243 0 (paperback)
ISBN 978 1 4744 9245 4 (webready PDF)
ISBN 978 1 4744 9244 7 (epub)

The right of Marie-Eve Morin to be identified as the author of this work has been asserted in accordance with the Copyright, Designs and Patents Act 1988, and the Copyright and Related Rights Regulations 2003 (SI No. 2498).

Contents

Acknowledgements	vii
List of Abbreviations	ix
Introduction: The Speculative Realist Challenge and the Limits of Phenomenology	1
1. The context: The speculative realist challenge	1
2. The limits of phenomenology: Being and sense	5
3. Merleau-Ponty and Nancy: Influence and resonances	13
4. Chapter breakdown	16

Part I – BODY

1 Merleau-Ponty, Descartes and the Unreflected Life of the Body	27
1. Reading Descartes: The relation between reflection and the unreflected	29
2. Sensing and self-sensing body of the *Phenomenology of Perception*	34
3. The problem of the *Phenomenology of Perception*: Tacit versus operative cogito	41
2 Nancy, Descartes, the Exposition of Bodies and the Extension of the Soul	50
1. Nancy's reading of Descartes: The *unum quid* against the modern subject	50
2. Nancy's bodies: Skin, sense, touch	60
3 Divergences: Unity versus Dislocation	70
1. Synthesis of the body schema or *partes extra partes*?	71

    2. Synaesthesia or dislocation of the senses? Self-touching or touching the outside?   75

Part II – THING

4 Things in the *Phenomenology of Perception*: The Paradox of an In-Itself-for-Us   89
    1. The order of the phenomena: Between being and appearance   90
    2. Answering the accusation of correlationism   94
    3. The limit of the answer in the *Phenomenology* and the move to ontology   98
5 Things after the *Phenomenology*: Merleau-Ponty's Cautious Anthropomorphism   104
    1. Sartre's things   105
    2. Merleau-Ponty's things   109
    3. Anthropomorphism as defamiliarisation   113
6 Nancy's Materialism and the Stone   119
    1. The freedom of the stone and the creation of the world   119
    2. The existence of the stone and its feeling hard   122
    3. Materialism, materiality, matter   126
    4. Thinking and things   134

Part III – BEING

7 Merleau-Ponty's and Nancy's Engagement with Heidegger   146
    1. Is Merleau-Ponty's late ontology Heideggerian?   147
    2. Merleau-Ponty between Husserl's *Wesenschau* and Heidegger's *Wesen*   150
    3. Merleau-Ponty between the negativism of doubt and the positivism of essences   154
    4. Merleau-Ponty's indirect ontology   157
    5. Nancy and Heidegger's withdrawal of Being   159
8 Two Ontologies of Sense   168
    1. Merleau-Ponty, *écart* and the flesh   171
    2. Narcissism and the reversibility of the chiasm   175
    3. *Écart* as encroachment or separation   178
    4. Conclusion: Two ontologies of sense for our time   183

Bibliography   189
Index   197

Acknowledgements

In winter 2013, at the request of my students, I taught a seminar on Merleau-Ponty. Up to that point, I had not delved seriously into Merleau-Ponty's thought and it is fair to say that reading – as well as teaching – Merleau-Ponty had a significant impact on my own thinking. My biggest debt of gratitude then is to my students, not only those who made their first foray into Merleau-Ponty's work with me in 2013, but also those who studied Merleau-Ponty with me in winter 2019. My understanding of Merleau-Ponty and my ability to explain his most complex ideas is indebted to our conversations. I am also grateful to all those who participated in our Nancy reading group in 2019 – Mackenzie, Júlia, Felix, Markéta, Jay – for reviving my enthusiasm for Nancy.

Along the way, there were many conferences and informal conversations with colleagues and friends, for which I am also grateful. Some parts of the following study have also been published in various forms. A much shorter version of Part I appeared as '*Corps propre* or *corpus corporum*: Unity and Dislocation in the Theories of Embodiment of Merleau-Ponty and Jean-Luc Nancy' in *Chiasmi International* 18 (2016): 353–70. An earlier version of Chapter 8 appeared as 'Flesh and *Écart* in Merleau-Ponty and Nancy', in Irving Goh (ed.), *Nancy Among the Philosophers* (New York: Fordham University Press, 2022). Chapter 5 appeared in an earlier version as 'Merleau-Ponty's Cautious Anthropomorphism' in *Chiasmi International* 22 (2020): 167–81. Some of the discussion of Nancy in Chapter 7 appeared in '"We Must Become What We Are": Nancy's Ontology as Ethos and Praxis', in Sanja Dejanovic (ed.), *Nancy and the Political* (Edinburgh: Edinburgh University Press, 2015). The beginning of the Introduction is adapted from 'Continental Realism – Picking Up the Pieces', with Vladimir Dukić, in Marie-Eve Morin (ed.),

Continental Realism and Its Discontents (Edinburgh: Edinburgh University Press, 2017).

My thanks also go to Carol MacDonald for her enthusiasm for the project and her renewed encouragement over the years and to all the staff at Edinburgh University Press for seeing this project through. Finally, the research for this study was supported in part by a research grant from the Social Sciences and Humanities Research Council of Canada.

Abbreviations

Works by Maurice Merleau-Ponty

CPP   *Child Psychology and Pedagogy: The Sorbonne Lectures 1949–1952*
MO   'Man and Object'
N   *Nature: Course Notes from the Collège de France*
NC   *Notes de cours 1959–61*
PP   *Phenomenology of Perception*
PoP   *The Primacy of Perception*
S   *Signs*
TFL   *Themes from the Lectures at the Collège de France, 1952–1960*
VI   *The Visible and the Invisible*
WP   *The World of Perception*

Works by Jean-Luc Nancy

A   *Adoration: The Deconstruction of Christianity II*
AR   'Merleau-Ponty: An Attempt at a Response'
BP   *The Birth to Presence*
BSP   *Being Singular Plural*
C   *Corpus*
C II   *Corpus II: Writings on Sexuality*
CW   *The Creation of the World or Globalization*
D   *Dis-Enclosure: The Deconstruction of Christianity I*
EF   *The Experience of Freedom*
ES   *Ego Sum*
FT   *A Finite Thinking*

GT   *The Gravity of Thought*
MM   *Marquage manquant (et autres dires de la peau)*
NMT   *Noli me tangere*
SW   *The Sense of the World*

Other works

AF   Quentin Meillassoux, *After Finitude*
BA   Tim Ingold, *Being Alive*
BN   Jean-Paul Sartre, *Being and Nothingness*
BT   Martin Heidegger, *Being and Time*
EC   Emmanuel de Saint Aubert, *Être et chair 1. Du corps au désir*
LEEE Emmanuel de Saint Aubert, *Du lien des êtres aux éléments de l'être*
MT   Jean-Paul Sartre, 'Man and Things'
OT   Jacques Derrida, *On Touching – Jean-Luc Nancy*
SC   Emmanuel de Saint Aubert, *Le scénario cartésien*
SEI   Jeffrey Cohen, *Stone: An Ecology of the Inhuman*
VOI   Emmanuel de Saint Aubert, *Vers une ontologie indirecte*

Introduction

The Speculative Realist Challenge and the Limits of Phenomenology

1. The context: The speculative realist challenge

The context for the present comparative study of Merleau-Ponty and Nancy is provided by the challenge that the speculative realist movement addressed to post-Kantian Continental thought in general, and phenomenology in particular. While the popularity of speculative realism as a movement might have waned since its inception in 2007, the challenge it raised against Continental thinkers remains important. Not only do Merleau-Ponty and Nancy, I will seek to argue, have the means to take up this challenge, but doing so allows us to bring to the fore the originality of their respective thinking.

As is well known by now, the speculative realist movement sprang out of a one-day workshop held at Goldsmiths College in April 2007, a little more than a year after the publication of Quentin Meillassoux's book *Après la finitude*.[1] The impetus for the original event was, as Brassier describes it, 'to revive questions about realism, materialism, science, representation, and objectivity, that were dismissed as otiose by each of the main pillars of Continental orthodoxy: phenomenology, critical theory, and deconstruction'.[2] 'Speculative realism' thus became, at least for a while, the name of a movement toward a revival of realist and materialist metaphysics as an attempt to counter what was seen as the dominance of a certain legacy of transcendental idealism in Continental philosophy, reflected above all in its focus on the subject, its critical limitation of knowledge to the phenomenal world, and its rejection of speculative metaphysics.

The various projects grouped under the banner of 'speculative realism' might not have as much in common as was first thought, except for their call to revive some form of realist metaphysics or another.[3] What interests me in the present study is not so much the positive philosophical programmes developed by the various thinkers grouped under this banner but rather the way in which they describe and challenge their common enemy: post-Kantian thought. Almost without exception, speculative realists maintain that 'things went grossly awry when Kant, having been roused from his dogmatic slumbers by the challenge of Humean scepticism, responded by announcing his "Copernican revolution" in epistemology'.[4] They are thus against any philosophical approach that emphasises subjective access to things, the finitude of human cognitive capacities, and the limitations of reason in its speculative use.

The clearest philosophical statement of this opposition can be found in *After Finitude*, where Meillassoux applies the term 'correlationism' to any philosophy that denies human access to the 'Absolute' – that is, to a 'reality' independent of human thought and interest. Meillassoux defines 'correlation' as 'the idea according to which we only ever have access to the correlation between thinking and being, and never to either term considered apart from the other' and 'correlationism' in general as 'any current of thought which maintains the unsurpassable character of the correlation so defined' (AF, 5). While Meillassoux distinguishes between different forms of weak and strong correlationisms, and also between correlationism and idealism, all correlationists are at bottom anti-realists: insofar as they maintain the unsurpassable nature of the correlation between thinking and being, correlationists reject any notion of the 'real' that would not already be reduced to its givenness to human beings. Or stated in terms of access: correlationists cannot legitimately say anything about objects independently of our mode of access to them. Since we cannot step out of our own mode of access, we lack the means of distinguishing 'between those properties which are supposed to belong to the object, and those properties belonging to the subjective access to the object'.[5] According to correlationism, 'thought cannot get *outside itself* in order to compare the world as it is "in itself" to the world as it is "for us", and thereby distinguish what is a function of our relation to the world from what belongs to the world alone' (AF, 5–6).

The ultimate aim of speculative realism, then, is to break philosophy free from its obsession with finitude and the limits of thought and renew the philosophical concern for the Absolute, for what is *not* in any way for us. If it is so urgent to undermine the wide, unquestioned acceptance of correlationist premises in Continental circles, it is not – or not merely – because correlationism is a misguided philosophical position. Rather, it is the unwillingness and the inability of correlationists to confront the challenges of our time that calls for speculative thought. From the speculative realist perspective, correlationists have turned towards human subjectivity and thought at the expense of the 'real world', while simultaneously condemning philosophical attempts to think the latter. According to the editors of *The Speculative Turn*,

> In the face of the looming ecological catastrophe, and the increasing infiltration of technology into the everyday world (including our own bodies), it is not clear that the anti-realist position is equipped to face up to these developments. The danger is that the dominant anti-realist strain of continental philosophy has not only reached a point of decreasing returns, but that it actively limits the capacities of philosophy in our time.[6]

More precisely, this unwillingness and inability of correlationists to confront the events of our time would be a direct consequence of three features of correlationist thought: its inevitable anthropocentrism, its aversion to the sciences, and its tolerance of fideism and the return of religious fundamentalisms. We will spend some time focusing on the first of these accusations in the second part of this study but for now, a short description of each and of their relation should suffice.

First, correlationism would be obviously anthropocentric because it reduces everything that exists to its being encountered by or given to human beings. Correlationism thus radically distinguishes the human being as the site of meaning or truth and as a consequence reduces all other beings to being merely objects at human disposal. Things are not worthy of concern in themselves since, unlike human beings, they are unable to enter into meaningful relations with their environment, or they are only worthy of concern once they become appropriated into the circuit of human thinking or manipulation. The study of these things 'in themselves' is thus left to the empirical sciences; all the while such scientific endeavour is denigrated as 'naïve' and 'non-philosophical'. Correlationists are averse not so much to the practice of the sciences but rather to scientism, that is, to a certain philosophical interpretation of the sciences as providing access to a real that is otherwise veiled. Science is simply another mode of access and can claim no privilege to 'get us out' of the correlation to the truth of the object 'as it is without us'. At the same time as they dismiss the power of science to give us access to the real, correlationists radically limit the claim of reason to access the Absolute, giving rise to 'fideism'. This is a problem especially for the correlationists who, like Heidegger, assert the contingency of the correlation itself. The structures of thought need not be the way they are, even though it is impossible for us to imagine them being otherwise. The strong correlationist's affirmation of the facticity of the correlation, according to Meillassoux, 'entails a specific and rather remarkable consequence: it becomes rationally illegitimate to disqualify *irrational* discourses about the absolute on the pretext of their irrationality' (AF, 41). As long as the religious person makes no claim to knowledge or to reason, she can assert whatever she wants about the Absolute. By restricting the scope of reason, correlationists surrender the ability to challenge irrational and even fundamentalist forms of religion, effectively giving them free rein over the Absolute, all the while maintaining a respectful distance.

In order to counter what they see as these three pernicious consequences of correlationist thought and do justice to a real that is independent of human beings, speculative realists argue for a renewal of 'speculation' in philosophy against Kant's critical philosophy.[7] Speculation as a method is supposed to be 'theoretically capable of disengaging objects from subjects in nonarbitrary ways, some of which approximate science fiction but none of which are, in the last analysis, fictitious'.[8] Speculation paradoxically liberates thinking from the categories of thought or from its own conditions of possibility. As Steven Shaviro explains: 'We need to subtract our own prejudices and presuppositions from any account we give of the world. And we need to create a new image of thought: one that is no longer modeled on, or limited to, anthropocentric parameters.'[9]

In what follows, I leave aside the question of whether or not the positive philosophical positions defended by various thinkers who have been identified as speculative realists in the broadest sense live up to their own standards and propose a philosophy that is able to tackle the problems of our time. I also do not defend phenomenology against the criticisms levelled against it in any sort of frontal and sustained way. In fact, such a defence, I take it, has already been successfully provided by Dan Zahavi.[10] Even though Zahavi's response is focused on Husserlian phenomenology, it is exemplary in its use of many, if not all, of the argumentative moves available to a so-called 'correlationist' in response to the speculative realists' accusations. Zahavi (1) admits that phenomenology is a form of correlationism, (2) admits that Husserl is a transcendental idealist, but (3) emphasises the fact that, of course, such idealism is not incompatible with scientific realism (and he does so by turning to Putnam to show that such a position is not an idiosyncrasy of Continental philosophy). He also (4) points out that scientific realism is not the only option when it comes to realism and that it itself comes under attack not only in phenomenology but also within more traditional philosophy of science, and (5) further reminds us that if one is attacking phenomenology from a scientific or metaphysical realist perspective, then this has already been done by analytic philosophy. Finally, he (6) claims that if we are looking for an affirmation of the reality of everyday objects (of the natural world), speculative realism 'fails miserably', or in other words, phenomenology is methodologically better equipped to account for the *real* world in its familiarity as well as strangeness. The exercise can be repeated for Kant, Heidegger and Derrida, as well as for Merleau-Ponty and Nancy.

But such a defensive response misses the question: does speculative realism make a difference within the 'traditional' Continental landscape? If we let our own thinking be challenged by it, do we then have to read the canonical texts differently? Do we see new threads in our favourite philosophers? Are we compelled to push them to answer new questions? Are we led to change the way in which we present their views? Do we leave them behind at some point?

Rather than adopting a defensive posture, I want to use the speculative realist challenge as a guiding thread to navigate the thoughts of Merleau-Ponty and Nancy. I enter their respective works with a series of questions I take from speculative realism: in what ways and to what extent are their philosophical positions able to displace the focus on human beings and their encounters with non-human entities? Do these philosophies have something to say about entities as they encounter each other outside of the purview of human beings? What do they have to say about the 'in-itself'? Is a positive discourse about the 'in-itself' possible, or is it an opaque, indeterminate glob that remains completely impervious to human thought? Of course, we might already feel that the worries raised by the speculative realists are foreign to the general concerns that give rise to Merleau-Ponty's and Nancy's thought, and we would not be completely wrong. One of the outcomes of my endeavour will certainly be to outline the ways in which Merleau-Ponty and Nancy transform and even undermine the terms of the speculative realist critique. Undoubtedly, we could be accused of approaching the works of these two thinkers armed with a series of questions and concepts that only risk distorting what is the most novel about their philosophies. My wager is that, as Derrida says at the beginning of '"Genesis and Structure" and Phenomenology', the introduction of 'the foreign substance of a debate' into our investigation 'may be efficacious, may surrender or set free the meaning of a latent process'. But as Derrida also warns, we must not forget that our investigation then 'begins with an aggression and an infidelity'.[11]

2. The limits of phenomenology: Being and sense

The disagreement – or we could even say misunderstanding – between speculative realism and phenomenology centres on the question of the limit, and more precisely on the relation between being and the limits of sense. For the phenomenologist, whether Husserlian or Heideggerian, the limits of sense are the limits of being.[12] Merleau-Ponty and Nancy, each in their own ways, challenge the collapse of being into sense as it is effected by phenomenology, yet they do so in a more subtle way than speculative realism in general. Rather than reinstating a strong divide between being and sense, one that we have the power and the duty to transgress, they displace and reassess both the place where the limits of sense are encountered and the role of the limit in sense-making.

Speculative realism, in a sense, still operates with a classical understanding of the limit as separating an inside from an outside: the disagreement with phenomenology then would concern the possibility of stepping out of the inside into the outside. In terms of sense and being, it would concern the possibility of encountering (or rather theorising) being apart from the limits of sense imposed by human experience, sensuous or cognitive. Indeed, if we look closely at the way in which Meillassoux describes his own project in *After Finitude*, we see that it is based on an appeal to a fairly classical understanding of the inside/outside divide. This is most obvious when Meillassoux speaks of the necessity to retrieve

> the *great outdoors*, the *absolute outside* of pre-critical thinkers: that outside which was not relative to us, and which was given as indifferent to its own givenness to be what it is, existing in itself regardless of whether we are thinking of it or not; that outside which thought could explore with the legitimate feeling of being on foreign territory – of being entirely elsewhere. (AF, 7)

Indeed, Meillassoux's framework remains Cartesian in that it reaffirms the divide between subject and object, or to be more precise between the subjective realm of everyday confused experience and the objective realm of science. Meillassoux, then, seeks to rehabilitate the '*glacial* world' of Descartes that made possible the Galilean and Corpernican revolutions, that is, mathematised science (AF, 115) and enjoins us 'to get out of ourselves, to grasp the in-itself, to know what is whether we are or not' (AF, 27).

Interestingly enough, the same sort of language was used earlier by the proponents of the linguistic turn in framing their own attack on realism. The insight of the linguistic turn can be expressed by saying 'it's language [or contexts, or interpretations, or what have you] all the way down'.[13] What this means differs greatly among philosophers but the basic insight is that we are bound to the structures of our linguistic, logical or conceptual schemes and have no direct, unmediated access to reality.[14] Truth, then, is measured by the coherence between our various propositions, and *not* by 'stepping out of our skin', as Rorty says.[15] Whatever can be thought or said, whatever conforms to our linguistic or conceptual schemes, is the world for us, and there is no sense of speaking of any other world. The anti-realists are trying to block the appeal to any kind of outside, hence undermining the whole inside/outside divide. At the same time, the way in which anti-realists speak – 'we are stuck *within* language', 'we cannot step *out* of our skin', and so on – already betrays the same kind of inside/outside dualism, or the mediational picture of knowledge, the realists use in their appeal to 'get outside'. As Charles Taylor points out: 'we find the [mediational] picture invoked within an argument that is meant to repudiate that very picture.'¹⁶ Husserlian phenomenology, on the other hand, is often presented as undermining exactly that conception of inside/outside divide that underlies the realism and anti-realism debate. Yet it does so, as I said above, by reducing being to sense, in a way that will be seen as problematic not only for speculative realism but also for Merleau-Ponty and Nancy.

The method of phenomenology as we learn from Husserl consists first of a suspension of our natural attitude called the *epoché*. In the natural attitude, we are focused on what is given and overlook its mode of appearance or givenness. Because consciousness is a movement toward objects, we tend to overlook the intentional relation between consciousness and what is given. To study objects in their givenness we need to put out of play the object-pull, refrain from following through with the 'arrow' that consciousness is. Thanks to this suspension, we are *led back* (*re-ducere* in Latin) and gain access to a forgotten or overlooked dimension of experience, that is, the consciousness–world relation. This is the phenomenological reduction. Reduction hence does not mean that something has been removed or that the object has been lost. In the reduction, I still have the whole of my consciousness with everything that is presented in it, but I suspend my judgement so that I can focus on *how* each object is presented as this or that, as real or illusory, and so on. Hence, we cannot say that the phenomenological reduction blocks our access to or leads us to disregard what is real in favour of what is merely thought. The phenomenologist can study what is real in its reality, but 'being-real' now means 'being given to consciousness in a certain way'. Being is a function of meaning, of givenness.

Husserl thinks that the phenomenological reduction if correctly and radically performed will necessarily lead to a transcendental reduction because consciousness – the dimension uncovered by the phenomenological reduction – cannot itself be a worldly thing that appears to consciousness. Such a circularity would lead us to transcendental realism and we would be committing the same mistake as psychologism. If we keep in mind the difference between the transcendental field uncovered by the phenomenological-transcendental reduction and the act-pole or ego-pole of any experience, which is always related to an object-pole, then we can start addressing the question of whether phenomenology does indeed overcome the inside/outside divide. Any difference between an inside and an outside, between what is immanent *in the act* and what is transcendent with regard to the act, is a difference that is only meaningful, and is only attested, within transcendental consciousness itself.[17] Being transcendent – being real in the sense of mind-independent – means, for the Husserlian phenomenologist, being given and attesting oneself as mind-independent in an intentional act. The differences between immanence and transcendence, between reality and fiction, between reality and ideality, are all differences in the mode of givenness of an object of experience.

Even though we can speak of what is 'outside' of or 'other' than the transcendental ego, of what stands against it (*gegenüberstehen*) as an object (*Gegenstand*), it makes no sense to speak of an outside of transcendental consciousness itself. Transcendental consciousness is a totality: it is open to everything that can be given to it, yet it is enclosed with limits. These limits are, for Husserl, the form of egoity and the form of presence.[18] There is no thought, no experience that is not experienced as 'mine' in living presence. This can be shown best if we look at the experience of the *alter ego*. That the alter ego is appresented means that it is given on the basis of a presentation (of its physical appearance) but is itself not presented. The alter ego does appear according to Husserl, but it appears as non-presence, as *Nichturpräsentierbar*. Thus we cannot say that the alter ego is not given. If this were the case, we could not even start making sense of the experience of an alter ego. But we also cannot say that the alter ego is given, if by that we mean that it is presented or intuited in originary presence. In terms of immanence and transcendence, this means that while the alter ego is 'outside' of my consciousness, it is so only 'within' my consciousness. That which I can never experience directly has to appear in some way within the field of my experience if it is to be anything at all for me so that we should distinguish between the whole of experienceable being (*alles erfahrbare Sein*) and what is experienceable in the original sense.[19]

In true Kantian fashion, then, the limits of experience are, for Husserl, the conditions of possibility of experience so that it makes no sense to ask what there would be beyond these limits. Without these limits, nothing would appear, and we could not even begin to adjudicate between what is real and what is not, or between what is originary and what is alien.[20] The limits of consciousness then for Husserl are the limits of what can be given. They are the limits of sense: 'If transcendental subjectivity is the universe of possible sense, then an outside is precisely nonsense. But even nonsense is always a mode of sense and has its nonsensicalness within the sphere of possible insight.'[21] The question 'what lies outside of the limits of sense?' is paradoxical. If we answer *Unsinn*, 'non-sense', then we are appealing to a modality of sense and are thinking of the limits between sense and nonsense as themselves given within the field of transcendental subjectivity. But what would it mean to understand the question as asking about what is absolutely beyond sense? The answer to such a question could only be '*Widersinn*', absurdity, so that even the question itself would be *widersinnig*, absurd: we could not even start making sense of what it is asking about.

In *After Finitude*, Meillassoux challenges the Husserlian reduction of being to sense by appealing to the problem of ancestrality and of the arche-fossil. An arche-fossil is 'the material support on the basis of which the experiments that yield estimates of ancestral phenomena proceed', an 'ancestral phenomenon' being a 'reality anterior to the emergence of the human species' (AF, 10). What the arche-fossil gives us to think is a time prior to manifestation or givenness, a time in which manifestation and givenness came to be. This, according to Meillassoux, means that if we take ancestral statements literally in their realist interpretation as statements about a referent that existed prior to any consciousness, we must necessarily admit that '*being* is not co-extensive with *manifestation*' and that 'what *is* preceded *in time* the *manifestation* of what is' (AF, 14). There is more to being than givenness. The phenomenologist of course already agrees. There are many things that are not given: the backside of the table, a tree that falls on an uninhabited island, and so on. But Meillassoux thinks that the arche-fossil gives us access to something different: not an unwitnessed event but an event that is in principle non-givable.

According to Meillassoux, the phenomenologist can only make sense of ancestral statements by distorting their literal meaning, turning them into subjective statements about the knowledge held by a community of scientists rather than objective statements about some entity that existed before consciousness. As Meillassoux points out, though, when scientists say something about the accretion of the earth they are not speaking about their own thoughts. Husserl would of course agree. After all, this was exactly his argument against psychologism. Because phenomenology does not reduce all givenness to intuitive givenness, what the arche-fossil would show is not being is not co-extensive to sense but rather that the realm of givenness or sense is not co-extensive with what is *urpräsentierbar* or *leibhaftig gegeben*. Meillassoux is mistaken, then, when he asserts that the referent of the statement about the arche-fossil (the earth before human consciousness) is unthinkable because it is non-givable. The referent is perfectly thinkable, and thinkable as non-intuitively givable, and this non-givability is part of its meaning. What the phenomenologist would point out however is that such empirical statements are only meaningful and verifiable, they only have a sense and a referent, insofar as there is a transcendental consciousness that constitutes both the meaning of the statement and the objectivity of the referent.

Yet, Meillassoux thinks that ancestral statements made on the basis of the arche-fossil are not merely empirical statements (see AF, 21–2). What they show rather is that the conditions of possibility of experience or the conditions of intelligibility have not always existed, that they have come to be in time and that science can tell us when this happens. If consciousness came to be at some point in time, then we cannot say that everything is within consciousness but rather that consciousness is but an event within being. We reach the limits of phenomenological discourse and must yield to the sciences to teach us about the conditions of possibility of phenomenology. The phenomenologist, for her part, would point out that the question of the coming-to-be of consciousness as a fact only makes sense within the domain of sense. The absolute priority of sense cannot be contested. As soon as consciousness comes to be, the domain of intelligibility and sense opens up and it becomes possible to question why there is what there is, including the consciousness that raises the question. Both the intelligibility or givenness of beings *and* the question of the limits of such intelligibility or givenness, of the before and the beyond, are given at once.

Heidegger, like Husserl, does, at least in *Being and Time*, also reduce being to meaning. Being does not name some entity in-itself beyond what is manifested or given. Rather it names the meaningful givenness of any entity so that it only makes sense to speak of the Being of entities within the space of meaning opened by Dasein's existence. This is why Heidegger can say that there is no Reality apart from Dasein because being-real is a meaning entities receive in relation to a Dasein that understands Being and hence can interpret this or that entity as real (see BT, H. 211–12). What we said above about the *Widersinnigkeit* of asking after what there is outside of or beyond this space of meaning also applies to Heidegger. Yet, at the same time, by moving the locus of this space of meaning from transcendental consciousness to Dasein as Being-in-the-world, by inquiring into the mode of Being of Dasein as such and by forgoing the transcendental and eidetic reductions as they are practised by Husserl, Heidegger is able to highlight two ontological characteristics of Dasein that were inaccessible to Husserl: facticity and finitude.

For Heidegger, the facticity of Dasein is the fact that Dasein is or occurs. Because its mode of Being is existence, however, Dasein does not occur as a mere fact within the world. Facticity names the 'that-it-is' of Dasein, its being thrown into its there, its being delivered over to its own being, without knowing 'whence' and 'whither'. Meillassoux then is not wrong to say that facticity names the inability to provide a reason for the correlation insofar as facticity names one side of our finitude, that is, our inability to reappropriate the limit that is our thrownness, to see it from the other side so to speak and provide a ground for it. We are always too late for our own birth, for the opening of our own 'there'. The other side of our finitude, of course, is death. Death for Heidegger does not name an event that will take place in the future and brings my life to an end, but rather a limit not to be surpassed. Of course, I can project myself beyond the future point of my demise, like I can project myself before the past moment of my birth, and imagine what there will be. The foreclosure of my horizon is not ontic but ontological. This is why the general term 'finitude' might be less misleading in discussing the issue. Finitude reveals the true meaning of possibility, that is, the meaning of possibility when it is not understood as lack of and on the way toward actuality.

Dasein exists as finite because its being is pervaded by 'not-ness', by limits that it relates to but cannot come back behind and gives to itself. Death and thrownness – which again are not to be confused with demise and birth as ontic events in time – are structures of the 'There', structures of the 'clearing' or 'space of meaning' in which Dasein find itself and to which it is exposed. As limits then they do not block my view and restrict what I have access to, rather they first make possible Being, that is, meaningful access to entities. In a similar way, the living present in Husserl is a horizon in the sense not of what blocks my view but of that upon which or in relation to which something can appear. The question of what lies on the other side of the horizon is unintelligible.

Meillassoux takes on Heidegger's view of limits, and of death more specifically, when he discusses the second decision of strong correlationism, namely the decision to assert the facticity of the correlation rather than absolutising it (which is what Husserl and Hegel do). There is no reason for the correlation: it could not have been, or it could have been otherwise. We cannot ask why it is and why it is the way that it is since that would require a point of view outside of the correlation. This decision, for Meillassoux, amounts to confining oneself 'to thinking the limits of thought, these functioning for language like a frontier only one side of which can be grasped' (AF, 41). The assumption behind Meillassoux's claim is that a 'limit' necessarily has two edges, an internal and an external one. While we see what is on this side of the limit, the limit also blocks our view on to what is on the other side. Strong correlationists would restrict themselves to meditating the internal limit of experience, leaving the other side to the free-for-all of irrational or religious beliefs. But as Hegel has shown, to posit a limit is already to posit another side and hence to transcend the limit. This is how Hegel overcomes the Kantian 'limit' between the world for us and its other side, the world in itself. By restricting himself to thinking only the internal edge of the limit, Heidegger is not ignoring Hegel's critique of Kant. Rather, he is radically recasting what is meant by limit: the possibilising limits that open the 'There' are limits that have no other side, no external edges.²² Yet, unlike Husserl's transcendental consciousness, the 'inside' here remains responsive to and responsible in the face of these limits.

While both Husserl and Heidegger have, from within their own frame of thought, perfectly sound responses to Meillassoux's demand to retrieve 'the absolute outside', a certain malaise remains, the feeling, as Meillassoux writes, of only ever having reached 'a cloistered outside' (AF, 7). The difficulty of raising the question of brute factuality within phenomenology and the paradoxical relation between being and sense or between fact and sense is perhaps best addressed by Derrida in his introduction to Husserl's 'Origin of Geometry'. The pure thatness of things – their 'wild singularity' – remains for phenomenology 'eternally the *apeiron*'.²³ It only appears as phenomenology's limit. Derrida explains:

> We pass from phenomenology to ontology (in the non-Husserlian sense) when we silently question in the direction of the upsurge of naked factuality and cease to consider the Fact in its phenomenological 'function'. Then the latter can no longer be exhausted and reduced to its sense by the work of phenomenology, even were it pursued *ad infinitum*.²⁴

If to the question 'Why are there things in their factuality?' phenomenology answers: 'So that sense can be transmitted', then phenomenology is confining facts to their phenomenological function. It speaks of the sense of facts and not of their factuality. By reducing fact to sense, phenomenology abandons pure otherness or brute factuality, in order to arrogate to itself the right to speak.²⁵ What remains, however, and what is felt, is a necessary delay between question and answer – or as Merleau-Ponty will say, between reflection and the unreflected. As Derrida writes: 'delay [*retard*] is the philosophical absolute, because the beginning of methodic reflection can only consist in the consciousness of the implication of *another* previous, possible, and absolute origin in general.'²⁶

If we come back to the larger context of this study, we can reframe the terms of the debate about the relation between an inside and an outside in terms of the appeal to realism. If we stick to the traditional metaphysical or epistemological definition of realism, which asserts the existence of a mind-independent reality and the passivity of knowledge, and locates truth in correspondence,²⁷ then neither Husserl nor Heidegger, neither Merleau-Ponty nor Nancy, will ever count as a realist and it is difficult to see how the issue of realism would even be relevant to their thinking. Yet, if we start from Crispin Wright's definition of realism as a mixture of modesty and presumption,²⁸ then the question of realism is not moot. According to Wright, the modesty of realism comes from the admission that we are not the measure of things and that our experiences and thoughts are answerable to an 'other' or an 'outside'. In other words, we are not 'Active Minds'[29] imposing our conceptual schemes on to an inert, meaningless outside. This modesty is coupled with the presumption that we can, if not represent and know, at least aspire to grasp and capture in thought or discourse a 'reality' that remains beyond such thought or discourse.[30] In Derridian terms, it is a question of navigating the paradox between an outside that would remain completely outside and 'the right to speak' about the outside that reduces it to a function of the inside. How to speak of an outside that is inscribed in the inside as absolute outside without falling into too much modesty or too much presumption? In this context who is too modest? Heidegger? Kant? Who is too presumptuous? Husserl? Meillassoux? Is Merleau-Ponty too modest in his early works? And does he become too presumptuous in his later works? Is Nancy too presumptuous from the start?

The relation between the inside and the outside, the way the outside is included while also resisting inclusion in the inside, as well as the relation between philosophy or reflection and non-philosophy is a central and constant concern for Merleau-Ponty. In this sense, by following the development of Merleau-Ponty's thinking, we can track the radicalisation of the paradoxical relation between being and sense. In the end, Merleau-Ponty will propose an ontology of sense, where sense is made within Being itself, yet one that also attempts to give 'wild singularities' or 'wild things' their due. Nancy's ontology, on the other hand, is situated from the start outside of the question of phenomenology and its reflective method. We could say that while Merleau-Ponty grapples with the limits of phenomenology, Nancy already situates his thinking beyond these limits. Yet at the same time, Nancy does propose an ontology of sense as well as a philosophy of experience. Putting Merleau-Ponty in conversation with Nancy will allow us to see more clearly the limits Merleau-Ponty does not want to cross.

3. Merleau-Ponty and Nancy: Influence and resonances

The decision to read Merleau-Ponty and Nancy together arises from a wager: that there are uncanny resonances between their oeuvres that can help us pinpoint more precisely the differences that remain irreducible between the two, highlighting the originality of each of their thinking. The goal is not to make a list of similarities and differences in order to then argue for the superiority of one over the other. Rather, I want to bring the two thinkers as close to one another as possible but without overlooking the irreducible differences between them in order to go beyond superficial similarities and differences and uncover the origin of their divergences.

The assumption is that this origin lies in philosophical commitments that are not always explicitly stated. More specifically, there is, in Merleau-Ponty's work, if not a posited unity, at least a desire for the One that has completely disappeared from Nancy's ontology, and this affects the way in which each conceives of sensing and sense-making more generally, as well as of the role of limits, differences or divergences within such sense-making.

I have just mentioned the uncanny resonances between Merleau-Ponty and Nancy, and I do think that anybody who sojourns in both oeuvres at the same time is bound to be struck by similarities in phrasing, images and ideas. Yet, I call these resonances 'uncanny' because unlike what one might expect, there is no direct influence of Merleau-Ponty's work on Nancy's thinking, and the references we find to Merleau-Ponty in Nancy's oeuvre remain sparse and often critical. There are however some interesting, if tenuous, indirect lines of influence.

Nancy moved to Paris shortly before Merleau-Ponty's death. During his time at the Sorbonne, Nancy worked closely with Canguilhem, who is well known for his criticism both of vitalism and of the reductionist approach to life, a criticism he recognises is indebted to Merleau-Ponty's first book, *The Structure of Behaviour*.[31] Yet, as Nancy says, Merleau-Ponty only belongs to his 'philosophical prehistory' (AR, 298). Nancy did read *The Structure of Behaviour* and the *Phenomenology of Perception* since these books were required readings in the philosophy programme, but this meant that his encounter with Merleau-Ponty's thought remained trapped within an 'academic horizon'. Despite his recent death, Merleau-Ponty was already an academic reference of the past for Nancy, one who, not unlike Sartre, did not belong to the contemporary landscape of the 1960s that marked the development of Nancy's thought.

It is through the encounter with Derrida that philosophy suddenly found, for Nancy, 'the actuality of its movement, of its act and gesture'[32] and that for the first time he heard 'the music of the present' (AR, 298).[33] It is through Derrida that Nancy took the measure of the event or rupture of Western philosophical thinking initiated by Nietzsche, Heidegger and Freud, and it is Derrida who enabled him to read Husserl. Nancy's reading of Husserl, unlike Merleau-Ponty's, begins with the posthumous fragment 'The Origin of Geometry' and is already mediated by Derrida's concern with the impurity of the origin. Here again, we could find an indirect line from Nancy to Merleau-Ponty, for whom the manuscript on geometry was also an important text, one to which he devoted a lecture course in 1959–60. Yet, Derrida never heard Merleau-Ponty lecture and his interpretation of the manuscript developed 'in total independence' from Merleau-Ponty's.[34]

More generally, these biographical anecdotes point to the fact Merleau-Ponty's and Nancy's thinking respond to different questions, move in a different milieu, and undeniably have a different feel. We must be careful not to let any superficial similarities or resonances obscure the more radical differences between their universes of thought. Nancy alludes to these differences when he describes his own universe as German and metaphysical, while Merleau-Ponty's universe would remain French and physical (AR, 299). Nancy summarises this difference between the French and the German climates with the following sets of oppositions: on the French side, we find a thinking of existence as life and flesh, a thinking of the 'participation in being' as being-in-the-world and 'inherence' of the self in the world. On the German side, we find a thinking of existence as Dasein and as the 'putting into play of the meaning of being in the being of *Dasein*', that is, a thinking of a 'distance opened within presence', of the 'transcendence of being as *Ereignis*'. As Nancy admits, the difference is 'as wide as it is narrow' (AR, 299), especially if we recall the importance of the body in Nancy's thinking.

If we now turn to the more direct textual evidence that would evince the influence of Merleau-Ponty on Nancy's thinking, the results are also disappointing. Indeed, there are only a handful of direct references to Merleau-Ponty in Nancy's texts, many of them epigraphs that do not give rise to any sustained engagement with Merleau-Ponty's ideas on Nancy's part. Others, which concern the role of self-sensing in the constitution of the self, are often critical. For example, in *Corpus*, Nancy is critical of the phenomenological analyses of self-touching insofar as they 'always return to a primary interiority' (C, 128).

One of the only positive mentions of Merleau-Ponty in Nancy's oeuvre is found in a short text titled 'Strange Foreign Bodies'. There, without mentioning Merleau-Ponty by name, Nancy speaks favourably of the figure of the chiasm, which points to the radical openness or exposure of the touching-touched body to the world. Nancy's affinity with Merleau-Ponty's thinking, then, would not be sought in the analyses of the lived body or the body proper but of a chiasm or torsion between inside and outside, one that teaches us that we are exposed 'right down to our most intimate depths' (C II, 82). Such is also the lesson Nancy finds in Merleau-Ponty's lecture notes on passivity and the notes on the Freudian unconscious, which he admits having read with interest. These notes show a displacement of the metaphysics of presence toward a thinking of the 'subject' as non-presence-to-self, as co-existence with the world and with others prior to the division between subject and object, and between ignorance and knowledge. At the same time, Nancy is not convinced. In the same text where he praises the lecture notes on passivity and on the Freudian unconscious, Nancy also quotes the following sentence from Merleau-Ponty's 'Eye and Mind': 'Vision . . . is the means given me for being absent from myself, for being present at the fission of Being from the inside – the fission at whose termination, and not before, I come back to myself', and confesses that this closure or return to oneself remains incomprehensible for him (AR, 299).

In what follows I will contest Nancy's own characterisation of his philosophical universe as metaphysical and Heideggerian by highlighting the role the body plays for him in sense-making and by distancing him from the Heideggerian limitation of sense-making to Dasein. At the same time, I do take seriously Nancy's concern with any kind of 'return to self' and seek to assess whether there is indeed such a return to self in Merleau-Ponty's philosophy, both early and late.

4. Chapter breakdown

The following study is divided into three parts, each staging an encounter between Merleau-Ponty and Nancy around a key notion in their respective work: Body, Thing, Being. Each part also introduces a conversation partner that serves as common interlocutor between Merleau-Ponty and Nancy: Descartes for the section on the body, contemporary realist and materialist thinkers for the part on things, and Heidegger for the section on ontology. While each part can be read more or less independently, there is also a natural progression not only in terms of a broadening of concerns from one particular kind of entity, the lived body, to things more generally, and finally to Being as such, but also in terms of the different periods of Merleau-Ponty's oeuvre we engage with, from the *Phenomenology of Perception* to the last unpublished manuscript and notes.

The first part of the present study contrasts Nancy's view of the body with Merleau-Ponty's description of embodied existence in the *Phenomenology of Perception*. Since both develop their thinking of the body against a certain Cartesianism but also through a non-dualist reading of the union of the soul and the body, the presentation of their respective notion of body requires an engagement with their reading of Descartes. Chapter 1 is focused on Merleau-Ponty's undermining of Cartesian dualism in his study of lived body and his attempt at tying reflection back to the unreflected life of the body. To get acquainted with the lived body I focus on the description of the experience of sensing and self-sensing in the *Phenomenology of Perception*, paying special attention to the kind of unity formed by the body's parts and by the system body–world. Finally, I also appeal to the immediate reception of Merleau-Ponty's project to show the problematic nature of Merleau-Ponty's project as it is carried out in the *Phenomenology*. It is in light of these critiques that Merleau-Ponty will be led to refine his method as well as his reading of Descartes.

Chapter 2 turns to Nancy's own reading of Descartes, which also focuses on the problematic relation between the union of the soul and the body on the one hand and the cogito on the other. Focusing on the performative utterance of the cogito, Nancy shows how this utterance consists in a double movement of withdrawal or distinction on the one hand and exposition on the other. Furthermore, such movement is only possible because what utters or opens itself in the cogito is not a substance but a body. The reading of Descartes allows us to propose a more careful interpretation of the notion of body in Nancy, one that does not merely focus on the spacing between bodies and their exposure to one another but also emphasises the spacing or differance of the body to itself.

Chapter 3 stages the first encounter between Merleau-Ponty and Nancy. While both Merleau-Ponty and Nancy situate the locus of sense-making processes in the body, for Nancy there is a priority of dislocation over unity and integration in both sensing and self-sensing. As a result, Merleau-Ponty remains ultimately more faithful to Descartes, in that he maintains the lived body as a third notion irreducible to either thought or extension, and hence necessitating its own way of being conceived. Nancy's reappropriation of the *partes extra partes*, on the other hand, ends up blurring the distinction between *Leib* and *Körper* in a way that is completely foreign to phenomenological analyses of embodied existence.

The second part of this study takes up this blurring of the distinction between my body and bodies in general more explicitly by turning to a discussion of the status of objects or things. Merleau-Ponty's and Nancy's conversation partners here are more directly a series of contemporary thinkers in the materialist or realist vein who take issue with anthropocentrism and anthropomorphism. Chapter 4 engages with the question of the status of objects or things in the *Phenomenology of Perception*. While even at this stage we can see that things for Merleau-Ponty are not merely correlates of human existence but retain some of their wildness and inhumanity, the issue at stake is the origin or root of this inhumanity. In the *Phenomenology*, it is a natural world whose status remains problematic, finding its place both within experience as correlate of perceptual life and outside of it as ground for all experiences. Again, as in Chapter 1, we are led to see the limitations of Merleau-Ponty's approach in the *Phenomenology*, limitations that will lead him to see the necessity of developing a new ontology, one that recasts traditional ontological dualism in order to account for the birth of sense in 'nature' or Being itself.

Chapter 5 focuses on Merleau-Ponty's engagement with Sartre's essay 'Man and Things' in the years following the publication of the *Phenomenology*. There Merleau-Ponty speaks of things in even stronger anthropomorphic terms than in the *Phenomenology*. Yet by bringing Merleau-Ponty's strategy in conversation with some recent thinkers in the new realist or materialist strand who propose a 'cautious' anthropomorphism as a process of defamiliarisation, we can show how anthropomorphic claims lead Merleau-Ponty toward an account of things that makes more and more room for their inhuman character. This discussion also prepares us to read some of Merleau-Ponty's more enigmatic claims about the flesh in the last chapter of this study.

Before moving to the question of Being more directly, Chapter 6 takes up the question of things now from the Nancean perspective. Because Nancy does not distinguish between the lived body and the bodies of things, we already know what things are from the discussions in Chapters 2 and 3. Things are bodies. Yet to really understand what this means we need to delve into Nancy's claims about the stone: the stone is free, the stone exists, the stone makes sense. In order to provide an interpretation of these claims that is not animistic or panpsychic, I bring Nancy's claims in conversation with recent materialist and realist thinkers in the Continental tradition. This allows us to specify the kind of materialism defended by Nancy and spell out what thinking means for such materialism. Ultimately, Nancy's materialism does not reduce thinking to a purely material process, nor does it attribute thinking or souls to material things. Rather it recasts sense as the 'inorganic' supplement of things, including this thing that thought is. In the end, Nancy, like Merleau-Ponty, undermines anthropocentrism and human exceptionalism in a way that resists both eliminative materialism and panpsychism, but that also resists, maybe more than Merleau-Ponty does, any form of vitalism.

The third part moves to Merleau-Ponty's later carnal ontology and proposes a more direct confrontation between the chiasmatic structure of the flesh and Nancy's understanding of being as differance and spacing. Before staging such a confrontation, however, I trace the influence of Heidegger on Merleau-Ponty's later thinking as well as on Nancy's in order to show how they both undo the metaphysical difference between *existentia* and *essentia* in favour of a thinking of existence or presence that is not pure positivity but includes a moment of negativity that is not the other of presence but its opening.

Chapter 7 takes up the question of the influence of Heidegger's thinking on Nancy and on the late Merleau-Ponty. With regard to the latter, I side with Saint Aubert, who argues that if Heidegger's work resonates with Merleau-Ponty as he develops his carnal ontology, it is because he finds in it something he was already on the way toward even if through a different path, namely a critique of the Cartesian-Sartrian of Being as plenitude and presence. At the same time, I also agree that Merleau-Ponty's appropriation of Heidegger is always mediated by his reading of Husserl and by his search for the opening of sense within the sensible itself so that Merleau-Ponty is not as close to Heidegger as it might appear at first glance. Developing Merleau-Ponty's own understanding of Being, we can see how it appropriates Heidegger's notion of *Wesen* but understands this *Wesen* also as depth and as the *Ineinander* of beings. As a result, Merleau-Ponty can critique Heidegger for proposing a direct ontology and can argue that, on the contrary, all ontology must be essentially indirect or interrogative. Nancy's own reappropriation of the later Heidegger's thinking of Being focuses on Heidegger's understanding of the withdrawal of Being as something that calls for a guarding or sheltering. While for Merleau-Ponty Heidegger would not escape the alternative between presence and absence because he would still try to express Being directly, for Nancy, Heidegger would fail because for him Being withdraws behind presence and as a result is kept in reserve as a kind of super-presence.

In their reading of Heidegger, both Merleau-Ponty and Nancy are looking for an understanding of negativity beyond the dichotomy of presence and absence. Being is neither positive (or determinate) Being, even one that would be withdrawn or hidden behind positive beings, nor is it nothing in the sense of a *nichtiges Nichts*. Both Merleau-Ponty and Nancy are looking for a principle of non-dialectical difference that allows for the emergence of sense within or right at Being itself.[35] In the final chapter of this study I stage a last encounter between Nancy and Merleau-Ponty, focusing now on Merleau-Ponty's understanding of the flesh as chiasm. The question at the heart of this chapter concerns the extent to which the flesh can be considered to be a differential principle. In order to approach this question, I revisit the phenomenon of self-sensing. Focusing on the doubling or chiasm at the heart of our carnal being – which constitutes a 'remarkable variant' or a 'prototype' of Being – I propose a reading of reversibility, mirroring and narcissism that emphasises both the ontological complicity and the non-coincidence of incongruent counterparts. In the end, however, and despite the fact that *écart* as divergence, spread or spacing is essential for sense in both Merleau-Ponty and Nancy, they defend different, if not incompatible, conceptions of this *écart*: as the place of encroachment and promiscuity or as unpassable limit.

Notes

1. An edited transcript of the event was published in the journal *Collapse*.
2. Brassier, 'Postscript', in Wolfendale, *Object-Oriented Philosophy*, 417.
3. The editors of *The Speculative Turn* admit that by the time they were putting together their collected volume in 2010, 'the group ha[d] already begun to break into various fragments'. See Bryant, Srnicek and Harman, 'Towards a Speculative Philosophy', in *The Speculative Turn*, 2. Jon Roffe calls speculative realism a 'Frankenstein's monster' and a 'hydra-headed beast'. See Roffe, 'The Future of an Illusion', *Speculations* IV (2013): 52.
4. Norris, 'Speculative Realism: Interim Report with Just a Few Caveats', *Speculations* IV (2013): 38. See also Bryant et al., 'Towards a Speculative Philosophy', 4.
5. Meillassoux, 'Time without Becoming', lecture given at Middlesex University, London, 8 May 2008.
6. Bryant et al., 'Towards a Speculative Philosophy', 3.
7. Bryant et al., 'Towards a Speculative Philosophy', 3. See also AF, 34 and Brassier, 'Postscript', 415. It should also be noted that Meillassoux is advocating a speculative materialism rather than a speculative realism, because absolute reality is an entity without thought (AF, 36–7).
8. Sparrow, *The End of Phenomenology*, 62. Sparrow never really specifies what distinguishes non-arbitrary from arbitrary ways of disengaging objects from subjects however.
9. Shaviro, *The Universe of Things*, 111.
10. Zahavi, 'The End of What? Phenomenology vs. Speculative Realism', *International Journal of Philosophical Studies* 24, no. 3 (2016): 289–309.
11. Derrida, *Writing and Difference*, 193.
12. While this is the case in *Being and Time*, it might not be true of Heidegger after the turn. We will discuss Heidegger's later works more closely in Chapter 7.
13. See Rorty, *Objectivity, Relativism, and Truth*, 100, 102 and *Truth and Progress*, 220.
14. See among others Davidson, *Inquiries into Truth and Interpretation*; McDowell, *Mind and World*; Putnam, *Reason, Truth and History*.
15. Rorty, *Truth and Progress*, 280.
16. Taylor, 'Merleau-Ponty and the Epistemological Picture', in Carman and Hansen (eds), *The Cambridge Companion to Merleau-Ponty*, 29.
17. See, for example, Husserl, *Cartesian Meditations*, §41.
18. These limits do not mean that consciousness is finite – quite the contrary: death is only an empirical event that befalls consciousness from the outside. See Lawlor, *Husserl and Derrida*, 128. This radical exclusion of death from the life of consciousness is complicated in Husserl's unpublished fragment on the origin of geometry. See Derrida, *Edmund Husserl's 'Origin of Geometry'*.
19. Husserl, *Ideas II*, §45.
20. Husserlian phenomenology is often interpreted as removing from Kant's philosophy the residue of the thing in itself that still plagues the critical project. See Ricoeur, 'Kant and Husserl', in *Husserl: An Analysis of His Phenomenology*, 175–201. It is also possible to argue that it merely clarifies the meaning of the 'reduction' of 'reality' to 'appearances', that is, the meaning of Kant's transcendental project. Against the two-world interpretation, which seems to be the interpretation Meillassoux relies on in his critique of correlationism, there is ample evidence that for Kant the thing in itself is not an elusive thing *beyond or behind* the object given in our experience. Rather it is part of the 'meaning' of phenomena, and hence something given within experience, right at the phenomenon itself. It is something (a 'thought-entity' or *ens rationis* as Kant says) we must necessarily posit in order to be able to make sense of our experience at all.

21. Husserl, *Cartesian Meditations*, §41.
22. Of course, Heidegger will become critical of the way in which he carried out his project in *Being and Time*. By linking the opening of the There to the ecstatic-horizonal temporality of Dasein, we are left with the impression that there is a genuine 'in-itself' and that we can ask about beings 'in-themselves', outside of or apart from their inclusion within the horizons opened up and projected by the ecstatic structure of Dasein's existence. For a clear discussion of the failure of the transcendental approach in light of the later *Contributions to Philosophy*, see Vallega-Neu, *Heidegger's 'Contributions to Philosophy'*, chapter 1.
23. Husserl, 'Philosophy as a Rigorous Science', cited in Derrida, *Husserl's 'Origin'*, 48.
24. Derrida, *Husserl's 'Origin'*, 151–2, n. 184, trans. mod.
25. On speech and silence in relation to the Other, see the critique of Levinas and of empiricism in 'Violence and Metaphysics', in *Writing and Difference*, esp. 155–6.
26. Derrida, *Husserl's 'Origin'*, 152.
27. At the beginning of his long study of the history of Continental anti-realism, Lee Braver provides a definition of realism by outlining the six defining features of the realism matrix and contrasting them with those of the idealist matrix; Braver, *A Thing of This World*, xix. See also 14–19.
28. See Wright, *Realism, Meaning and Truth*, 1–2.
29. The term is used by Braver in 'A Brief History of Continental Realism', *Continental Philosophy Review* 45, no. 2 (2012): 261–89.
30. Following Wright, a slide toward the pole of modesty always leads to scepticism, whereas too much emphasis on presumption ultimately leads to idealism.
31. See the Preface to the Second Edition in *The Normal and the Pathological*, as well as *The Knowledge of Life* and *La formation du concept de réflexe aux XVIIe et XVIIIe siècles*.
32. See 'On Derrida: A Conversation with Sergio Benvenuto', *Journal of European Psychoanalysis* 19, no. 2 (2004): <www.psychomedia.it/jep/number19/benvenuto.htm>. Derrida was the assistant of Paul Ricoeur, who supervised both Nancy's *diplôme* and doctoral theses. It is unclear how much contact Nancy had with Derrida while at the Sorbonne, but they knew each other's works from afar before becoming closer collaborators and friends in the early 1970s. See Derrida's letter to Nancy from 22 April 1969 in Peeters, *Derrida: A Biography*, 216.
33. See also Nancy in Peeters, *Derrida*, 217.
34. See Peeters, *Derrida*, 128.
35. 'Right at' translates the expression '*à même*', which is frequent in Nancy's work. While the phrase is sometimes also translated as 'just in' or 'within', such a translation might mislead one into thinking that one has to do with an immanent totality within which sense is made, losing the emphasis on the idea of opening, difference or self-differentiation. The translator of *The Sense of the World* opts for 'along the edge of', which can also be misleading insofar as it gives the impression that the in-itself, along the edge of which sense is made, is a totality with only one edge. See, for example, SW, 62 and also CW, 7.

Part I
BODY

We start our study of Merleau-Ponty and Nancy in the context of the new realist challenge with a discussion of the body because it is embodied existence that, for both, undoes the Cartesian presuppositions that are still at work in the appeal to materialism or realism.

Meillassoux's framework is emblematic in its Cartesianism insofar as it reaffirms the divide between thought and object. To be more precise, the divide that interests Meillassoux is not so much that between mind and body, *res cogitans* and *res extensa* – even if he also reaffirms that divide in separating the worlds of matter, life and thought – but rather that between the realm of everyday confused experience and the realm of science. This is clearest in Meillassoux's call, at the beginning of *After Finitude*, for a rehabilitation of the distinction between primary and secondary qualities, between those properties that belong to the subject-object relation and those that belong to the object itself independently of the subject (see AF, 11–13). The call to get to the great outdoors is a call to get to Cartesian nature and its primary qualities. Meillassoux seeks to rehabilitate the '*glacial* world' of Descartes that made possible the Galilean and Corpernican revolutions, that is, mathematised science (see AF, 115–16). This world is indifferent of human beings' concerns and is stripped of all its concrete properties. It is the opposite of the phenomenological life-world that remains, for Husserl, the foundation of all our scientific truths.

What is missing from Meillassoux's defence of a Cartesian in-itself is an engagement with the Sixth Meditation, the one where Descartes returns to everyday experience and its life-world and asserts the substantial union of what had been previously separated, soul and body. Turning to the lived body – or to remain within the Cartesian framework for now, to the substantial union of the soul and the body – is the first step toward a displacement both of what counts as 'real' and of how our everyday lived experience is conceived. The opposition between the world as it is in itself and the world as it is experienced, between realism and correlationism, is predicated on the difference between the *res cogitans* and the human being as lived body or as union of soul and body. Taking this strange 'object' that is the lived body as our starting point for ontology, then, shakes up the Cartesian framework that is still at work in the call toward a realist turn in Continental philosophy.

Chapter 1 develops Merleau-Ponty's description of the unreflected life of the body as it appears in the *Phenomenology of Perception*. My engagement with the descriptions of embodied life, and specifically of the sensing and self-sensing body, is embedded in the broader question of the relation between reflection and the unreflected as it arises in the context of Merleau-Ponty's engagement with Descartes. While Merleau-Ponty seeks to integrate the teachings of the union of the soul and the body within a new philosophy rather than relegating them to the realm of everyday life, he will come to see the limitation of the reflective, phenomenological method in accomplishing this task. This will lead Merleau-Ponty to reject the tacit cogito of the *Phenomenology* and propose, in his last lecture course, a new reading of the cogito as operative cogito.

Chapter 2 turns to Nancy's own reading of Descartes in *Ego Sum*. Undoubtedly, Nancy's engagement with Descartes is less developed than Merleau-Ponty's, yet there are a few enlightening parallels, especially concerning the relation between the meditator's doubt, the discovery or utterance of '*ego sum*', and the union of the soul and the body. Nancy proposes a reading of the cogito, or rather of '*ego sum*', that allows us to understand the double movement of existence as withdrawal and exposure. Since it is not a substance but a body that opens itself and utters 'ego', Nancy's reading of Descartes allows us to develop his notion of the body not as a mass but as a differance.

After having discussed both Merleau-Ponty's and Nancy's notion of embodied existence, I stage, in Chapter 3, a more explicit dialogue between their respective conceptions of embodied existence. Again, the focus is on the role of sensing and self-sensing in the 'constitution' of the body and its relation to the world. Despite the proximity between the two thinkers, I show that Nancy reverses the Merleau-Pontian priority of unity over dislocation, which is also the priority of interiority over exteriority or of the moment of reappropriation and integration over the moment of alienation and separation. While the difference from Merleau-Ponty is quite subtle and can be seen as a slight shift in emphasis rather than a complete opposition, it does have at least one wide-ranging consequence, which we turn to in the next part of this study, namely, the impossibility for Nancy of maintaining the phenomenological distinction between my own body as it is experienced from the first-person perspective and other extended bodies.

Chapter 1

Merleau-Ponty, Descartes and the Unreflected Life of the Body

Many commentators position Merleau-Ponty's philosophy in stark opposition to Descartes and speak of Merleau-Ponty's fundamental discovery of the lived body as a 'victory over Cartesianism'.[1] While this affirmation is not completely false, some commentators also acknowledge that Descartes is not merely Merleau-Ponty's adversary. Sara Heinämaa, for example, claims that Merleau-Ponty finds in Descartes 'a fruitful discussion on the mind-body compound'.[2] Indeed, by describing the union of the soul and the body as a third notion irreducible to both extension and thought, one that necessitates its own, distinct way of being conceived, Descartes also provides Merleau-Ponty with some of the tools necessary to overcome Cartesian dualism. Saint Aubert also qualifies Merleau-Ponty's relation to Descartes as ambivalent and shows how Merleau-Ponty finds his own premises in what he calls the 'Cartesian tremor [*le tremblement cartésien*]' (SC, 21, 38). Descartes, then, plays a double role throughout Merleau-Ponty's thinking: he is both the thinker who is criticised for his 'ontology of the object' and the one who provides the tools to overcome this same ontology. What we find in Merleau-Ponty then is never a straightforward rejection of Descartes's thinking, but rather a criticism of the Cartesian – i.e. dualistic – premises that are still at work in our thinking today.

Merleau-Ponty's ambivalence toward Descartes's philosophy is explicit, for example, in his criticism of vision as the 'thought of seeing' against which he will develop, with the help of Gestalt psychology, his own phenomenology of perception. While Descartes's *Dioptrics* remains an important text for Merleau-Ponty,[3] we would be wrong to consider that the Cartesian theory of perception is merely a *historical* curiosity for Merleau-Ponty. Early on, Merleau-Ponty denounces 'the pseudo-Cartesianism of scientists and psychologists [who] consider perception and its proper objects as "internal" or "mental phenomena", as functions of certain physiological and mental variables'.[4] Furthermore, it is not as if vision in act was completely absent from Descartes's philosophy. But as with the union of the soul and the body, vision in act is an enigma that doesn't trouble Descartes's philosophy because it belongs to everyday life and not to philosophy. It cannot be conceived; it can only be exercised or practised (see PoP, 176).

Descartes also figures prominently in the 1956–7 and 1957–8 lecture courses on nature. The point of departure of Merleau-Ponty's study of nature in these lectures is the Cartesian idea of nature, that is, nature as extension, as essence revealed by the understanding. This study then leads to the rediscovery of nature as 'an enigmatic object, an object that is not an object at all; it is not really set out in front of us. It is our soil [*sol*] – not what is in front of us, facing us, but rather, that which carries us' (N, 4). But again, Merleau-Ponty underlines Descartes's hesitation in relation to the human being as a soul-body composite, which does not fit within his conception of nature as extension. While Descartes does encounter in the lived body a phenomenon that should lead him to question his ontology, he chooses to reject this experience outside of the realm of philosophy instead (see N, 19–20). Despite the fact that the 'experience of existence is irreducible to the view of it in pure understanding', this experience ultimately 'cannot teach us anything which might be contrary to understanding' (TFL, 70).

For Merleau-Ponty, the interesting question is whether the reversal from the perspective of nature as extension to that of the lived body – which is also the reversal from natural light to natural inclination – that occurs between the first five and the last of Descartes's *Meditations* compromises the unity of philosophy or not. If it does, then the question is whether it is possible to integrate the teachings of natural inclination within a new philosophy rather than rejecting them to the obscurity of everyday life. Ultimately, this question is that of the relation between reflection and the unreflected, which already preoccupies Merleau-Ponty in the *Phenomenology of Perception*, but becomes more and more important after the 1946 presentation at the Société française de philosophie published under the title 'The Primacy of Perception and Its Philosophical Consequences'. In order to show how Merleau-Ponty comes to see the limitation of the phenomenological approach to reflection in its relation to the unreflected, I first present Merleau-Ponty's circular reading of Descartes's meditation and then review his description of embodied life in the *Phenomenology*. We will then be in a position to turn to the issues raised against Merleau-Ponty's approach in the discussion that followed the 1946 presentation and show how they ultimately led Merleau-Ponty to a more Nancean understanding of the cogito.

1. Reading Descartes: The relation between reflection and the unreflected

The best way to highlight the originality of Merleau-Ponty's reading of Descartes is to place it side by side with Martial Gueroult's influential *Descartes' Philosophy Interpreted According to the Order of Reasons*. Gueroult's two-volume study of Descartes was published in 1953, so not only after the *Phenomenology* and 'The Primacy of Perception', but also after the 1946–7 course on the union of the soul and the body, and so did not exert any direct influence on the development of Merleau-Ponty's reading. Still Merleau-Ponty read Gueroult's work with interest.[5] The critiques he raises against Gueroult's reading underline what is at stake for Merleau-Ponty, namely, the relation between reflection and the unreflected.

In *Descartes' Philosophy Interpreted According to the Order of Reasons*, Gueroult famously defends the coherence of Descartes's project: his rationalism, even if not absolute, remains rigorous.[6] Reconstructing the argument of the *Meditations* according to the order of reasons means presenting it as 'an orderly linkage of truths' that goes from the most simple to the most complex.[7] But as Gueroult undertakes this project, he is forced to recognise various 'schisms' or 'breaks' within this linkage so that what we expected to be a unilinear linkage resolves itself into a *nexus rationum*, a node of reasons. The multiplications of the chains give rise to intersections or crisscrossings, to intersections of intersections, to quadruple and six-fold nexuses. Yet, despite this growing complexity, the nexus remains, on Gueroult's reading, 'single and unified'.[8]

Merleau-Ponty remains ultimately unconvinced by Gueroult's argument in favour of Descartes's rigorous rationalism. In the second course on the concept of Nature, Merleau-Ponty borrows from Maurice Blondel the idea of an ontological diplopy to speak of the alternation between natural light and natural inclination, between an ontology of the object and an ontology of the existent (TFL, 89; see N, 125–31). Merleau-Ponty then describes his own project using the analogy of the two monocular images of which binocular vision takes possession in depth perception. Speaking of the oscillation between positivism and negativism, between naturalism and humanism, between the truth of being and the truth of appearances, Merleau-Ponty writes in the summary of the lecture course:

> The back and forth of philosophies from one perspective to the other would not involve any contradiction, in the sense of inadvertence or incoherence, but would be justified and founded in being. All one could do is to ask the philosopher to admit this phenomenon and think it, rather than merely

suffering it and occupying alternatively two ontological positions, each of which excludes and invites the other. (TFL, 90, trans. mod.)

The problem with Descartes is that he undergoes this oscillation without being able to affirm it as the truth of ontology.[9]

What interests Merleau-Ponty, then, contrary to Gueroult, is not rebuilding the Cartesian system 'according to the order of reasons' but taking up the tensions within this system productively, playing up its 'discordant unity' in order to find a new ontological beginning (see SC, 21). The greatness of Descartes, for Merleau-Ponty, is that we find in his work 'not only a philosophy of understanding for the understanding' but a philosophy

> that encompasses, besides the sphere of truths of the understanding, the obscure sphere of unreflected existence. This philosophy does not deem false everything that is only doubtful, does not impose upon our affirmation about being the critical conditions that enclose us definitively in the being-posited [*l'être-posé*]. It collects every testimony about being prior to the one given by the understanding.[10]

The greatness of Descartes, then, is that he carves out a space for natural inclination and its teachings, and acknowledges the specific kind of evidence or clarity found within it.

For Descartes the confusion at work in our experience of the union of the soul and the body is not attributed to the weakness of our understanding. It is an essential or substantial confusion attributed to the mixture between two substances. For Descartes, then, this confusion has its own clarity, a clarity that is obfuscated by any method that seeks to purify or analyse. The analytic method, which disentangles what is substantially united in the union, Merleau-Ponty states, 'renders unintelligible' (VI, 268).[11] While this analytic method is found in Descartes, it is not the only one according to Merleau-Ponty:

> The experience of one's own body, then, is opposed to the reflective movement that disentangles the object from the subject and the subject from the object, and that only gives us thought about the body or the body as an idea, and not the experience of the body or the body in reality. Descartes was well aware of this, for in a famous letter to Elizabeth he distinguishes between the body as it is conceived through its use in life and the body as it is conceived by the understanding. (PP, 205)

Despite this recognition, the status of the non-distinct clarity of what is confused always remains problematic in Descartes's philosophy.

Here, Merleau-Ponty is again positioning himself against Gueroult, who does not see any contradiction in claiming that we obtain clear knowledge of the nature of the sensible *as obscure and confused*. Rather than accepting this priority of knowledge by means of ideas over factical or living knowledge, Merleau-Ponty emphasises the contradiction that consists in 'guarantee[ing] this living knowledge or "natural inclination" that teaches us the union of the soul and the body . . . through the divine truth that is nothing other than the intrinsic clarity of the idea'. Merleau-Ponty continues: 'perhaps Descartes's philosophy consists in taking up this contradiction' (PP, 44). The tension between Descartes's philosophy of the understanding (natural light) and his 'philosophy of existence' (natural inclination), between reflection and the unreflected, forms the core of Descartes's thought, according to Merleau-Ponty. While on Gueroult's reading the understanding dissolves the unreflected into reflection, on Merleau-Ponty's, 'when Descartes says that the understanding knows itself to be incapable of knowing the union of the soul and the body, leaving the task of knowing this union to life, this signifies that the act of understanding is given as a reflection upon an unreflected that it absorbs neither in fact nor in principle' (PP, 44).

It is the resistance of the unreflected to reflection, a resistance that appears, however, only to reflection, that Merleau-Ponty will underline by proposing a reading of Descartes that seeks to integrate unreflected and reflective life, the union of the Sixth Meditation and the cogito of the Second Meditation, by proposing a circular reading of the *Meditations* that is not unlike the one we will find in Nancy. In this circular reading of the *Meditations*, the experience of the union of the soul and the body is not relegated to unreflected life but finds its place within reflection as the ground from which reflection arises and upon which it rests.[12] This is why Merleau-Ponty will insist on the facticity of reflection rather than on the discovery of the thinking thing, a discovery that remains incapable of explaining why I sense and perceive in the first place.

Merleau-Ponty's puzzle is that of the beginning: why does the meditator begin to meditate? In his lecture course on the union of the soul and the body in 1947–8, Merleau-Ponty explains this puzzle in the following way:

> If we take the methods of the First Meditation seriously, are we not led to consider the Sixth as an aberration? And conversely, if we take the Sixth Meditation seriously, how were the methods of the First possible? . . . If the union of the soul and the body is a confused thought, how was I able to discover the Cogito? And if I discovered the Cogito, how can I be the unreflective subject of the Sixth Meditation?[13]

The answer lies in the relation of interdependence between reflection and the domain of the unreflected, from which reflection itself emerges.

Merleau-Ponty, like Nancy, sees the union of the Sixth Meditation, not as the last step in the reconstruction of the edifice of knowledge, but as the experience that underlies meditation and doubt, and to which the meditator returns, in order to live and dwell in it, after he has explored it methodically. There is something before and after the 'series of reasons', and this something is called 'existence'. This is why Merleau-Ponty will say, in his 1960–1 lecture course, that for Descartes 'there is a truth of the false and a falsity of the true'. There is a truth to what is an illusion from the point of view of the understanding, hence, the necessity to study pre- and post-methodic experience, and not only the 'acquired thoughts' of the *Meditations* (VI, 273–4).

In the *Phenomenology*, Merleau-Ponty had already explained this relation between meditation and pre- or post-meditative experience as follows:

> Reflection is not absolutely transparent for itself, it is always given to itself in an *experience* . . . it always springs forth without itself knowing from whence it springs. . . . But if the description of the unreflected [*l'irréfléchi*] remains valid after reflection, and if the 'Sixth Meditation' remains valid after the 'Second Meditation,' then, reciprocally, we know this unreflected itself only through reflection and it must not be placed outside of reflection like an unknowable term. Between myself, who is analyzing perception, and the self who is actually perceiving, there is always a distance. But in the concrete act of reflection, I cross this distance; I prove, by doing it, that I am capable of *knowing* what I was *perceiving*; I overcome [*je domine*, 'I overlook'] in practice the discontinuity of these two I's; and, in the end, the *cogito* would have the sense not of revealing a universal constituting power or of reducing perception to intellection, but rather of observing this *fact* of reflection that simultaneously overcomes [or overlooks] and maintains the opacity of perception. (PP, 45)

This dense passage gives us an insight into Merleau-Ponty's own method, which he calls radical reflection in contrast to the 'intellectualist' philosophies of reflection, including Husserl's phenomenological-transcendental reduction. As Merleau-Ponty explains in the *Phenomenology*, 'For intellectualism, reflection involves putting sensation at a distance or objectifying it and causing an empty subject to appear across from sensation who can survey [*parcourir*] this multiplicity and for whom it can exist' (PP, 250; see also VI, 44).

Transcendental phenomenology, according to Merleau-Ponty, is always at risk of turning into such a philosophy of reflection. After having traced the world that is supposed to contain consciousness as an object of psychological study back to the perceived world (world as intentional correlate) and then realised that consciousness is co-extensive to the world (discovery of the transcendental field), transcendental phenomenology reduces perceptual consciousness to intellection and turns perception into the active constitution of the meaning of the perceived. Transcendental philosophy discovers in reflection a transcendental ego, which it posits as having always already been there, doing its constitutive work behind the back of empirical consciousness. Transcendental philosophy, as Merleau-Ponty says in the *Phenomenology*, finds truth in the 'inner man', *l'homme intérieur*. But for Merleau-Ponty, 'there is no "inner man," man is in and toward the world, and it is in the world that he knows himself. When I return to myself from the dogmatism of common sense or of science, I do not find a source of intrinsic truth, but rather a subject destined to the world' (PP, lxxiii).

It is in order to immunise himself against such intellectualist or idealistic interpretations of the phenomenological-transcendental reduction that Merleau-Ponty will radicalise reflection. If Merleau-Ponty calls his reflection radical, it is not because it would be complete in the sense of succeeding in dissolving the unreflected into reflection. On the contrary, that kind of 'absolute' reflection never reaches the kind of completion it claims to achieve because it necessarily ignores the facticity of its own beginning in the unreflected. Transcendental reflection thinks it can reduce fact to essence and incorporate its own beginning within itself without remainder to reach a transcendental sphere purified of the mundane. But in doing so, reflection forgets *itself* as fact. It forgets that there is always a delay between the unreflected (the already-there) and reflection, or between being and meaning, between the facticity of silent experience and the philosophical speech that articulates its latent meaning. By seeking to ground itself only in itself and be the condition of its own possibility, reflection thinks its possibility has always been given in advance and forgets its *real* origin, or dismisses it as irrelevant.

What a radical reflection uncovers is the dependency of reflection on the unreflected: 'Reflection is only truly reflection if it does not carry itself outside of itself, if it knows itself as *reflection-upon-an-unreflected*, and consequently as a change in the structure of our existence' (PP, 63). This is what Merleau-Ponty meant in the passage above when he said that I overlook or survey '*in practice*' the discontinuity of the two 'I's, the I that lives straightforwardly in the world and the I that reflects and knows itself as the one who perceives this or that, or the union of the Sixth Meditation and the cogito of the Second Meditation. Because reflection is a factical experience, it can hold together both the unreflected and reflection; it guarantees that reflection is not intellectualist or idealist thought, a *pensée de survol* detached from its roots in the factical life-world, but rather a reflection *of* the unreflected.

If reflection is to be possible, the unreflected must already be opened to knowledge. If reflection is to be a fact, it cannot give rise to an instance or power that is completely detached from factical life. This is why Merleau-Ponty will famously claim that 'the most important lesson of the reduction is the impossibility of a complete reduction' (PP, lxxvii). The reduction does not teach us that the natural attitude is an illusion and that only a thinking purified of the mundane is true. Rather it allows us to see the natural attitude, our unreflected life, as such. Rather than speaking of the reduction as a withdrawal from the world that leads us back (*re-ducere*) to its ground in transcendental consciousness, Merleau-Ponty will famously use the image of loosening the thread that attaches us to the life-world. The phenomenological reduction is not for Merleau-Ponty 'the formula for an idealist philosophy' but 'the formula for an existential philosophy', that is, a philosophy that is nothing but the 'ever-renewed experience of its own beginning' in the unreflected and the description of that experience (PP, lxxviii, trans. mod.). As we will see, Merleau-Ponty will come to realise the shortcomings of his understanding of radical reflection after the *Phenomenology of Perception*, which will lead him to return to Descartes. But for now, let us turn to the description of the unreflected life of the body as it is presented in the *Phenomenology*.

2. Sensing and self-sensing body of the *Phenomenology of Perception*

In the *Phenomenology of Perception*, Merleau-Ponty seeks to criticise objective thought without falling back into transcendental phenomenology. By the end of *The Structure of Behaviour*, we had learn to study behaviour not as a fact to be measured, observed and recorded but as a meaning to be deciphered. A form or a Gestalt is a totality whose properties are not the sum of those which its isolated parts would possess; it is a set of relations that has a meaning that is not explainable by the mere combination of its parts. How does the Gestalt as meaning arise? From the organism itself. Merleau-Ponty's study of behaviour is a direct critique of naturalism and scienticism, of nature understood as parts external to one another entering in purely linear causal relations with each other. But it can easily lead to the opposite misunderstanding: if a Gestalt is a structure that has meaning, then it requires a consciousness to exist. The danger would be to find the source of meaning in a transcendental consciousness that constitutes its sense. Gestalt psychology would lead directly to Husserlian phenomenology. What Merleau-Ponty needs to show if he is to avoid the trap of transcendental phenomenology is that the 'consciousness' that enters into meaningful relation with the world is not a constituting consciousness: it is not a detached spectator, fully in possession of itself.

Hence the *Phenomenology of Perception* undertakes a criticism of both sides of what Merleau-Ponty calls objective thought. For objective thought, the world is already finished, it is extended parts outside parts. The consciousness that encounters this world, if it cannot be merely another part of this world (that would be transcendental realism), can only be an interior wholly transparent to itself. There is an essential complicity between what Merleau-Ponty calls empiricism (for which everything is an object and every event in the world can be explained through causal interaction between material things) and intellectualism (for which the world is a meaningless in-itself, and meaning is constituted by a consciousness that is not of the world, that surveys the world and that is fully transparent to itself). Both necessarily miss the lived body, which will be the focus of the first part of the *Phenomenology*, and because they miss the way of being of this body, they are unable to explain our primordial, pre-reflective, pre-predicative being in the world: perception, sensing, but also habit, all the compartments that are studied in the second part of the *Phenomenology*. By studying the peculiar ways in which the lived body shows up in experience, we will be led to discover an ambiguous being which undermines the categories of object and subject used to describe it.

How then is the body that I call my own experienced? In the *Cartesian Meditations*, Husserl already points out the way in which my 'animate organism' (*Leib*) is 'uniquely singled out' in my own experience: my lived body is the only experienced object to which I ascribe fields of sensations, in which I rule and govern immediately, and which is reflexively related to itself.[14] Merleau-Ponty finds in traditional psychology a similar list of characteristics used to distinguish the lived body from other objects: the lived body is a permanent feature of experience, is affected from the inside, has kinaesthetic sensations, and can reflexively relate to itself in double sensations. Looking at these phenomena, Merleau-Ponty will show how they undermine the Cartesian ontological categories of object and subject used to explain them.

The phenomenon that interests us particularly here is that of double sensations. It is worth noting that the experience of self-touch plays a minimal role in the *Phenomenology*. It is mentioned briefly in a discussion of the psychologist's interpretation of the kind of permanence attributed to my own body, which is for Merleau-Ponty of a radically different order from that of permanent objects: 'To say that my body is always near to me or always there for me is to say that it is never truly in front of me, that I cannot spread it out under my gaze, that it remains on the margins of all of my perceptions, and that it is with me' (PP, 93). I cannot observe my lived body. When I see my eyes in the mirror, I see 'the eyes of someone who is observing' and can 'barely catch a glimpse of my living gaze' (PP, 94).

The same happens when my left hand touches my right hand while it is palpating an object:

> The right hand, as an object, is not the right hand that does the touching. The first is an intersecting of bones, muscles, and flesh compressed into a point of space; the second shoots across space to reveal the external object in its place. Insofar as it sees or touches the world, my body can neither be seen nor touched. What prevents it from ever being an object or from ever being 'completely constituted' is that my body is that by which there are objects. It is neither tangible nor visible insofar as it is what sees and touches. (PP, 94)[15]

Turning then to the classical psychologist's use of double sensations to distinguish my own body from other objects in the world, Merleau-Ponty again shows how the psychologist focuses on the right phenomenon but misinterprets it because insofar as she is a scientist, she assumes that what she studies is an object for her. She takes herself as lived body out of the equation, and even if she were to turn her investigating gaze back on to herself, she would only encounter herself as object. As a result, the characteristics of this strange object that is my body are only '*contents* of consciousness that make up our representation of the body' (PP, 98). They do not alter the ontological status of the body as an object like any other.

Indeed, while it was said in the passage above that the right hand touched is an object, in appealing to double sensations the psychologist should recognise that this is not quite true. Even though it is never simultaneously touched and touching, the hand can 'alternate' between the functions of 'touching' and 'being-touched' and in this passage can recognise the object touched (the hand as 'package of bones and muscles') as the same living hand that is actively involved in exploration. When I touch my right hand with my left hand, the right hand 'also has this strange property, itself, of sensing' (PP, 95). When my body attempts to touch itself touching, it sketches, as Husserl says, 'a sort of reflection'.[16]

In self-touching, we have to distinguish between two different phenomena: reversibility and doubling. Reversibility is a characteristic of all touching. Touching a table, for example, means being-touched by the table. In Husserl, this reversibility is described as a modification in the 'direction of attention'.[17] Husserl also emphasises the fact that the touched sensations that are the reverse side of the touching activity are always localised in some part of my lived body. This will turn out to be important for the experience of self-touching. What the reversibility of touching teaches me is that I am only able to touch something because I can also be touched. The touching, sensing body is *of* the thing it is trying to grasp or make sense of. Here we have an ambiguous being, one that is passive in its activity (touched when it palpates) and active in its passivity (actively feeling what it undergoes). We will return to this phenomenon of reversibility in the last chapter of this study since it forms the core of Merleau-Ponty's later ontology. Anticipating one of Merleau-Ponty's more radical departures from Husserl's analysis of the phenomenon of reversibility, we can already point out that Merleau-Ponty will want to apply the same reversibility found in the experience of touch to vision. Husserl for his part is clear that 'What I call the seen Body is not something seeing which is seen, the way my Body as touched Body is something touching which is touched'.[18] The eye in the mirror does not see but the touched hand touches. Hence for Husserl the sense of touch is essential to the original constitution of my lived body in a way that vision cannot be, whereas for Merleau-Ponty the reversibility of vision will mean that vision is also made from within the visible world. If this weren't the case, there would be no depth perception since there is depth only for a perceiver who is situated with regard to what she is trying to perceive.

Let us now turn to the second moment in the phenomenon of self-touching: the doubling of reversibility. Imagine that you can touch things but not touch your 'touching instrument' as it is palpating things. If this were the case, some layer of the constitution of your lived body would be missing. When I touch my left hand while it is itself palpating an object, I am confronted with my own exteriority as *my own*. Here we have a sort of reflection as the appropriation of what shows up as other or as exterior (my left hand is other than, exterior to, my right hand) as my own (but the left hand is also me because it feels from within what the right hand explores from without). It is because my body is experienced from the inside and from the outside at the same time that it is a lived body, a *Leib*, and not just a *Körper*. This experience of self-touching, then, does not just add a new property to the physical thing I touch – it's smooth, it's cold – but rather turns it into a *Leib*.[19] In and through my right hand I sense the external thing at the same time as I sense this right hand itself: I experience both the objective features of the thing (it is smooth, it has this shape) and the subjective features of my own hand (it moves, it feels pressure). This is reversibility.

We have doubled sensations in each part of the lived body, in the right and the left hands, so that each part is itself *leiblich*. For Husserl, as well as for Merleau-Ponty, double sensations effect the synthesis of the internal and external perspective on my own body and produce a kind of proto-reflection. It is not just that the body can alternate between subject and object, but that it can (almost) experience itself as subject. The question is how this self-reflection happens. Even though Husserl is describing the primordial constitution of my lived body in experience, he also posits the primacy of the transcendental ego as what constitutes the lived body and hence guarantees the synthesis of the two sides of the experience into the constituted object: 'my body'. Merleau-Ponty on the other hand is trying to describe the experience of my lived body without appealing to a transcendental or constituting power. He is looking at the birth of 'self-consciousness' in that experience of bodily reflexivity, a reflexivity that is strictly impersonal since it is prior to the constitution of the personal ego and of language. As we will see, Merleau-Ponty will appeal to a tacit cogito, the role of which will be to ensure that I am not a thing (since I am not wholly unaware of myself) and hence that I am still able to say 'I', even though I am never wholly transparent to myself.

The first part of the *Phenomenology* is about my experience of my lived body – how I 'have' or 'hold' this body. Merleau-Ponty starts the second part by asserting that 'The theory of the body schema is implicitly a theory of perception' (PP, 213). It is the body described in the first part of the book who engages in the world, who perceives, senses and 'knows' in habit. The focus of the second part of the book, then, is on the relations between the lived body and the world, that is, on the anonymous level of experience underneath the conscious experience of an ego, where an 'I' intends or aims at an object. The phenomena described here also allow us to clarify the way in which I hold my body in these pre-reflective comportments and will help us address the issue of the unity of the body through the body schema, an issue we will return to when we turn to the comparison with Nancy.

In the first part of the *Phenomenology*, Merleau-Ponty has already shown how the lived body is an ambiguous being, always passive in its activity and active in its passivity. The same ambiguity will pervade the body's relation to the world. At the level of our embodied existence, body and object are engaged in a 'dialogue' (PP, 134) or a dialectical process of solicitation and response (PP, 222). The sensible world solicits or motivates my movement and a certain tacit decision with regard to that solicitation then opens up a visual field. The perceived responds to my exploration, which is itself but a response to its solicitation, a gearing of my body into the world. Here is how Merleau-Ponty phrases this relation:

> Without the exploration of my gaze or my hand, and prior to my body synchronizing with it, the sensible is nothing but a vague solicitation. . . . Thus, a sensible that is about to be sensed poses to my body a sort of confused problem. I must find the attitude that will provide it with the means to become determinate and to become blue; I must find the response to a poorly formulated question. And yet, I only do this in response to its solicitation. My attitude is never sufficient to make me truly see blue or truly touch a hard surface. The sensible gives back to me what I had lent to it, but I received it from the sensible in the first place. (PP, 222)

No sensing without a sense that presents itself, but no sense presents itself without my engagement with and my gearing into it. This is the meaning of the expression *co-naître*: coming to presence together in a relation of co-determination. This also means that it is not possible to say which side acts and which suffers, which gives sense and which receives it. This co-determination Merleau-Ponty will infamously name 'communion' (PP, 221). The carnal exchange between my body – or more precisely what Merleau-Ponty will call the body schema – and the world does not annul the distance or difference between them. My carnal existence lives with and from the sensible; it does not possess or assimilate it. But there is a certain resonance or vibration that propagates itself between them.

In the *Phenomenology*, the body schema is responsible for both the specific unity of the human body and the way in which my body is implicated in the world. It is the integration of the body schema that allows for coherent relations with the world and the other, while the relations to the world and to the other also allow for the unceasing restructuration and enrichment of the body schema. The body schema then is not an image or sketch of the objective body but the way in which my body (my body and all its appendages: cane, feather of the hat, and so on) is at my disposal in movement as an articulated whole. It is the kind of awareness I have of my lived body in praxis, which is not a thetic consciousness of my physical body as assemblage of parts but the way in which the world is able to attract and polarise my whole body by inscribing in it durable powers – what Merleau-Ponty will later call pivots or hinges.

The kind of integration found in the body schema explains phenomena of substitutions: the ant substituting another leg for the cut-off one, for example (PP, 80), or the generality of habits: the organist adapting to a new instrument (PP, 146). This is because the body schema is not the synthesis of my body parts in objective space but a system of equivalences (PP, 142). The body schema is the way I install myself in the world by installing it in me. Through habituation, I can integrate things in my body schema so that they become, like the blind person's cane, a quasi-organ. I can also develop new ways of moving or responding to the world that will become part of my general style and will be readily transposable to similar but non-identical situations. This system of equivalence also explains the intra- and intersensorial cohesion of my experience of my own body: the passage within one sense between its active and passive side (PP, 153) as well as the passage between the senses and between sensation and motion (PP, 243–4). The body schema is a coherent system in which the senses can respond to each other.[20]

The unity of the body found in sensorial and habitual life is a unity of envelopment or implication, similar to that of a work of art (PP, 153). The body is a 'knot of living significations'; what unifies this 'knot' is not an intelligible idea but the fact that it is involved in one 'single gesture' (PP, 153). Later, in the Nature lectures, Merleau-Ponty will appeal to the metaphor of the melody to describe the unity of the organism.[21] Here again, Merleau-Ponty is trying to move past a mechanistic understanding of the organism as *partes extra partes* without falling into a vitalism or teleology that appeals to a transcendental or metaphysical principle to guide the development of the organism from without, so to speak.[22] For Merleau-Ponty, the organism is rather a macroscopic 'envelop-phenomenon' (or envelopment-phenomenon, *phénomène-enveloppe*) whose unity or unification is similar to that of a musical theme or a style (see N, 183; see also PP, 100–1). The organism is a structured whole whose totality is everywhere and nowhere and whose unity is not to be sought behind its parts but rather *between* them (N, 213). The parts of the organism are neither exterior nor interior to one another but reciprocally resound with one another. As a result, there is a certain cohesion of the whole, but it is 'without concept' (VI, 152).

At the end of the analysis of the body in Part 1 of the *Phenomenology*, Merleau-Ponty draws the conclusion of his discussion of the experience of one's own body in terms of the Cartesian tradition. Contrary to this tradition, which 'purifies simultaneously the common notions of body and of soul by defining the body as a sum of parts without an interior and the soul as a being directly and fully present to itself', establishing 'a clarity within us and outside of us', the experience of one's own body 'reveals to us an ambiguous mode of existence' whose 'unity is always implicit and confused' (PP, 204–5). While Merleau-Ponty will always remain critical of a certain Cartesian dualism and what he calls the ontology of the object, he nevertheless seeks to integrate both the truth of the union and the truth of dualism in his description of embodied experience. As we explained earlier, the assumption is that while the truth of the union is, in some way, the truth of our embodied pre-reflective life, it is no less the case that doubt, reflection and dualism likewise find their impulse in this embodied life and must hence be explained on that basis.

This can be done if we take seriously Descartes's rejection of the metaphor of the pilot in the ship so that we do not understand the union as a composite of a thinking substance and an extended substance. As Sara Heinämaa rightly points out: 'body as part of the union should not be confused with body as the extended substance; and the same holds for the soul: as part of the union it is not merely the principle of thinking.'[23] The duality of the union should not be confused with the ontological dualism between thought and extension, or between subject and object. It makes no sense to ask how an intellect can move a piece of extended matter;

such a question is based on an equivocation between the body thought of from the third-person perspective (piece of extended matter obeying causal laws) and the body as it is lived in sensible experience.[24]

Rather, the relation between body and soul must be understood on the model of expression, provided we don't understand expression as the accidental conjunction of a thing and a sense, a word and a meaning. The movement of existence that accomplishes the union is similar to the movement of expression that accomplishes sense (PP, 91). The means of expression are not added to a fully formed sense after the fact as a simple way of carrying it outside, but contribute to shaping the sense itself. This means that a sense is only fully itself in its manifestation or expression. When the union between soul and body is understood along these lines, then it means that the terms of the union can never be completely separated without each ceasing to be what it is, in the same way that a joy that lacks the means of expressing itself withers away without ever really crystallising as joy, while jumping and laughing without joy are merely empty, senseless gestures.[25] The thought that, because of tiredness, illness or timidity, for example, cannot express itself, that is, the thought that experiences the resistance of the body, never reaches itself as clear thought. On the other hand, the body which, 'by a play of mechanisms which its past life has built up', 'limits itself to mimicking intentions which it *does not have any longer*'[26] – as does, for example, the hand of Proust's dying grandmother, which keeps thrusting the blankets aside, still performing personal gestures, even though personality itself is disintegrating – is no longer fully a body. If the relation of expression allows us to overcome *ontological* dualism and prevents us from positing the results of analysis as the explanation of unreflected experience, it also explains the duality of union, and the origin of the distinctions of its components: the tired, sick body resists expression, the intention does not succeed in expressing itself, or the body moves itself without intention or sense. 'In these cases of disintegration', Merleau-Ponty writes, 'the soul and the body are apparently distinct; and this is the truth of dualism.'[27]

3. The problem of the *Phenomenology of Perception*: Tacit versus operative cogito

In 1946, shortly after the publication of the *Phenomenology of Perception*, Merleau-Ponty was invited to give a presentation at the Société française de philosophie, in which he summarised and defended the main results of the book and which was subsequently published with the discussion that followed as 'The Primacy of Perception and Its Philosophical Consequences'.

This text is important because the objections raised during the discussion and the misunderstandings upon which they are based were integral to Merleau-Ponty's growing awareness of the shortfalls of his thesis.[28]

Saint Aubert divides these objections into two sets. On the one hand, Bréhier and Hyppolite do not see the link between the description of perception, which would only have a psychological import, and the new ontology of sense Merleau-Ponty seeks to develop (PoP, 39). By seeking to draw ontological conclusions about meaning from a description of perceptual meaning, in other words, by seeking a philosophy within the primacy of perception, Merleau-Ponty would destroy or at least distort what it means to philosophise (PoP, 27–31). Merleau-Ponty's 'doctrine of perception', according to Bréhier, can only be lived; it cannot be formulated into a theory, or rather, it destroys itself as soon as it is formulated into a theory (PoP, 29–30). Or rather, it would be 'better expressed in literature and in painting than in philosophy'; it 'results in a novel' (PoP, 30). Merleau-Ponty replies to Bréhier by appealing to the idea of expression: 'It is to begin the effort of expression and of what is expressed; it is to accept the condition of a beginning reflection' (PoP, 30). The solution then is to be found in the notion of expression.

While Bréhier and Hyppolite raise the spectre of empiricism and psychologism, and reaffirm a certain 'absolute' or 'idealist' understanding of philosophy to ward off this spectre, Beaufret, representing the Heideggerians, intervenes to defend the phenomenological perspective. But in doing so, Beaufret voices the opposite worry: not that Merleau-Ponty's research is merely psychological and remains trapped in empiricism, but rather that it remains stuck within a certain form of intellectualism. The objection here is not that Merleau-Ponty went too far in the direction of a phenomenology of perceptual life but rather that he did not go far enough. This is the Heideggerian objection to Husserlian phenomenology: its phenomenological descriptions should lead to relinquishing the category of the subject and the vocabulary of subjective idealism. By remaining bound to Husserlian phenomenology and its vocabulary, Merleau-Ponty would be unable to effect the more radical rethinking of subjectivity demanded by the result of his phenomenological descriptions.

In other words, the *Phenomenology* would not have succeeded in grasping the paradox or 'good ambiguity' of expression, but would have remained entangled in a philosophy of consciousness and hence in a bad ambiguity (PoP, 11).[29] As such, it could only cast the living body as both subject and object, oscillating between the two traditional categories, or as a 'mediator' (PP, 146) between consciousness and the thing, without being able to develop the specific way of being of the body itself in a positive way.[30] Consequently, Merleau-Ponty's descriptions of perception or of sensing also remain caught in a bad dialectics, oscillating between passivity and activity, receptivity and creativity. Of course, in the *Phenomenology*, the description of perceptual experience did acquaint us with a being that is passive in its activity and active in its passivity, a being who is never sovereign with regard to the sense of its experience without either being fully one with the world, a thing among things. Within a bad ambiguity or oscillation, however, the question of the *passage* from one mode to the other, from the unreflected silent life of the body to the reflective, articulated life of 'thought', remains unaddressed. How is the being who is open to itself and to the world able to reflect upon its own experience and ultimately express the meaning of these experiences in language? The puzzle remains intact.

One of the problems with the *Phenomenology*, then, is that its method, despite all we said about radical reflection and the incomplete reduction, remains underdeveloped. The status of the phenomenologist's assertions, the relation between the 'immediacy' she is trying to describe and her linguistic descriptions, remains unclear. What is needed is this 'phenomenology of phenomenology' (PP, 382) announced in the *Phenomenology*, one that explicitly takes up the problem of phenomenology's power to return to and express our unreflected life. Without such a 'phenomenology of phenomenology', the relation between language, especially philosophical language, and the foundation or ground that exceeds it remains unclear.

In the *Phenomenology*, Merleau-Ponty attempts to 'solve' this problem, unsuccessfully as he will come to recognise, by appealing to a tacit cogito.[31] The tacit cogito is this silent contact of myself with myself, the role of which is to explain the possibility of reflection and language, the passage from unreflected life to reflection and thematisation. As we said above, if reflection is to be a fact, it cannot give rise to an instance or power that is completely detached from factical life. This means that Merleau-Ponty must propose a different reading of the cogito, one that does not give rise to a Cartesian thinking thing or a Husserlian transcendental ego. As Merleau-Ponty writes in the Preface to the *Phenomenology*, 'The true *Cogito* . . . recognizes my thought as an inalienable fact and it eliminates all forms of idealism by revealing me as "being in the world"' (PP, lxxvii). The spoken, reflective cogito we find in Descartes gives me, by means of words and significations, the idea of myself as a thinking thing, but not this 'contact with my own life and my own thought' which is 'prior to speech' (PP, 424). The tacit or silent cogito, by contrast, is supposed to allude not to an empirical or transcendental immanence but rather to 'the profound movement of transcendence that is my very being, the simultaneous contact with my being and with the being of the world' (PP, 396). The tacit cogito explains how I am neither completely foreign to myself (in which case it could never come to know what I think) nor completely transparent to myself (in which case there would be no difference between the movement of existence which throws me into things and the reflection that gives me back my act and there would be no need to reflect to see whether I *really* think, desire or see what I think I think, desire or see). Merleau-Ponty's cogito then stays with the phenomenon:

> there is consciousness of something, something appears, there is a phenomenon – such is the true *cogito*. Consciousness is neither the thematization of self, nor the ignorance of self, it is *not hidden* from itself, that is, there is nothing in it that is not in some way announced to it, even though it has no need of knowing it explicitly. (PP, 310)

Merleau-Ponty's appeal to a 'tacit cogito' is not entirely successful at explaining this reintegration, however. As he says bluntly in a note from January 1959: 'What I call the tacit cogito is impossible' (VI, 171). As we said above, if reflection is to be possible, the unreflected must already be opened to being known or thematised. But that tacit cogito cannot explain this openness or this passage because it merely retroactively posits and hypostasises a primordial, pre-reflective experience that is only accessible from within language.

The problem becomes glaring near the end of the section on the cogito where Merleau-Ponty states: 'the tacit *Cogito* is only a *Cogito* when it has expressed itself' (PP, 426). But the question is: what is the tacit cogito prior to its expression? Is it a cogito or not? Merleau-Ponty needs the tacit cogito to be pre-reflective and pre-linguistic, but he also needs it to open on to reflection and language and be the inexhaustible ground of all my expressions. With the silent or tacit cogito Merleau-Ponty is trying to name an ambiguous mode of self-experience, without developing the mode of being of this ambiguity. Rather he merely posits 'the world of silence' as what one sees when one looks back from the world of already spoken language (see VI, 171). Silence here is merely the absence or negation of all that will arise from reflection: object, idea, signification. The challenge is to think this 'world of silence' as 'zero of being which is not nothingness' (VI, 260), rather than as negation of language. The question that needs to be taken up is that of a logos of the world of silence, a wild or vertical logos.

The objections raised in 1946 – the necessity to elaborate the relation between the primacy of perception and the new ontology of sense, as well as the necessity to relinquish the vocabulary of Husserlian phenomenology and its dualism – percolate for a while, until Merleau-Ponty finds in the notion of expression a way of addressing them, explicitly for the first time in his lecture course at the Collège de France, 'Le monde du silence et le monde de l'expression'. By turning to Saussure and understanding all sense as diacritical difference between non-positive units, Merleau-Ponty will be able to show more clearly how pre-linguistic perceptual experience is already expression and how linguistic expression, though it breaks the silence, remains shrouded in silence. By developing his notion of expression Merleau-Ponty will be able to accomplish what was missing in the *Phenomenology*, namely connect the chapter on speech to the chapter on the cogito (see VI, 176). Expression will be neither pure creation nor pure reproduction, neither a 'saying without a said', a pure *énonciation*, nor a 'said without saying', a pure *énoncé*, but a paradoxical or ambiguous doing in which 'a threshold is crossed'.[32] Expression will give us the 'good ambiguity' the *Phenomenology* was after, 'a spontaneity which accomplishes what appeared to be impossible when we observed only the separate elements' (PoP, 11), that is, the unreflected, silent life of perception on the one hand, and the spoken, significative life of reflection on the other.

This does not mean that the cogito will disappear from Merleau-Ponty's thought, but the existentialist reading of the cogito he will propose will be more explicitly opposed to the idealist (Husserlian-Sartrian) reading phenomenology inherits from Descartes. This is most explicit in the last few sessions of his 1960–1 course on Cartesian ontology. There, the 'presence of self to self' of the tacit cogito is explicitly thought in terms of opening and non-concealing, of a 'not nothing' that is also not some 'thing'. At this point, Merleau-Ponty's reading of Descartes starts to resonate with Nancy, for whom what comes to utter itself and distinguish itself in '*ego sum, ego existo*' is a certain indistinction of embodied life, but one that was not a mass, but already spacing and to-itself.

In order to prepare for the parallel with Nancy, let's look a little bit more closely at some important passages from this lecture course.[33] As in the *Phenomenology*, Merleau-Ponty's reading does not see in the 'I think' the guarantee that I am, but rather sees the 'I think' as arising out of the movement of existence. Here again, Merleau-Ponty positions himself against Gueroult's reading, for whom the individuality and lived nature of the cogito is an empirical fact, an experience that allows us to grasp the intelligible necessity that is the condition of possibility of this empirical experience (see NC, 260). Gueroult's reading ignores the fact that in the order of the *Meditations* there is a priority of the I for-myself over the I in-itself, of existence over essence. For Merleau-Ponty, then, there is a priority of the lived, operative, existing cogito, the certainty of which cannot be guaranteed by relying upon thought as a substance.[34]

This operative – or vertical or 'thick' – cogito is the ego that I *am* and that I find in the utterance prior to any idea I can have of myself (NC, 244, 247). Contra Gueroult, then, the ego of '*ego sum, ego existo*' is not (yet) the idea of myself as thinking substance, a simple nature or an essence, but a certain non-concealing or presence to self as an opening *to*:

> I am – what am I? *Cogitatio* – This means a being open to, disposed for . . . An opening (*facultas cogitendi*) – Opening that is not simply gaping hole [*béance*], *nichtiges Nichts*, that is not free to remain gaping, even as it is free to think this or that: even the nothing transforms itself into something for it: thought. *Res cogitans* is not substantialist construction, but way of saying that this opening to . . . something is not a zero of being, that this appearance, this presentation of someone to myself and hence of myself to myself is sufficient to constitute a being, and of a completely new type – Not an opaque in-itself, but a 'true thing', i.e. truly a thing and a thing of truth. (NC, 251; see also 266–7)

The cogito opens a third domain of being

> between immediate being and negation, the domain of the not nothing, of the something – Between 'what one sees' and 'what one negates' or rather containing both: I am, I exist, not as a being that is all positive, in itself, not as a pure refusal, rejection or nihilation [*néantisation*], but as *aliquid*, different than the nothing [*néant*], as the one to whom all of this appears, being of appearance, of *Erscheinung*, to whom it is manifest that . . ., or at least who is manifest to itself, who is not hidden from itself. For it doesn't yet know who or what it is . . . (NC, 257)

What Merleau-Ponty has retrieved from Descartes is most obviously the union of the soul and the body as a third notion irreducible to both extension and thought, one that necessitates its own, distinct way of being conceived. It is this notion that provides Merleau-Ponty with some of the tools to overcome Cartesian dualism. This is so because Merleau-Ponty situates the description of the union within the broader methodological question of the relation between the unreflected and reflection, of the beginning of doubt and reflection in embodied everyday life. This requires that the body – or the union, that is, the body that is sensing and self-sensing – not be understandable as extension, but as already open to itself and to others. Thought begins in the body because the body already 'thinks', or reflection begins in the body because the body already 'reflects'. Merleau-Ponty first conceives of this opening or contact of self to self of the body in terms of a tacit cogito but later abandons this idea in favour of a vertical or operative cogito. As we will see in the next chapter, in his engagement with Descartes, Nancy will develop this idea of an operative cogito as opening, and more specifically as the opening of the mouth that utters *ego sum*. A mouth: that is, the opening of the body.

Notes

1. Kwant, *The Phenomenological Philosophy of Merleau-Ponty*, 11. See also Bannan, *The Philosophy of Merleau-Ponty*, 51–7; Madison, 'Flesh as Otherness', in Johnson and Smith (eds), *Ontology and Alterity in Merleau-Ponty*, 29–31; Moran, *Introduction to Phenomenology*, 404; Dillon, *Merleau-Ponty's Ontology*, chapter 1; and Carman, *Maurice Merleau-Ponty*, 52–3 and *passim*. I agree with Isabelle Thomas-Fogiel who writes that 'It seems that even Merleau-Ponty's most acute commentators do not take seriously [Merleau-Ponty's] desire to find the premises of his own theory in Descartes'. See Thomas-Fogiel, 'Merleau-Ponty: De la perspective au chiasme, la rigueur épistémique d'une analogie', *Chiasmi International* 13 (2011): 387, my translation.
2. See Heinämaa, 'From Decisions to Passions: Merleau-Ponty's Interpretation of Husserl's Reduction', in Toadvine and Embree (eds), *Merleau-Ponty's Reading of Husserl*, 135. The claim is further developed in her 'The Living Body and Its Position in Metaphysics: Merleau-Ponty's Dialogue with Descartes', in Zahavi et al. (eds), *Metaphysics, Facticity, Interpretation: Phenomenology in the Nordic Countries*, 23–48.
3. *The Dioptrics* was also the book found opened on Merleau-Ponty's desk at the time of his death.
4. Merleau-Ponty, *The Structure of Behavior*, 192.
5. Upon the publication of his work, Gueroult sent a copy to Merleau-Ponty, who had just been appointed to the Collège de France. Merleau-Ponty seemed particularly interested in the first chapter of the second volume, 'De l'existence des choses matérielles. Le *nexus rationum* de la VIe *Méditation*', which Merleau-Ponty analysed in his lecture course on dialectics in 1955–6. See SC, 34.
6. See Gueroult, *Descartes' Philosophy*, vol. 2, 236–7. See also N, 17.
7. See Gueroult, *Descartes' Philosophy*, vol. 1, chapter 1.2.
8. See Gueroult, *Descartes' Philosophy*, vol. 1, 167. On the reduplication of the nexus, see vol. 2, chapter 21, section 3. The essence of the *nexus rationum* is an important question because it is the proposed solution to the problem of the so-called Cartesian circle, according to which the demonstration of the existence of God depends on the cogito, whose evidence depends on the existence of God. We will see below that Merleau-Ponty, who lectured on the 'Cartesian circle' during his course on dialectics in 1956, also proposes a kind of (but ultimately different) circular reading of the *Meditations*.
9. Soon after their appearance, however, the references to the ontology of the existent and to ontological diplopy disappear and the emphasis is put solely on the ontology of the object against which Merleau-Ponty now develops his own ontology. See SC, 35–6. See also VOI, 124–8.
10. Note from Merleau-Ponty dating probably from autumn 1957 and cited in SC, 36 (my translation).
11. See also: 'Broadening of natural light, which will recognize a "purity" of sentiment that would be clouded by the understanding. There is a truth of the false and a falsity of the true. This means that "the sensuous man" justified by the Sixth Meditation refutes the purification of the first two, would need to begin the path anew' (NC, 225–6).
12. On this circular or dialectical reading, see: 'There is something after the series of reasons. This, circularity and dialectic – by opposition to linear – by opposition to the manifest attitude of Descartes: philosophy and non-philosophy without encroachment or conflict, philosophy giving us reasons not to philosophize anymore' (NC, 225–6). By dialectics Merleau-Ponty means 'a thought that doesn't erase its traces, doesn't forget its path, where the path co-defines the truth, where the "conclusion" is not truer than the pathway, where the end is also the beginning and vice versa' and not 'in the sense of sending oppositions and differences flying' (NC, 225).
13. Merleau-Ponty, *The Incarnate Subject*, 35.

14. Husserl, *Cartesian Meditations*, §44.
15. The reference for the expression 'completely constituted' is to Husserl's second volume of *Ideas*, which was unpublished at the time. As the translator of the *Phenomenology* notes, the passage Merleau-Ponty is alluding to is probably the following: 'The same Body which serves me as means for all my perception obstructs me in the perception of it itself and is a remarkably imperfectly [*unvollkommen*] constituted thing.' See Husserl, *Ideas II*, 167.
16. Though the exact phrase is not found in the original German or the English translation, in §44 Husserl does speak of the animate organism (*Leib*) as 'reflexively related to itself [*auf sich selbst bezogen*]'. See Husserl, *Cartesian Meditations*, 97.
17. Husserl, *Ideas II*, 154.
18. Husserl, *Ideas II*, 158.
19. Husserl, *Ideas II*, 152.
20. The role of the body schema will evolve over the course of Merleau-Ponty's career. In the *Phenomenology*, Merleau-Ponty focuses on the structural and cognitive dimensions of the body schema, leaving its affective or libidinal dimension underdeveloped. Starting from 'Le monde du silence et le monde de l'expression' in 1953 and through a more thorough study of Paul Schilder, Merleau-Ponty will discover the intercorporeal and libidinal nature of the body schema, which will lead him to the discovery of a general regime of the *Ineinander* and of promiscuity. On the development and evolution of Merleau-Ponty's notion of the body schema, see EC, 70–5 and the whole section A. We will come back to the transformation of the body schema in the 1950s in the comparison with Nancy.
21. The example of the melody is borrowed from Jakob von Uexküll. See N, 173–4. There is no citation for the passage but we find the metaphor of the melody throughout von Uexküll's *Theory of Meaning*. Uexküll speaks of an organ as a melody and an organism as a symphony. He also describes the relation of 'fitness' between the organism and its *Umwelt* in terms of harmony and counterpoint and calls for a 'theory of composition' of nature.
22. Even when the guiding principle is thought to be immanent to the organism, it acts as if from the outside since it anticipates something that is not yet given in the organism itself, e.g. an ideal end-state. This is what Merleau-Ponty will call a retrospective ontology, one that posits the result retroactively as the cause, as having always already been at work in the organism.
23. See Heinämaa, 'The Living Body', 28.
24. Hence the frustration Merleau-Ponty expresses at Alquié's criticisms in his 1947 article 'Une philosophie de l'ambiguïté'. See VOI, 28–31, esp. n. 4. Alquié accuses Merleau-Ponty of eluding, by appealing to a phenomenal body, the real question which is that of the relation between consciousness (*la conscience*) and the objective body (*le corps objectif*). As a result, Merleau-Ponty would fall back into subjective idealism and remains unable to take into account scientific objectivity. Alquié gives the example of a chemical sedative that calms anxiety whether the patient knows or not what she is absorbing. Here the objective body affects consciousness and it is this relation that, according to Alquié, needs to be explained. But Merleau-Ponty has already replied to this objection both in *The Structure of Behaviour* and in the *Phenomenology of Perception*, especially in the chapter on the phantom limb (PP, 75–90). The physiological and the psychical are integrated into the movement of existence as being-in-the-world. Our existential attitude is the sense (in the sense of both meaning and direction) of a physiological fact, the way this fact is lived and acquires sense for me. If the physiological fact is removed then the 'psychical phenomenon' dissipates because the basis for the existential project has been removed, but this does not mean that the physiological basis produces or explains the psychical phenomenon. The issue revolved around the concept of 'sense', which Merleau-Ponty wants to understand without appeal to a constituting consciousness.

25. See Waelhens, *Une philosophie de l'ambiguïté*, chapter 2, esp. 52.
26. Merleau-Ponty, *The Structure of Behavior*, 209.
27. Merleau-Ponty, *The Structure of Behavior*, 209.
28. See VOI, 21–35, chapter 1, §1 'Merleau-Ponty face à ses critiques'.
29. See Waldenfels, 'The Paradox of Expression', in Evans and Lawlor (eds), *Chiasms: Merleau-Ponty's Notion of Flesh*, 93–4.
30. See, among others, 'Consciousness is being toward the thing through the intermediary of the body' (PP, 140).
31. The first person to describe Merleau-Ponty's philosophy in terms of ambiguity is Ferdinand Alquié in the article mentioned above. See also Waelhens, *Une philosophie de l'ambiguïté*.
32. Waldenfels, 'The Paradox of Expression', 92. For a comprehensive reading of Merleau-Ponty's oeuvre through the notion of expression, see Landes, *Merleau-Ponty and the Paradoxes of Expression*. Landes's interpretation of Merleau-Ponty's notion of expression is influenced by Nancy's idea of the exscription of sense. Landes thinks of 'good ambiguity' in terms of exscription, where he seems to read the pair inscription/exscription as corresponding to the difference between explicit and latent content. On my reading, the pair replaces, for Nancy, the traditional dichotomy between intelligible meaning and material support. Following Derrida's notion of arche-writing or trace, if we say that sense is exscribed while significations are inscribed, we mean that the materiality of sense cannot be sublated or that sense happens in materiality's turning inside out and touching 'sense'.
33. See especially the two versions of the 27 April session, NC, 244–64.
34. Merleau-Ponty is not the first to point out the personal or existential dimension of the cogito in the *Meditations*. On this issue he often refers to Jean Laporte's assertion according to which Descartes wrote 'cogito' and not 'cogitatur' (see NC, 251). See Laporte, *Le rationalisme de Descartes*, 97–8, n. 4. A decade later, in his review of Gueroult's *Descartes selon l'ordre des raisons*, Alquié will make a similar point: 'M. Gueroult is wary of the affective, reduces spirituality to intellectuality, universalizes the cogito, ignores any ontological experience, and tends to correct Descartes's vocabulary in that way. . . . His cogito is a thinking I in general [*moi pensant en général*], and not a concrete I.' See Alquié, 'Notes sur l'interprétation de Descartes par l'ordre des raisons', *Revue de Métaphysique et de Morale* 61, nos 3/4 (1956): 417. In the same year, in *Descartes, l'homme et l'œuvre*, Alquié develops this ontological experience at the heart of the cogito. Against the commentators who import post-Kantian concerns into their reading of Descartes and following Laporte, Alquié points out that Descartes didn't write '*cogitatur*, or *est cogitatio* or *est intellectus*', or even '*sum cogitatio*', but '*sum res cogitans*': I am a thing that thinks (94).

Chapter 2

Nancy, Descartes, the Exposition of Bodies and the Extension of the Soul

Descartes is not as major a figure for Nancy as he is for Merleau-Ponty. Indeed, even though Descartes is mentioned in shorter texts on the body and the soul, such as *Corpus*, 'On the Soul' or 'The Extension of the Soul', the only in-depth treatment of Descartes is found in the 1979 book *Ego Sum*. On the other hand, the meditations on the body Nancy undertakes in *Corpus* are made possible by the thinking of *ego* as *unum quid* and as the union of the soul and the body undertaken in *Ego Sum*. Indeed, it is in the earlier text, in a meditation on the mouth, that we encounter Freud's famous posthumous note 'Psyche is extended, knows nothing about it' for the first time, a statement to which Nancy returns in almost all his writings on the body. Developing Nancy's understanding of the body then requires a detour through the earlier text on Descartes. We will see how Nancy proposes a circular reading of Descartes's *Meditations* not unlike Merleau-Ponty's, but also how he radicalises further Merleau-Ponty's later reading of the cogito as vertical, operative cogito. The passage through *Ego Sum* also helps in warding off certain misinterpretations concerning Nancy's concept of body, namely the overemphasis on 'exposition' or 'exposure' at the expense of a certain 'distinction' or 'withdrawal', as well as the exclusive focus on the spacing between bodies (or parts of bodies) at the expense of the spacing or différance at the heart of the body.

1. Nancy's reading of Descartes: The *unum quid* against the modern subject

The issue at the core of Nancy's reflection on Descartes is the problematic return of the Subject Nancy diagnoses in the philosophical situation at the time, one in which the 'deconstruction' of the Subject was in full swing. It had become commonplace at the time to speak of the Subject as an effect – of the text, of history, of power, and so forth – and believe that one had in so doing overcome the metaphysics of the Subject and left Descartes behind.

If we follow the Heideggerian interpretation and see the Cartesian cogito as the inaugural moment of modern metaphysics, then we can see how such a Cartesian conception of the Subject is already disrupted, 'deconstructed', by the discourse of psychoanalysis, and especially Lacanian psychoanalysis. Yet, as Nancy had shown in *Le titre de la lettre*, his first book, published in 1973 and co-written with his colleague and long-time friend Philippe Lacoue-Labarthe, the Lacanian discourse inadvertently reconstitutes the Subject it seeks to disrupt and overcome. Lacan does show that the 'Subject' is not the Cartesian subject fully transparent to itself in all of its utterances: the gap that is opened between the subject of the statement (the 'shifter') and the subject who speaks or utters the statement leads to the impossibility for the subject of identifying himself with himself without a detour through the Symbolic or through language. The speaking subject is in fact a spoken subject, the locus of the signifier, and not the master of meaning.

What Nancy and Lacoue-Labarthe show, however, is that despite all the displacements Lacanian psychoanalysis still presupposes the value of subjectivity and develops a theory of the subject, albeit a negative theory of a split subject. The lack or gap at the heart of the subject becomes the foundation of a subject certain of itself as non-coincidence,[1] and psychoanalysis becomes the scientific discourse that masters this subject. In *Ego Sum*, Nancy reasserts this position toward both traditional and contemporary psychoanalysis, which 'obstinately reinvest[s] the position of a discourse of the subject, according to both possibilities of this genitive' (ES, 7). While psychoanalysis problematises the Cartesian subject, it does nothing to undermine 'the *imperium* of the subject' (ES, 6). Nancy also claims that such reconstruction of the Subject is not exclusive to psychoanalysis but pervades contemporary 'theory':

> From all sides, then, whether as the unconscious, or as history, language, machine, text, body, or desire (and everywhere where the subject is declared to be simple effect-of-subject), these new subjects have so far only produced the aggravation, or in a simpler and more massive way, the exacerbation of the *status* of the Subject: the consolidation of the *substratum* as such, which *substrates itself*, if one may say so, all the more and all the better now that it claims to sink deeper outside of the figure of the conscious subject, of the subject as creator or as master. (ES, 13)

The lesson is that any theoretical discourse, no matter how subversive, always produces a subject: the subject of the discourse, in both senses of the genitive. It is in this context that the necessity of a detour through Descartes makes itself felt for Nancy. Why? Because the collapse of the Subject, or rather the collapse of its substance, is already inscribed in its Cartesian inauguration. Already in Descartes, the Subject does not stand firm and needs to be propped up.

By following Descartes's writings, by following the twists and turns by means of which Descartes attempts to make the subject (or make himself as the subject of his own discourse) visible, Nancy's goal is to go 'back to the instant of a foundation, that of the Subject – in order to lend an ear to what only the foundation can make audible, because it triggers it and brings it about: the whisper of the subject that utters itself there, and collapses there' (ES, 11). Nancy's wager is that it is at the moment of the foundation of modern subjectivity, a foundation which always already includes all the possibilities of its exhaustion, that another thought of 'the subject' is possible. This 'subject' speaks, but he is not the speaking subject or the subject of the utterance; he is not even the neuter, impersonal *ça* of *ça parle*. Rather this 'subject' is *ego*, a mouth that opens and says, in turn, *dum scribo, larvatus pro Deo, mundus est fabula, unum quid*. Of course, the pronouncement that interests us here the most is *unum quid*, a 'certain something one'. The phrase is found both in the synopsis of Descartes's *Meditations* and in the Sixth Meditation and is normally translated as 'a kind of unit' or simply 'a unit'.[2]

In 'Unum quid', the last chapter of his 1979 *Ego Sum*, Nancy claims, as Merleau-Ponty did before him, that Descartes is not a Cartesian dualist, at least not if one understands by this term that there is an *ontological* demarcation between the soul and the body. Descartes does not elaborate the problematic relation between a thinking thing and a body-object. What we find in his texts, under the guise of the union between the soul and the body, is a description of 'the impossible experience of the human being that the thinking of the Subject is compelled to reach, but which it cannot face' (ES, 110). For Nancy, then, Descartes is not the founder of humanism, of anthropology, or of the human sciences (ES, 109), or rather he makes possible the thought of another *humanitas* 'that remains exorbitant for this humanism to which we still belong – even if against our own *body*' (ES, 110). *À notre* corps *defendant*: against our own will or reluctantly. But if we can only belong reluctantly to humanism, it is because our body resists the humanism that also takes its roots in Descartes – in a misunderstanding, inevitable as it may be, of Cartesian thought – and against which Heidegger also calls for another thought of the humanity of the human. For Nancy, Cartesian humanism can be overcome neither by 'a thinking that pretends to be of the body, or of the absence of subject' nor by 'a thinking of the subject as a structural, historical, or fictional effect' (ES, 110). It is not a question of moving away from the Subject, but rather of returning to the experience of the subject in the moment of its first articulation, an experience that necessarily implies a body.

Nancy's reading of Descartes, then, does not only draw from the Sixth Meditation a way of thinking the human being or the lived body; it additionally attempts to show, as Merleau-Ponty did in his last lecture course, that the *ego* of the cogito is not, *pace* Heidegger, the self-certain subject (ES, 99). Indeed, Heidegger interprets the Cartesian cogito as the moment of the self-grounding and self-positing of the subject of thought and knowledge. Heidegger takes the cogito to be the inaugural moment of modern metaphysics, where the 'I' becomes the *sub-jectum*, the underlying subject of representation. At this point, certainty becomes the measure of truth and truth becomes the adequation between representations within the subject and objects that stand before it.[3] Nancy's reading of Descartes disrupts this Heideggerian reading by showing that the ego is not the thinking substance, but rather the gaping mouth that unfounds the subject in the very moment of its foundation. One could say that the uttering of *ego cogito* represents, for Nancy, the moment of the self-foundation or self-creation of the subject. Such a 'subject', however, would not be substance but rather ex-istence – an existence that is, as we will see, necessarily ex-tended.

Rather than speaking of '*the* Cogito' – that is, the deduction of my own existence through methodical doubt – Nancy focuses on the uttering '*ego sum, ego existo*' as it is produced in the Second Meditation. The evidence that 'I exist' is not based on a logical proof or a deduction, a proof that would be conducted by a pre-existing ego. Rather the evidence lies in, and is one with, the utterance of the ego. As such, the phrase 'the uttering of ego' is ambiguous and oscillates between a subjective and objective genitive: is ego the subject of the uttering or is it the object of the utterance? While it seems that the ego must pre-exist the expression of its existence – first I exist and only then can I utter 'I exist' – when we hear the expression in the objective genitive where what is enunciated is the ego, it is implied that the ego is the *result* of an enunciation and hence not itself the enunciator. There is no underlying, pre-existing enunciator that precedes the utterance. Emphasising the objective genitive, Nancy, then, will read *ego sum* as a sort of pure performative, that is, a performative without underlying substrate or subject (ES, 84–5). What passes itself off as a constative utterance, as the expression of a prior existence, in fact lets this existence come about or come to itself. A subject, a true and living subject, Nancy says, never takes place, never happens. Yet the uttering of *ego* happens. This *ego* '*is* not', Nancy writes. It is 'neither a nature, nor a structure of subject, not even it [*ça*]. But something that nevertheless makes up the very act of *ego*, its self-position in the form of: it withdraws *itself*, and this *happens* to it, at the extreme point of its fabulation – of its *saying*' (ES, 87). Before the subject of the *énoncé* (the I that is spoken of in the statement) and the subject of the *énonciation* (the I that speaks), there is the verb, *énoncer*, an action without subject, the opening of a gaping mouth that articulates 'ego' (see ES, 85, 111). In this opening of the mouth, in this articulation of the 'o', ego produces its own distinction from everything else, that is, it produces itself as distinct.

'*Ego sum*', we could say with Derrida but changing a bit the context in which he used the term, is a kind of teleiopoetic uttering. In *The Politics of Friendship*, the word 'teleiopoetic' names the movement of a sentence that begins at the end, travels at infinite speed, 'advances backwards . . . outruns itself by reversing itself . . . outstrips itself [*se gagne de vitesse*]'.[4] A teleiopoetic utterance is one where the subject who seems to be pre-existing the utterance is in fact made possible by the utterance itself. Such utterances are impossible since the sentence must already have reached its end before it can set itself in motion.[5]

If we were to follow Derrida further, we could speak of the mystical foundation of the authority[6] of the *ego* as the author of its own saying or of its own fable. No foundation sustains *ego*, or, as Nancy will say in *Ego Sum*, ego 'supports itself with nothing [*se soutient de rien*]' (ES, 109–10). We will never find, underneath the ego that comes to utter '*ego sum*', an 'ego in general', an 'egoity' that sustains the uttering, but only the 'each time' and each time 'such and such' of a singular utterance. Descartes indeed ties the evidence of the ego first only to its performance: 'this proposition, *I am, I exist*, is necessarily true whenever [*quoties*] it is put forward by me or conceived in my mind' (AT VII 25). Without underlying substance or substrate, this means for Nancy that ego is a 'spasm or convulsion', a punctual, local inflection (C, 25).

For Nancy, then, the path of Descartes's *Meditations* is the path by means of which this 'spastic' ego assures itself of itself by assuring itself of the distinction between substances. The purpose of the latter is to sustain the originary distinction that ego *is* by guaranteeing that it, ego, has the nature of a thing, and not merely that of a spastic stance at the extremity of its utterance (ES, 100). To assure itself of itself, ego must bind its discrete utterances and install 'continuous space, the indistinctness of the *times* of existence' between them (C, 27).

Following the path of the *Meditations*, which leads from doubt, to the uttering of ego, to the distinction between substances, and finally to the *unum quid*, Nancy will connect the *ego* of the Second Meditation with the *unum quid* of the Sixth Meditation, and distinguish both from the thinking substance. In order to defend the plausibility of this reading – which is similar to the one proposed by Merleau-Ponty and seeks to answer the question: how is it that the meditator begins to meditate? – we must focus on the first step of the *Meditations*, the passage from doubt to the uttering of the ego. This passage, according to Nancy, leads to the ego's exception from the 'world' and effects a torsion or reversal of the inside and the outside. This reversal is probably best laid out by Antonia Birnbaum in her text on Nancy's reading of Descartes titled 'To Exist Is to Exit the Point' (C, 145–9). During the stage of doubt, I seem to retreat from the outside world into the interiority of thought. But, Birnbaum writes, 'in cutting itself off from the world, the "auto" of auto-affection and the "I" of the "I am, I exist" don't regain an interiority closed in upon itself but experience themselves in the concentrated extremity of thought' (C, 147). Here is the torsion or inversion: the 'outside' world as extension is an interiority, that is, it is the world *within* which I exist indistinctly, or as Merleau-Ponty would say, pre-reflectively. Such a world has no outside worthy of the name: everything finds itself 'in' it, including myself. Hence it would make more sense to speak of the so-called 'outside world' as an absolute inside. But during the time of doubt, the ego 'determines exteriority by exempting itself from everything that renders it [the ego] present to the inside of the world' (C, 147). The ego strips itself off of every possible way of experiencing the world and hence of experiencing itself as inside that world. The subject *se retranche*: withdraws, cuts itself off, retreats or hides behind a fortification.

While this exemption from the world looks like a withdrawal from exteriority into intimate self-presence, like a *retranchement* or withdrawal from a deceiving world to a solid and stable interiority, by calling the subject to which it gives rise 'abysmally intimate' (ES, 87), Nancy in fact introduces an excess in the movement of withdrawal so that the interior to which the subject is thought to withdraw does not form a ground but itself withdraws deeper and deeper, further and further away from any ground. The word 'intimacy' is the superlative of *intus*: the most *intus*, the most interior, the innermost. 'It is the inner', Nancy writes,

> such that there is no deeper or higher inner. But the depth in question has no ground: if there were a ground, somewhere it could be grounded or founded (in whatever sense), and it (or he or she) could not even enter into relation. This is because a ground assures and fixes a being on its proper substance. The intimate is always deeper than the deepest ground. (C II, 18)

This movement of *retranchement* or withdrawing, which is also a movement of distancing or distinction since it gives rise to *ego*, does not lead to a protected interiority but to an exteriority. The excess pushes the withdrawal to the outermost extremity of the interior, to the point where this interiority falls outside of the world. Nancy writes of the cogito:

> Thus, the *extremity* constitutes, in all respects, the position and the nature of the *cogito*. *Extremum* is the superlative of *exterum*: the extremity is that which is most exterior. It is, *of all the things that are interior*, the one that is farthest out [*le plus à l'extérieur*]. In all extremity, not only do the interior, the inside, or the property of a being reach their limit, the ultimate point of their completion and of their closure, but they also exceed this closure and undo their own completion. (ES, 79, my emphasis)[7]

In uttering '*ego sum, ego existo*', ego withdraws away from the absolute inside that we call the outside world into an 'inside' where it calls itself 'ego'. At the extreme point of this withdrawal, ego distinguishes itself as the *extremum*, the most exterior of all the things that are inside the world. It is as such that the I is a point without extension or, in Descartes's vocabulary, a non-extended thinking thing.

According to Nancy's reading, it cannot be the thinking substance of the Second Meditation that utters 'ego' but only the *unum quid* of the Sixth Meditation. As Nancy writes:

> *Unum quid*, a something that is neither-soul-nor-body, opens its mouth and pronounces or conceives: *ego sum*. . . . [S]omething – unum quid – opens (it would therefore have the appearance or shape of a mouth) and this opening articulates itself (it would therefore have the appearance of discourse, hence of thought), and this articulated opening, in an extreme contraction, forms: *I*. (ES, 107; cf. C, 25)

In order to defend his interpretation, Nancy underlines an addition made in the French version of the *Meditations*: 'it is certain that this I, *that is, my soul, by which I am what I am*, is entirely and truly distinct from my body' (see AT VII 78, AT IXa 62). Nancy explains: 'At the same time, *I* am distinct from my body (insofar as I am a thing that thinks), and this *me* is only me insofar as it constitutes that by which "I am what I am," which does not exclude that *I* perhaps be something more than that *by which* I am *what* I am' (ES, 95). What the Sixth Meditation shows is that I am so intimately linked (*arctissime conjunctum* and *quasi permixtum*) to what I am *not* that I am more than what I essentially am. Nancy concludes: 'What *I am* – the whole and veritable being of what *I am* and that affirms itself as existing in the statement of this existence and without having to examine "whether the mind is distinct from the body" – must be distinguished from that *by which* I am what I am' (ES, 96). The thinking substance, then, is distinct not only from the extended substance but also from the I-subject-of-the-utterance of its own existence. There are, hence, two distinctions: that between me and my body and that between two things that are mine, two sides of me (ES, 96–7).

It might be easier to accept the claim that it is the *unum quid* and not the *res cogitans* who utters '*ego sum*' once we understand how the uttering of ego, which produces the ego's distinction from everything else, leads me to cover over the evidence that it is I, *unum quid*, who says 'I am'. We find a hint in 'The Extension of the Soul', where Nancy explains by way of everyday examples that resonate with the anonymous level of experience described by Merleau-Ponty: 'When I struggle or breathe, when I digest or suffer, fall or jump, sleep or sing, I know myself only as being that which [*cela qui*] struggles or sings, grimaces or scratches itself: that, rather than someone [*cela, et non celui*], or at any rate not as an ego distinct from every other thing. That, then, instead of someone, or someone who is only that' (C, 139–40, trans. mod.). Here I cannot even say that what is known is *my own* body. There is only the indistinction between myself and the struggle itself: 'The more effective this identity is, the more indistinct it is, and the less there is to know, properly speaking. The less, therefore, is there knowledge of a "body proper" [*corps propre*] since the structure [*l'instance*] of propriety or property has vanished' (C, 140, trans. mod.). As soon as *unum quid* distinguishes or affirms itself by uttering 'ego', it produces something proper, an I that can say 'I', and ob-jects the body, that is, throws it in front of itself. At this point, it can affirm that this body is its own, but only because it is effectively not its own body – as effective or operative indistinction – but holds the body at a distance.

If *unum quid* can, out of a state of indistinction, come to utter 'ego' and affirm itself as existing, it is according to Nancy because from the start it does not have the structure of substantial presence but that of the to-itself (*à-soi*). The to-itself denotes for Nancy the movement of existence as being-towards itself so that, in accordance with Derridian differance, there is no self at the origin of this movement. Rather, the self is an effect of the movement toward an exteriority that it can never fully reappropriate or fold back into itself. This inappropriable exteriority is the limit upon which the self is exposed to itself and to others, a limit that properly belongs neither to the inside nor to the outside. While it is true that exposure at the limit is a central tenet of Nancy's ontology, interpreters have a tendency to overemphasise exposure and gloss over the fact that this exposure – which we could also call sensibility (both intelligible and sensible) – is the result of, or is made possible by, the withdrawal of any ground that opens, spaces or extends any being. The movement of *retranchement* in which I distinguish myself, insofar as it does not lead to a ground but to an abyssal intimacy, is necessarily tied to exposition as the turning toward the outside of the existent, which we recall is the inside of the world. What is most inside is not some me that would finally coincide with itself but always something more or other than me that exceeds any identity, distances me from myself, and opens me up to relation. Without this spacing or this opening of extension, there would be only a black hole. What is would collapse upon itself and would not succeed in coming to presence.

Substantial presence is, according to Nancy, precisely such a black hole: the negation of presence-to-self, the point without extension, non-extension concentrated in itself (C, 75). Existence, on the contrary, is a rupture of presence, or in Nancy's words, the 'hollowing out of [pure] presence, which is the possibility and even the most proper nature of its *coming*', its presentation 'in the difference with itself' (GT, 64). The distancing of self-coincidence as the most interior is 'coexistence of the origin "within" itself, a coexistence of origins', which means that being-with is not the 'secondary dispersion of a primordial essence' (BSP, 12). When we emphasise the movement of withdrawal or distinction that is concomitant to the expression of *ego*, we understand why exposition is not a melting or blending together: it is always the other side of a distinction. It is such double movement of contact/separation or entanglement/disentanglement that forms the basis of Nancy's thinking of singularity and that runs the risk of being forgotten if one overemphasises the category of 'exposure' in Nancy's work.[8]

This understanding of existence as to-itself explains the importance Nancy attaches to the figure of the mouth in his reading of Descartes.[9] Playing on the double meaning of areal, Nancy speaks of the areality of the mouth: the mouth is an area the ontological status of which is beyond the opposition real/unreal/ideal. The area of the mouth is a dislocation that opens an incorporeal gap, a difference within continuous space or within the extended substance. The mouth is the abyss in which the subject ruins itself. Why? Because it is in a sense impossible to say that the mouth belongs to me, that it is mine. 'The subject', Nancy writes,

> ruins itself and collapses into this abyss [the mouth]. But *ego* utters itself there. It externalizes itself there, which does not mean that it carries to the outside the visible face of an invisible interiority. It means, literally, that *ego* makes or makes itself into *exteriority*, spacing of places, distancing and strangeness that make up a place, and hence space itself, primordial spatiality of a true *outline* in which, and only in which, *ego* may come forth, trace itself out and think itself. (ES, 112)

In the opening of the mouth, the inside is thereby 'turned on itself, extravasculated, exogastrulated, exclaimed, expressed and thrown – not "outside" but "as the outside"' (C II, 88). It is not that I, in the uttering, carry what was hidden inside of me to the outside. As for Merleau-Ponty, expression is not a secondary movement that carries outside what already existed inside. Hence, rather than speaking of an outside of me, we should speak of a 'me-outside', of me as outside, especially when the exclamation *I am, I exist* seems to come out of my deepest heart of hearts. 'Not "outside me"', Nancy writes,

> because in truth the only inside is not 'me' but the gaping in which a whole body gathers and pulls itself together in order to find a voice and announce itself as 'self,' reclaim itself and call itself, desire itself in desiring the echo that will perhaps come back from the other bodies around it. (C II, 88)

The mouth is extension, then, but of a completely different kind than the one theorised by Descartes under the heading of the extended substance. It is this mouth that allows Nancy to make sense of Freud's puzzling claim in a posthumously published note from 1938: 'psyche is extended, knows nothing about it.'[10] At the same time, Descartes could not be completely oblivious to this extension. While we seem to have, in Descartes, pure extension on the one side and pure cogitation on the other, Nancy notes that 'thought is sensing [*la pensée est sentante*]' (C, 131). This means both that sensing is a mode of thinking, and that thought thinks because it senses itself thinking. In order to sense itself thinking and to know itself as that which thinks, and hence to really think (since there is no thinking that is not also aware of thinking), thought has to encounter an obscurity or opacity, an exteriority that makes it sensing/sensible. If thought were only thought, if it were purely luminous, clear and transparent, it would not sense anything, and it would not sense itself think. Hence it would have no way of knowing itself as something that thinks. As Nancy says: 'The *psyche* is first psyche by its *extension, partes extra partes*, and by the opacity to itself in which it remains with respect to this exteriority-in-itself, or with respect to the *to*-itself that constitutes it' (GT, 83). The soul knows itself and is present *to* itself thanks to its being opened to and touched by something extended that it cannot think or know (see C, 21).

Conversely, it is by being opened to thought, penetrated by it in some non-spatial way, that the body senses itself. A body insofar as it senses itself as body cannot be a mass closed upon itself – the black hole we mentioned above. Nancy gives the example of the organs: when I am healthy, I do not feel my stomach or my heart; they are silent. Here we can speak of an interiority or an intimacy, which is not of the order of what can be sensed but rather of the mass (C, 129). When I feel my stomach, it is both from the outside and as an outside (*c'est du dehors*) (C, 128). This is what is at stake in the word 'soul'. The soul 'doesn't represent *anything other* than the body, but rather the body outside itself, or this other that the body is, structurally, for itself and in itself (C, 126). What we have to think is not an opposition between body and soul but the soul as 'the body's difference from itself' (C, 126). The soul is the fact that *there is* a body, this body. The soul is the presence of the body, 'its position, its "stance," its "sistence" as being *out-side* (ex)' (C, 128). In sum, the relation of body and soul, their union if one will, is not a relation between two things or two substances, since each is nothing but the ontological spacing or opening-*to* of the other.

2. Nancy's bodies: Skin, sense, touch

The simplest characterisation of bodies in Nancy's ontology is that bodies are 'places of existence' (C, 18) and 'systems of openings' (MM, 33). Already in the discussion of Descartes above, we saw that bodies are not substantial things, dense masses closed upon themselves. Bodies, Nancy writes in *Corpus*,

> aren't some kind of fullness or filled space (space is filled everywhere): they are *open* space, implying, in some sense, a space more properly *spacious* than spatial, what could also be called a *place*. Bodies are places of existence, and nothing exists without a place, a *there*, a 'here,' a 'here is,' for a *this*. (C, 15)

Everything that exists exists in a place that it opens or spreads out. To return to Antonia Birnbaum's phrase: 'to exist is to exit the point', hence to be spread out, distended, open.[11] Nancy gives the example of a newborn baby – but we should remember that the phenomenon described, as well as the concept of singularity, is not limited to human beings but applies to each body in each and every place: 'when a baby is born, there's a new "there." Space, extension in general, is extended and opened. The baby is nowhere else but *there*. It isn't in a sky, out of which it has descended to be incarnated. It's spacing; this body is the spacing of "there"' (C, 132–3). Incarnation, or what Nancy will also sometimes call carnation, does not mean that what was at first merely ideal or imaginary now comes to occupy a place, but rather that a place opens itself or spaces itself out. A body exists without origin or end: a body arrives here without coming from anywhere, without going anywhere, and without holding anything in reserve: 'like an image coming on a movie or a TV screen – coming *from* nowhere behind the screen, *being* the spacing of this screen, existing as its extension – exposing' (C, 63; see C, 199, BP, 187).

The body as spacing and place of existence is extended but at the same time Nancy will say that it cannot be reduced to being completely in exteriority since in that case we would be inanimate objects (MM, 37). In the vocabulary of the *Phenomenology of Perception*, mechanistic or physiological explanation of the body cannot account for the phenomenon of the lived body and its meaningful relation to the world. Nancy writes: 'With the body, it is a question of the outside. Of an outside that would suppose an inside. What is remarkable and introduces a sort of sensible dualism, it's that we feel that there is some inside [*du dedans*]' (MM, 37). We have an outside that is not mere extension and an inside that is not a constituting consciousness. But then the question is: what is this 'interiority' that resists reduction to mere extension or objectivity and defeats mechanism and empiricism from the start? We already know the answer to this question: "There is ego, that is, "all the inside"' (MM, 38). But this ego is nothing but its uttering, an uttering that goes through the opening of the mouth right at the body itself. The body opens and utters 'ego'. It is the body that says 'I' but it says 'I' not as Cartesian extension but as opened extension.

Here we encounter the second characteristic of the body: a system of openings. In *Ego Sum*, the mouth was emblematic of the opening and it reappears in the discussion with Nicolas Dutent in *Marquage manquant (et autres dires de la peau)*. What happens in the mouth is 'the convergence and deployment . . . between the body and the soul' (MM, 29), between the outside and the inside. In *On Listening*, Nancy had proposed a similar description of the ear that listens: 'To be listening is to be *at the same time* outside and inside, to be open *from* without and *from* within, hence from one to the other and from one in the other.'[12]

At this point, it is useful to distinguish between two different meanings of spacing at play in Nancy's understanding of the self as body. First there is the spacing or diaresis at the heart of any self so that there is, properly speaking, no self-presence prior to any differentiating: the self has always already started by altering itself and can never catch up with what would be a pure origin to coincide with itself. Existence, then, denotes not the presence of the thing, but the coming of what is to-itself. At the level of the originary spacing or opening of the to-itself, we cannot speak either of a 'self'-relation or of a relation to 'another'. Rather

> it is a matter of a diaresis or a dissection of the 'self' that precedes not only every relation to something other but also every identity of the self. In this diaresis, the other *is* already the same, but this 'being' isn't confusion, still less a fusion: it is the being-other of the self in as much as neither 'self' nor 'other,' nor some relation between them can be given to them as an origin. It is less than and more than an origin: the to-itself as the appropriation of what cannot be appropriated in its *to*-being – of its sense. (FT, 7, trans. mod.)

The movement (or the *sense*) of the to- or toward-, which is an effect of the spacing (otherness, exteriority) at the heart of the self, turns the existent toward the outside and exposes it on its limit or edge, which both separates it from and joins it to other things. Hence for Nancy, the spacing is double. First there is the originary spacing at the heart of the self, the différance, to use Derrida's term, that rends any self and means that I am always already affected with some otherness or exteriority, that I always come too late. Then, there is the spacing between things, the limit or edge upon which they are exposed, upon which they sense each other, and which belong properly neither to the inside nor to the outside. This limit does not enclose but rather is the place where the opening takes place. A limit that would enclose would have to have only an interior edge, its exterior edge being absolved from any contact with an outside. Such a limit would merely limit and not open on to anything other. On the other hand, if there were no limit, no closure at all, then there would be nothing, no place of differentiation where something can come to presence in its distinction with anything else.

As system of openings, then, the body exists as limit. This means that the mouth is not a hole but a limit between inside and outside, itself neither inside nor outside. It is the place where the body spaces itself out and exposes it. Of course, we should not reduce our understanding of the body as opening to its cavities. For Nancy, the skin is also an opening in the sense of a limit as place of exposition. The body 'is a skin, variously folded, refolded, unfolded, multiplied, invaginated, exogastrulated, orificed, evasive, invaded, stretched, relaxed, excited, distressed, tied, untied. In these and thousands of other ways, the body *makes room* [donne lieu] for existence' (C, 15).

The skin is the body insofar as it is turned toward the outside and exposed. While the skin seems to separate inside from outside, body from world, in fact the body neither is nor has an inside if by that we mean some content that would be hidden underneath the skin: 'The skin is therefore not a container for a content because, precisely, the content is not a pile of guts with which there is little to do. The skin is the ultimate and first form in as much as it is turned toward the world. The skin is the form of the body' (MM, 79). Note that this is exactly how Nancy, following Aristotle, has described the soul, namely as the form of the body. Yet for Aristotle, form means organisation. For Nancy, the soul doesn't form – that is, organise – the body; rather the body draws the form or outline of the soul. The skin assures us 'that this body is entirely there within it, that it is itself this body and consequently that it is its soul'.[13]

This tension between inside and outside right at the skin itself is perhaps best explained in the few paragraphs that Nancy adds to the 2006 Russian publication of '58 Indices on the Body' and which he titles 'Le corps: dehors ou dedans'. Note the absence of a question mark. It is not a question of figuring out whether the body is an outside or an inside but of explaining how the body is both – and hence not what we normally take to be either an inside or an outside. Nancy writes:

> A body opens and exposes, it opens and exposes itself. A body, through all its skin and all its openings, ex-poses an 'inside' that is nowhere, that is neither 'in' it nor 'outside' of it, but that it itself is . . . *insofar as it is 'itself' only in the pulsation* [battement] *of its being-exposed.* This exposition is but another name for *ex-istence*.[14]

If the body as skin is a surface 'without thickness' because there is no inside to accede to that would be the truth of the surface, we should not be too quick to give a 'superficial' reading of this surface, since Nancy also adds that it is nevertheless 'the sign of an infinite depth'. The skin is an *envelope* not in the sense of a container, but in the sense of the promise of an infinite development, the promise that 'it will never stop extending itself, offering itself, deepening itself'.[15]

The emphasis on the skin might leave us with the impression that the body is a unified whole, yet Nancy understands neither the skin nor the body as an organised or functional whole since such an organisation would preclude the kind of diaresis that allows the body – and each zone of the body – to be exposed and, through this exposure, to sense itself and others. For Nancy, the body does not have 'parts, a totality, functions, or finality. It's acephalic and aphallic in every sense [or direction], as it were' (C, 15). The body is divided into zones, which disseminate its purported unity so that the zoned body is 'discontinuous, fragmentary, part of the logic of a non-unity' (C II, 100). The zone, Nancy writes, 'represents a distinction, a differentiation not only with regards to the extension of the body but also with regards to its finality and its construction. It is a sort of deconstruction, or even an access to struction – the chaotic heaping up rather than the coherent assemblage.'[16] In this context, Nancy often refers to Freud's claim, in the 'Essay on Infantile Sexuality', according to which the whole body – Freud says any region of skin or mucous membrane – can become an erogenous zone. Pleasure 'gives access to unity in the zone, leaving behind a presumed or assumed unity (integrated, perceptive, organised) in favour of a fragmented unity [*unité éclatée*], that is to say, a unity that is brilliant in its explosion [*en son éclat, éclatante*]' (C II, 100, trans. mod.). It is important to underline this lack of totality, organisation and function, since it will turn out to be one of the differences between Nancy's account of the body and Merleau-Ponty's. For Nancy, sense-making is inorganic, even disorganised. With Nancy, then, we have to do with a different notion of envelop than the one used by Merleau-Ponty when he calls the organism an 'envelop-phenomenon', even if both are linked in some way to depth. This lack of unity or organisation will ultimately lead Nancy to prefer to speak of corpus, instead of speaking of *the* body, or even worse, of my *own* body:

> Corpus: a body is a collection of pieces, bits, members, zones, states, functions. Heads, hands and cartilage, burnings, smoothnesses, spurts, sleep, digestion, goose-bumps, excitation, breathing, digesting, reproducing, mending, saliva, synovia, twists, cramps, and beauty spots. It's a collection of collections, a *corpus corporum*, whose unity remains a question for itself. Even when taken as a body without organs, it still has a hundred organs, each of which pulls and disorganizes the whole, which can no longer manage to be totalized. (C, 155)

Nancy's understanding of sense and of sensing follows from his understanding of the body as fragmentary and de-totalised. Playing on the double meaning of spacing we discussed above, sense, exactly like existence, is what happens on the limits between bodies, or between zones of the 'same' body, thanks to their 'inner' diaresis or distension. First, there is sense only for a self that ex-ists or is essentially *to* itself.[17] In fact, any coincidence of a return to self would destroy sense: 'Sense depends on relating to itself as to another or to some other. To have sense, or to make sense, to be sensible [*être sensé*], is to be to oneself insofar as the other affects this ipseity in such a way that this affection is neither reduced *to* nor retained in the *ipse* itself. On the contrary, if the affection of sense is reabsorbed, sense itself also disappears' (FT, 6, trans. mod.).

Yet what Nancy emphasises throughout his work is how this 'inner' distension turns the existent inside out, so to speak, and exposes it at its limits or edges. Sense then belongs to neither the inside nor the outside, but is always an experience of the limit. It happens not in appropriating or assimilating the other, making myself other or making the other my own, but rather in approaching the limit so that one touches and is touched by the outside. If Nancy sometimes says that the body in touching passes to the limit, he never says that the body passes the limit in the sense of crossing over and reaching the other side. The passage to the limit, on the contrary, 'does not cross [*ne franchit pas*] but brushes [*frôle*], touches, and in touching lets itself be touched by the outside' (C II, 94). Or again: 'Touching never does away with the distance between us, but it metamorphoses the spacing [*écart*] into an approach. Not a contact, but a coming. Not a presence but an apparition. Not a "being there" but a manner of "passing through," of haunting, of frequenting . . .'[18]

Given that Nancy understands sense-making on the model of touch, we can say that all sense-making is a form of sensing, and more specifically of touching. 'Sense *is* touching,' Nancy writes (FT, 110), so that Derrida will speak of a quasi-transcendentalisation or ontologisation of touch in Nancy (see OT, 275). In its quasi-transcendental function, touch is not one of the senses. Rather,

> Touch is nothing other than the touch or stroke [*la touche*] of sense altogether and of all the senses. It is their sensuality insofar as it is sensed and sensing. But touch itself – inasmuch as it is a sense and consequently inasmuch as it senses itself sensing, or more than that, inasmuch as it senses itself sensing itself, since it only touches by touching also itself, touched by what it touches *and* because it touches it – touch presents the proper moment of sensuous exteriority; it presents it *as such and as sensuous* [comme sensible]. What makes for touch is 'this interruption, which constitutes the touch of the *self-touching*, touch *as self-touching*.' Touch *is* the interval and the heterogeneity of touch.[19]

Touch acts as a figure of interruption: it necessarily includes a moment of obscurity, or untouchability, which limits each sense's or each sensation's appropriation of what is sensed. Contact is always interrupted, or better: contact is interruption itself.

Despite the emphasis on interruption, Nancy does recognise in the passage above that touching the other is also touching oneself touching. Yet Nancy has a tendency to focus on the first of the two moments of self-touching we discussed in relation to Merleau-Ponty, reflexivity, rather than the second one, doubling. Let us recall that it is thanks to the second moment that the body effects a sort of 'proto-reflection'. Focusing on the first moment, on the fact that as touching I am also always touched, allows Nancy on the contrary to emphasise the exteriority at play in touching: in touching I relate to myself solely from the outside and as an outside (see C, 128). Rather than saying that sensing the other presupposes self-sensing, a minimal contact of self to self, Nancy speaks, on the contrary, of 'a "self-sensing," a "self-touching" that necessarily passes through the outside – which is why I can't sense myself without sensing otherness and without being sensed by the other' (C, 133). To emphasise the priority of exteriority and otherness in touching, Nancy will prefer to speak of a self-touching you (or a feeling oneself touching you, *se toucher toi*), of a self-touching skin (or a feeling oneself touching skin, *se toucher peau*), rather than a self-touching oneself (C, 39; see OT, 278).

In *On Touching*, Derrida calls the philosophy Nancy is attempting to develop an 'absolute, irredentist, and post-deconstructive realism' (OT, 46). By calling Nancy's post-deconstructive realism 'irredentist', Derrida offers a double criticism of Nancy's thinking of touch and of the body. First, irredentism points to the fact that in touch, there is always a certain desire to master or assimilate what is on the other side of the border upon which, or at the limit of which, touch happens. Second, it points to the fact that such a desire to assimilate is predicated on an assumed homogeneity. In engaging with the philosophical tradition's understanding of touch, Derrida wants to show how this tradition participates in what he famously calls the 'metaphysics of presence', which he defines as 'The enterprise of returning "strategically," "ideally," to an origin or to a priority thought to be simple, intact, normal, pure, standard, self-identical, in order then to think in terms of derivation, complication, deterioration, accident, etc.'[20] In *On Touching*, Derrida demonstrates how the 'haptological' strand of this tradition is implicated in the metaphysical gesture insofar as it thinks touch in terms of identity, homogeneity, immediacy and self-presence, even when it emphasises a certain interruption or distance. This is what Derrida's reading of Merleau-Ponty shows.[21] The question addressed to Nancy is: is his post-deconstructive realism also implicated in this metaphysical gesture? Derrida's response is ambivalent. Nancy's thinking of touch is, on Derrida's own admission and as we mentioned above, 'neither intuitionistic nor continuistic, homogenistic, or indivisibilistic. What it first recalls is sharing, parting, partitioning, and discontinuity, interruption, caesura – in a word, syncope' (OT, 156). Yet, Derrida worries that in *succeeding* to interrupt itself, this interrupted touch still presupposes the propriety and integrity of a self-contained body whose self-touch or self-sensing is itself immediate, that is, without detour through an irrecoverable exteriority. Even though for Nancy to touch is always to touch a limit rather than to penetrate into or merge with what is on the other side, and hence to touch the intangible, Derrida worries that this thinking of the intangible as that which is touched renders, despite all denegation, the intangible accessible (OT, 38; see OT, 295–6).[22] Furthermore, such thinking of touch as touching of the intangible or untouchable finds its roots in Christianity so that Nancy, according to Derrida, would still be the heir of this tradition. Christianity is the religion of desire to make the intangible, invisible God *present* in the mystery of the Incarnation, and then of the Eucharist. Christianity desires the presence of God as body that can be touched.

Nancy will contest Derrida's understanding of Christianity in ways that echo his reading of the union of the soul and the body in Descartes more than a decade earlier. In the Eucharist, we do not participate in or touch the Spirit that would be made present in or by the wafer any more than the Incarnation of God consists in the presence of the Spirit in a physical body. God's presence in the world as a body or as wafer does not mean that the Absolute has fallen into the world, that the Idea has materialised itself and is now available to be sensed or touched. It only means that the Intangible is not hidden in a beyond but is, here and now, this 'other' body, that is, not a pure physical body but the body of sense, or the body that is opened to or passible of sense. The mystery of the Incarnation then teaches us about the irreducible ambiguity of all bodies as flesh – matter and spirit in the same 'body'. The body is neither the prison of the soul nor the expression of a hidden interior, nor is it a full presence. It is, as we learned from our discussion of *Ego Sum*, an open or gapping presence, an extension or a spacing. Christianity then is neither the thought of the separation of body and spirit nor that of their fusion but rather the understanding of flesh as the contact–separation between these two dimensions.

Nancy develops this Christian understanding of the two-dimensional body in *Noli me tangere*, a book that addresses Derrida's worries about the Christian underpinning of the relation between touch and the metaphysics of presence more directly. The phrase *noli me tangere* refers to a scene in the Gospel of John, where Jesus instructs Mary Magdalene, at the moment when she recognises that the Gardener outside of Jesus's tomb is in fact the Risen Christ himself, not to touch him. How should we understand this interdiction to touch in light of what Derrida said about Christianity as the religion of touch?

To understand this interdiction of touch at the moment just before the Ascension, Nancy will start by questioning the ontological status of the resurrected body. Death cannot be, for Christians, the separation of the soul and the body, in which case there could not be any resurrected *body*, any glorious body of the Ascension. Rather than a division between a body and a spirit we have two bodies, or more precisely, two dimensions of the same 'thing here': the glorious body of the Ascension and the body of mortal flesh. According to Nancy, the former is the raising up of the latter, its pivoting to the vertical.

It is upon the background of this understanding of death and resurrection that the interdiction against touching the resurrected body must be understood. To want to touch Christ would be to think of resurrection in terms of resuscitation, a beginning anew of presence. But the truth of the resurrection, for Nancy, lies not in the renewed presence of Christ but in the departure of presence: 'Just as [a presence] comes, so it goes' (NMT, 15), and this is the law of its sense or its touch. 'To touch him or to hold him back would be to adhere to immediate presence, and just as this would be to believe in touching (to believe in the presence of the present), it would be to miss the departing [*la partance*] according to which the touch and presence come to us' (NMT, 15). The interdiction of touch concerns only this full presence of a body that would be fully in this world or of this world. The interdiction of touch then allows for another dimension to be touched, 'this dimension from which alone comes *glory*, that is, the brilliance of more than presence, the radiance of what is in excess of the given, the available, the disposed [*déposé*]' (NMT, 17). This other dimension is not another world, but again the opening of this world. This point must be underscored since it allows us to understand what it means to live a Christian life, that is, to be *in* the world but not *of* the world

(John 17: 14–16). It does not mean to take leave of the world in favour of a spiritual interior or a heaven, but to live in proximity to that which is not of this world and yet is not an alternative world. It means 'to think and feel the world according to its opening', that is, according to its irreducibility to relations of force or to values defined by given common measures (A, 40). To clarify the kind of opening that belongs to the world, Nancy redeploys a motif he developed in *Ego Sum*. The opening of the world 'belongs to the world, as the mouth belongs to the body' (A, 28). As we have already seen, the mouth is not somewhere else than 'in' the body; it cannot be reified or detached from the body whose opening it is. At the same time, the mouth is not a piece of extension in the Cartesian sense; rather, it opens extension to the outside.

What is at play in Christianity then is two ways of being in the world. There is nothing but the world, yet it is possible to relate to *either* according to its all-encompassing and enclosing givenness, *or* according to its 'opening, rift, play, or risk' (A, 24). Nancy calls these two dimensions the horizontal-mundane and the vertical-divine (A, 39). Here we find interesting resonances with the later Merleau-Ponty. Against the idea of a world that is fully accessible, spread out in front of me, Merleau-Ponty deploys the motif of verticality to speak of the world *of* which I am, a world in depth, a world that contains openings and lacunae. We would be wrong, however, to think that Merleau-Ponty's emphasis on my belonging to the world contradicts Nancy's affirmation that I am in the world but *not of* the world. Both Nancy and Merleau-Ponty are looking for a mode of being-in-the-world that is not that of a detached spectator observing a world that is fully accessible, and both think our 'embeddedness' in the world not in terms of objective presence (empiricism) but in terms of opening, depth and *écart*. We will return to this point in the last chapter of this study.

Notes

1. As Lacoue-Labarthe and Nancy write in *The Title of the Letter*, 'even the gap of the *shifter* operates almost as a sort of confirmation of the subject adhering to its own certainty through the certainty of its noncoincidence to itself' (121).
2. See AT VII 15 and 81. I use the translation by John Cottingham, Robert Stoothoff and Dugald Murdoch of *The Philosophical Writings of Descartes* in two volumes (Cambridge: Cambridge University Press, 1984). The French version, for its part, of the Meditations has '*une même chose*' and '*un seul tout*'. See AT IXa 12 and 64. For Nancy's reading of this passage, see ES, 89–90.
3. See, among others, Heidegger, 'Metaphysics as History of Being', in *The End of Philosophy*, 28–30.
4. Derrida, *The Politics of Friendship*, 32.
5. See Derrida, *The Politics of Friendship*, 77. An example of such sentences is found in the American Declaration of Independence: 'we, the people', who will only come to

be at the end of the Declaration, anticipate our own independent existence in order to be able to declare it; 'we' will have been the one who uttered the sentence only once the sentence is completed. See Derrida, 'Declarations of Independence', *New Political Science* 7, no. 1 (1986): 7–15.
6. See Derrida, 'Force of Law', in Cornell, Rosenfeld and Carlson (eds), *Deconstruction and the Possibility of Justice*, esp. 11–15.
7. In *Being Singular Plural*, we find a similar torsion of inside and outside, but instead of the inside being what is the most outside, the farthest out, it is the outside that is the most inside: 'in an inside more interior than the extreme interior, that is, more interior than the *intimacy* of the world and the intimacy that belongs to each "me." If intimacy must be defined as the extremity of coincidence with oneself, then what exceeds intimacy in interiority is the distancing of coincidence itself' (BSP, 11–12).
8. About contact/separation, see BSP, 5, 91, 97. About entanglement/disentanglement, see Nancy's discussion of ipseity in 'Eulogy for the Mêlée', in BSP, 145–58.
9. See, among others, ES, 103, 111–12 and C, 25. See also OT, 20–1, 24–5.
10. Freud, *The Standard Edition of the Complete Psychological Works*, vol. 23, 300. The original has a comma between the two clauses and the English translation a semi-colon. Nancy refers to Freud's note, among other places, at the end of *Ego Sum* (ES, 110), throughout *Corpus* (C, 21, 95–7 and *passim*) and in 'The Extension of the Soul' (C, 144). Derrida discusses Nancy's reading of the note in *On Touching*; see especially OT, §1.
11. In one of his lectures at Marc Bloch University in Strasbourg in 2000–1, Nancy mentioned a story by Italo Calvino found in the Cosmicomics series called 'Tutto in un punto', 'All at One Point'. In it, the narrator, Qfwfq, recounts how in the beginning everybody inhabited one single point with all the absurdities such a claim entails. For example, though the narrator says that they were all packed like sardines, 'in reality there wasn't even space to pack us into. Every point of each of us coincided with every point of each of the others in a single point, which was where we all were' (Calvino, *Cosmicomics*, 43). And the cleaning lady 'had nothing to do all day long, not even dusting – inside one point not even a grain of dust can enter – so she spent all her time gossiping and complaining' (44).
12. Nancy, *On Listening*, 12.
13. Nancy, 'Rethinking Corpus', in Kearney and Treanor (eds), *Carnal Hermeneutics*, 80, trans. mod. The first part of this text, titled 'Essential Skin', is a translation of the text of a conference given in Quito in November 2013. The text is published in Spanish as 'Pial essential' in *Dar Piel* and some excerpts appear in French in MM; see MM, 77. On the notion of skin, see also Nancy's recent *La peau fragile du monde*, esp. 143–9.
14. Nancy, 'Le corps: dehors ou dedans. Cinquante-huit indices sur le corps', *Siniy divan* 9 (2006): 109, my translation.
15. Nancy, 'Rethinking Corpus', 80, trans. mod. See MM, 77; C, 151.
16. Nancy, 'Rethinking Corpus', 83, trans. mod. See also Nancy, 'Of Struction', *Parrhesia* 17 (2013): 1–10.
17. On the parallel between the structure of the self and the structure of sense as referral, see Nancy, *On Listening*, esp. 8–9.
18. Nancy, 'Rethinking Corpus', 81, trans. mod.
19. Nancy, *The Muses*, 35, trans. mod. The quotation at the end of this passage is from the first version of Derrida's 'On Touching', 'Le toucher: Touch/To Touch Him', *Paragraph* 16, no. 2 (1993): 127.
20. Derrida, *Limited Inc*, 93.
21. See OT, §9 Tangent III. The problem becomes especially glaring when, while supposedly commenting on Husserl's *Ideas II*, Merleau-Ponty erases the difference between self and other and assimilates the handshake to self-touching. See OT, 189–92. See also James, *The Fragmentary Demand*, 121–30.
22. We will return to the question of the untouchable or intangible as the 'place' where touching happens when we discuss the chiasm in Merleau-Ponty in Chapter 8.

Chapter 3

Divergences: Unity versus Dislocation

Let us pause here and relate more explicitly what Merleau-Ponty says of one's own lived body to Nancy's thought of the body. Both find in the *unum quid* of the union a description of the body that overcomes the ontological dualism of pure mind and pure matter. Yet there are obvious differences in their thinking of the body. The question is: what do these differences amount to? And more generally for our study: what do they tell us about phenomenology, especially in its Merleau-Pontian transformation? There are many ways in which we could cast the differences between Merleau-Ponty's and Nancy's thinking of the body. We could say, for one, that the difference is one of obscurity versus clarity. While Merleau-Ponty's lived body is transparent, expressive, shot through with sense, Nancy's bodies appear to be impenetrable and dense. Of course, it is not unproblematic to qualify the lived body, especially in Merleau-Ponty, as transparent or shot through with sense. After all, Merleau-Ponty ends the first part of the *Phenomenology of Perception* by reminding us that it is the reflective attitude that 'purifies simultaneously the common notions of body and of soul' and 'establish[es] a clarity within us and outside of us', whereas 'the experience of one's own body . . . reveals to us an ambiguous mode of existence' (PP, 204). At the same time, the impenetrability or obscurity attributed to Nancy's bodies does not prevent these bodies from making sense; it is rather the condition of their sensing and sense-making. The difference then lies in their respective ways of conceiving of sense and sensing. In what follows, I want to cast this difference in terms of a priority of unity over dislocation, which is also the priority of interiority over exteriority or of the moment of reappropriation and integration over the moment of alienation and separation. In order to clarify how this priority plays out, I propose to go through two main areas of comparison. First I compare the kind of unity attributed to the body schema with Nancy's description of the body as corpus, and second I compare the kind of synthesis experienced in sensing to Nancy's pluralisation of bodies of senses, focusing more specifically on the experience of self-touching. I want to suggest that the lived body is experienced as a kind of unity while Nancy's corpus is constituted by a fragmentation that is never mended, and that this difference spreads to the body's relation to the world.

To be clear, I am not claiming that Merleau-Ponty posits the body as a metaphysical unity: the unity of the lived body is an achievement of intentional life, one that arises out of a certain material exteriority and is always prone to disintegration. A failure or lapse (*défaillance*) of sense is always possible, as Merleau-Ponty says in 'Man and Adversity' (S, 239). I am also not saying that the descriptions of embodied life in Merleau-Ponty are phenomenologically inaccurate. In truth, I take them to be more accurate than Nancy's at the phenomenological level. What I hope to show, however, is that Nancy takes things in a different direction because for him there is something more at stake than a mere description of the lived body as it is experienced.

1. Synthesis of the body schema or *partes extra partes*?

In the *Phenomenology of Perception*, Merleau-Ponty rejects the Cartesian conception of space as extension *partes extra partes* both as a description of the space occupied by the lived body and as a description of the space in which the lived body moves and senses. In terms of the lived body, rejecting the metaphor of the pilot in the ship to explain the relation between the soul and the body also means rejecting a conception of their relation in terms of spatial location. If the soul is not in the body like a captain in the ship, this means for Merleau-Ponty that the soul is neither hidden in some non-spatial point in the body, nor is it the piece of extension that is located closest to the soul. The soul is spread out throughout the body. Since both soul and body occupy the same piece of extension, the union – the lived body – is not explicable in terms of Cartesian space.

One of the key points of Merleau-Ponty's analyses in the first part of the *Phenomenology* is to make us grasp the kind of unity proper to one's own body against a conception of the body as constituted of parts in external relations with each other. To the Cartesian *partes extra partes*, Merleau-Ponty opposes the body schema, the synthesis of my own body. As we saw in our discussion of the body schema, the body is not made of parts that stand in external relations to one another but rather is a space of implication or envelopment. The body schema is the way in which my body is at my disposal in movement as an articulated whole. It is the implicit unity of my body that underlies my gesture and is responsible for its natural, flowing character. We also mentioned how Merleau-Ponty explicitly distinguishes this unity of envelopment or implication of my own body in the body schema from any kind of collection or assemblage.

Of course, Merleau-Ponty recognises the possibility of a disintegration of the body schema. In the discussion of anosognosia, for example, when a patient experiences her arm as a long, cold snake, or when another patient ties his arm to his body so that he does not lose it (PP, 149–50), we see the body itself falling into pieces, literally, *partes extra partes*. Yet, Merleau-Ponty also specifies that the rejected or ob-jected body part cannot be completely so since the patient still knows where to find the cold snake or the falling arm.

For Nancy, on the contrary, the *partes extra partes* describes the relation between bodies and between parts of bodies. While Descartes thinks the 'extra' as undifferentiated void, for Nancy the extra is the place of differentiation, of the articulation of one body or one part of the body with and against another (C, 97; see also C, 29, 143). For Nancy, space is always and everywhere filled, a body always opening on to another, more or less subtle body. If this filled space does not collapse into a mass, if it 'spaces itself out' and gives place to existence, it is because of the extra that articulates bodies against bodies, and parts against parts. Yet, unlike Merleau-Ponty, Nancy's articulations do not form a coherent whole by implication or envelopment. Articulation, Nancy writes in a different context, 'is only a juncture, or more exactly the play of the juncture . . . without the mutual *play* . . . ever forming into the substance or the higher power of a Whole'.[1] Nothing oversees or sustains the spacing of the *partes extra partes*; no Subject subtends and gathers the *partes* (C, 39–41). This allows Nancy to claim that a body 'doesn't have an outside or an inside, any more than it has parts, a totality, functions, or finality' (C, 15), that 'a body is never *completely whole*' and that 'there's no experience of *the* body' (C, 101).

Hence, rather than taking Nancy's description of his heart transplant in *L'intrus* as the story of the disintegration of his own body through the intrusion of something foreign in it – not only the intrusion of the heart of a stranger, but first of all the intrusion of a disease that rendered his own heart inoperative and hence foreign – we should instead learn from this text that the body 'itself' is always a stranger, always foreign not only to 'me' but also to itself. As Diane Perpich puts it: '*L'Intrus* ultimately suggests that there is never a single moment when the body falls to pieces and is no longer one's own; that is, there is no threshold that the body approaches and having crossed over it is no longer recognizably one's own body. Rather, the law of intrusion is that the alterities of the body are always multiple and multiplying.'² Rather than thinking of his own body as the site of identity and integrity and equating illness with intrusion and loss of ownness, Nancy ends up claiming all the strange foreigners that invade his proper body as integral to his 'own' identity:

> I am the illness and the medical intervention; I am the cancerous cell and the grafted organ; I am the immune-depressive agents and their palliatives; I am the bits of wire holding together my sternum; and I am this injection site permanently sewn into me below my clavicle; just as I was, for that matter, already these screws in my hip and this plate in my groin. I am becoming like a science-fiction android, or the living-dead, as one day my youngest son says to me. (C, 170)

We might be tempted to read this affirmation as a reclaiming of identity and integrity and reduce it to Merleau-Ponty's Marcellian affirmation 'I am my body',³ but we would, I think, be missing the radicality of what Nancy is trying to think. The intruder is not some other whom, in a Hegelian fashion, we would have to tame, appropriate and learn to recognise as our own. Intrusion is not some event that befalls a body that was previously whole and integral; rather it is the *most proper* state of the body. Hence, when I say that *I am* the intruder, it is not because I succeeded in appropriating that intruder so that I now identify with him/her/it; rather *I am* the intruder, because it is thanks to this strangeness and foreignness that my body is and always remains for itself and for me that I can say 'I' at all.

Furthermore, such strangeness is not a function of traumatic experiences such as Nancy's heart transplant, though these certainly make it more conspicuous. Even the body that we normally consider to be healthy and whole contains exteriority within itself. In *Being Singular Plural*, Nancy speaks of the stone as a foreign body that is both out there, in what we call the 'outside world', and within my own body, as the 'quasi-minerality of bone' (BSP, 18). The stone within my own body does not lose its strangeness and foreignness because it now belongs to my own body as if this integration would endow the stone with the power of intentionality and expression. The stone in my body remains an exteriority so that I cannot really call this body my own by opposition to the other bodies in the world, the stone for example. Exposition then is not limited to the exposition of a living body, a flesh, to the outside world; it is already played out within the body itself.

Of course, even though the body schema is, for Merleau-Ponty, responsible for the cohesion of the lived body, this should not lead us to underemphasise the fact it is also thanks to the body schema, insofar as it is a system of equivalences, that I open on to the world and others. In the *Phenomenology*, the incompletion and openness of the body schema is discussed mostly in the context of habit formation. The process of habituation consists in the double movement of prolongation (dilatation) of the body schema into the world and integration of the world into the body schema. While the integration of the body allows for its relation to world and other, these relations in turn lead to a permanent restructuration of the body schema.

The unity of implication or envelopment that characterises the body schema for Merleau-Ponty also spreads to the world in which the lived body senses and moves. The breach or gap in the body that makes it both sensing and able to be sensed – that is, self-sensing, sensing itself from the inside and from the outside at the same time – also opens the self to this outside that is the world. A self-sensing self can sense the other – since it already senses 'itself' also as other, that is, from the outside. Yet, even at this level, Merleau-Ponty has a tendency to close the circle of self-sensing on to an interiority. In describing my contact with the outside in sensing as communication and communion, Merleau-Ponty has a tendency to reduce that alterity of what is sensed so that it is neither foreign nor strange.[4] What I open on to, what I 'gear into', as Merleau-Ponty often says, is something that is adequate to, or commensurate with, the powers of my body: the books on my shelves are reachable, rocks are climbable, pianos are playable. The world and I form a harmonious system. Indeed, in the *Phenomenology*, Merleau-Ponty describes the world as a totality – albeit an open one – and speaks of the unity of the subject and the object – albeit a presumptive one:

> We have the experience of a world, not in the sense of a system of relations that fully determines each event, but in the sense of an open totality whose synthesis can never be completed. We have the experience of an I, not in the sense of an absolute subjectivity, but rather one that is indivisibly unmade and remade by the course of time. The unity of the subject or of the object is not a real unity, but a presumptive unity within the horizon of experience. (PP, 228)

In the 1950s, as he is delving into child psychology and psychoanalysis and deepening his understanding of the body schema through a renewed reading of Paul Schilder, Merleau-Ponty comes to put more emphasis on the dynamism of incorporation between, and the originary entanglement or *Ineinander* of, body schemata. If we follow the development of the logic of incorporation after the *Phenomenology*, we can see that Merleau-Ponty also abandons the idea of a 'body proper' or of a body that I can properly call my own. Indeed, in a working note dated from 1960, Merleau-Ponty writes: 'Bodily schema = system of these equivalences. Neither projection nor introjection: two systems that communicate (235) in the form of an *Ineinander* or a *Verflechtung*. "Commerce" of bodily schemata (235). One should not start from *my body* [*Ne pas partir de* mon corps].'⁵ Rather one needs to start from the system self/other, from their originary intertwinement. There is, as Merleau-Ponty will say, an equivalence between *renter* and *sortir*, going out of oneself and coming into oneself. One becomes oneself only in the movement toward the other through projection/introjection of their own body schema so that the more I am able to relate to the other – the more the other is structured or differentiated for me – the more I am myself, and vice versa (see VOI, 238–41). While Merleau-Ponty will never go as far as Nancy and affirm that the self is essentially dislocated, we will see when we turn toward the later work how he will come to emphasise more and more a certain alienation or detour through exteriority at the core of the experience of sensing and self-sensing.

2. Synaesthesia or dislocation of the senses? Self-touching or touching the outside?

The system of equivalences of the body schema not only serves to integrate the parts of the body into a whole and assure the coherence of the body in relation to various tasks, that schema is also responsible for the cohesive integration of various sensory and kinetic experiences. A mode of sensory experience translates into other modes without having to pass through reflection or representation because each sensation is a certain mode of movement or behaviour of the whole body (PP, 243–4). This relation of envelopment explains, among other things, how I can recognise my gait on a screen even though I have never seen it from the outside (PP, 150–1). The motor or kinaesthetic sensation calls or evokes a visual sensation. It also explains cases of synaesthesia, where a patient sees a sound or hears a colour. As Merleau-Ponty notes, in these cases, the patient is not saying that '*he has a sound and a color at the same time: it is the sounds itself that he sees, at the place where colors form*' (PP, 238).

Rather than treating synaesthesia as the exception, Merleau-Ponty recognises that it is the rule of sensing: we see the fragility of glass, the softness of cotton, the weight of iron, and we hear the hardness of the cobblestone, to use a few of the examples Merleau-Ponty mentions (PP, 238–9). But Merleau-Ponty is not reducing all differences between the senses to a general and indeterminate regime of sensations. Each sense does have its own field or its own space, but the different sensory domains 'gear into each other' (PP, 231), allowing passage and translation. Sensory experience in the narrow sense, that is, the experience that isolates one sense from the whole, like the experience of one monocular image,

> is unstable and wholly unknown to natural perception, which is accomplished with our entire body all at once and opens onto an inter-sensory world. Like the experience of the sensible quality, the experience of isolated 'senses' takes place only within an abnormal attitude and cannot be useful for the analysis of direct consciousness. (PP, 234)

It is a mistake to try to explain our sensuous experience starting from isolated, punctual sensory experiences and distinct senses and then ask how they can be synthesised so as to constitute *my* experience of *the* world. Rather, when we focus on our natural experience, we find not an 'epistemological consciousness' that effects an 'intellectual synthesis', but rather a 'synergetic system of which all of the functions are taken up and tied together in the general movement of being in the world, insofar as it is the congealed figure of existence' (PP, 243, trans. mod.). It is to name this synergetic system that Merleau-Ponty appropriates Herder's phrase and calls 'man' a *sensorium commune* (PP, 244).

For Nancy, on the contrary, the plurality of the senses cannot be collected into a systematic whole. Not only is there no intelligible or sixth sense into which all the sensible senses would find their truth and no transcendental sense that would be the condition of possibility of sensing, but there is also no system of the senses. On this point Merleau-Ponty might agree. But there remains for Merleau-Ponty a body schema, and this schema effects the synthesis of the senses and turns the perceived object into an intersensorial object. This is true even if the integration is never completed (PP, 242–3). For Nancy, on the other hand, sensing is always a spacing:

> Sense *is* a distance [*un écart*]: the distance between a subject and itself, or between one subject and another, or the distance, within the same subject, between those distinct subjects that are the (organs of the) senses. This is why we cannot look for some final compenetration [*compénétration*] of the senses in a synesthesia, any more than we can absorb the different senses within some intelligible assumption. We can never say 'the' sensible in the singular: there are only sensibles, there are only sensibilities.[6]

In *The Muses*, Nancy uses a passage from Deleuze's book on Francis Bacon to explain the relation between the plurality of sensations, their 'existential communication'. Sensations communicate because each 'is directly plugged into a vital power that exceeds all domains and traverses them'.[7] The idea of a 'vital power' into which all sensations would be plugged sounds strange in Nancy's mouth. And indeed, Nancy immediately adds: 'it must only be noted that the "originary unity of the senses" that is invoked here proves to be nothing but the singular unity of a "between" of the various domains of sensation and that the existential communication happens only in the element of the "outside-of-itself" [*hors-de-soi*], of an ex-position of existence.'⁸ In other words, Nancy insists again on the discretion – in the mathematical sense – of sensations, each time this colour, this taste, this sonority, on the exteriority in which they stand with regard to one another and on the unbridgeable limit between them that is the place of their 'communication'.

Turning to the sense of touch more specifically and to their respective analyses of self-touching, we find the same emphasis on integration and unity on Merleau-Ponty's part and on dislocation and spacing on Nancy's. As we mentioned in the Introduction, when Nancy picks up the phenomenological analyses of self-touching in *Corpus*, he points out that these analyses 'always return to a primary interiority' (C, 128). Indeed, in the *Phenomenology*, Merleau-Ponty takes up Husserl's analyses of self-touching in *Ideas II* and adopts its conclusion that the body effects, in its attempt to touch itself touching, a sort of reflection, a synthesis of two different perspectives I have on my body: from the inside and from the outside. Of course, in the end there is no touching of the touching, and it is indeed in preserving this distance or gap between the two touching hands that there can be an experience of 'doubling' – else there would only be one undifferentiated touching. Yet, it is this imminent protoreflection, this minimal folding back upon itself of my body, that allows me to call *this* piece of extension my *own* body. As Derrida writes: 'This detour by way of the foreign outside . . . is . . . what allows us to speak of a "double" apprehension (otherwise there would be one thing only . . .) and what allows me, after undergoing this singular experience . . . to say "this is my body"' (OT, 175). The experience of self-touch is what puts me in touch with or makes me present to myself, so that the loop of the touching-touched closes itself upon a sort of interiority. Never does the distance between touching and touched undermine the integrity of my own body.⁹

On the contrary, Nancy's thinking of touch always puts the emphasis on the spacing or interruption between the touching and the touched. In the same way that Derrida shows in *Voice and Phenomenon* how hearing-oneself-speak in immanent soliloquy cannot take place in the immediacy of an instant – an instant that, in order to guarantee self-presence, would have to be without dimension and hence without exteriority – Nancy introduces differance at the heart of touch. As a result, any self-touching-itself that would lead back to an interiority is always deferred. Here, Merleau-Ponty might agree, insisting as he does on the imminence of coincidence. Yet this deferral of self-presence is for Nancy the result of a more originary and more radical difference or spacing 'within' touch 'itself' or within the 'self' that is supposed to touch itself somehow.

In his discussion with Nicolas Dutent, Nancy refers explicitly to Merleau-Ponty: 'The hand touches itself while touching the pen or the keyboard. Merleau-Ponty thought a lot about what it means to touch oneself: To touch oneself is to relate to oneself from the outside, to be to oneself one's own outside [*son propre dehors*]' (MM, 45–6). As we mentioned in the previous chapter, Nancy does not distinguish between the two moments found in self-touching. Indeed, his example is not Merleau-Ponty's: it is not a hand touching the other hand while the latter palpates the table but simply one hand touching a pen or a keyboard. Because Nancy never actually discusses the quasi-reflection that happens in the doubling of self-touching, he misses what is specific about it: in it, I become *Leib*, I can say '*this* is my body'. Nancy on the contrary can affirm that touching – whether oneself or another, this makes no difference – happens solely 'from the outside' and never from the inside.

Nancy seems to reverse the phenomenological priority of the self. Rather than saying that sensing (the other) presupposes a self-sensing body (*Leib*), Nancy writes, on the contrary, of 'a "self-sensing," a "self-touching" that necessarily passes through the outside – which is why I can't sense myself without sensing otherness and without being sensed by the other' (C, 133). If he speaks of a self-touching-you or a feeling oneself touching you (*se toucher toi*), very simply, it is because there is no 'I' that bridges the distance between hand and hand, between I and you. Yet if there is sensing, there must be a minimal moment of reappropriation. There must be a self, even if this self is an effect of a primary difference. The matter at issue then is whether in the 'touching oneself as another' there is a priority of the self – so that everything returns to a primary interiority – or whether there is a priority of the 'other'. Of course, the kind of 'primary interiority' Nancy thinks he can find in Merleau-Ponty is not Husserl's transcendental ego: the unity of the organism is found between its parts. Nancy's point is that this 'between', insofar as it is conceived as implication or envelopment, leads back to a certain interiority.

At this point, I hope to have shown the sense in which we can speak of the unity of the lived body and of experience in Merleau-Ponty and the way this kind of unity is more radically undermined in Nancy's emphasis on fragmentation and plurality. This difference can be traced back to their respective engagements with Cartesian extension as *partes extra partes*.

Indeed, attention to the lived body in its relation to its environing world is what allowed Merleau-Ponty to overcome both subjectivism and objectivism, that is, both a concept of the soul or consciousness as a pure, non-extended interiority, and a concept of the body, and bodies in general, as exteriority, as extended *partes extra partes*. These are linked: only a non-situated, disincarnate subjectivity would have access to a purely extended world. For Merleau-Ponty, the *partes extra partes* is linked to the position of overview that a Cartesian seer (*un voyeur* and not *un voyant*) occupies, who deploys his monocular gaze on to the world and establishes a projection that flattens all depths. The space of vision is here without any surprise: everything is visible, laid out in front of the gaze. Merleau-Ponty's rejection of space as *partes extra partes* is a consequence first of his emphasis on the situatedness of the seer who is of the visible so that the visible envelops her, as well as of his emphasis on binocular vision, on this synthesis of incompossible images that let us see not depth itself, but in depth.

The lived body is the first 'here', a place in space that is unlike any other and from which space opens up meaningfully and unfolds for me. As a consequence, space is not first and foremost a system of relations between objects seen from nowhere or from everywhere at once. Existential space is always meaningfully orientated; it always has a *sens*, a direction and a meaning (PP, 263–4). Furthermore, since it is the space in which I am implicated and by which I am enveloped, existential space includes perspectives, and hence lacunae and obscurities. Against Cartesian space, which is exteriority as such, each part standing in external relation with every other, Merleau-Ponty will speak of an inside of the outside. This 'inside' are the latencies and pregnancies of existential or lived space, so that when Merleau-Ponty speaks of the inside of the outside, we should not think of this invisible or this shadow as something hidden in some inaccessible other realm, but rather as that which gives the outside – the visible – its relief and consistency – its reality – and upon which the visible opens so that there is always more to see.

As we have already seen, Nancy reappropriates the Cartesian *partes extra partes*, understanding the extra not as undifferentiated void, but as the necessarily plural places of differentiation and articulation between parts of the bodies and between bodies themselves. As a result, not only are bodies more radically plural and fragmented for Nancy than they are for Merleau-Ponty, but so is the world itself. For Nancy, the world is neither *cosmos*, 'a world of distributed places, given by, and to, the gods', nor *res extensa*, 'a natural cartography of infinite spaces with their master, the conquistador-engineer, a place-taking lieutenant for vanished gods' (C, 39). After *cosmos* and *res extensa* comes *mundus corpus*, the world of bodies: 'a world where *bodies initially articulate space*. If bodies are not in space anymore but space in bodies, then the world is spacing, tension of place' (C, 27). The world of bodies is but the articulation and spacing of the *partes extra partes* without anything left to sustain it, where this spacing or articulation is not reabsorbed into a self or a subject that would be called *the* world. Nancy calls this world a 'prodigious *press* [presse] of bodies' (C, 41).

Of course, Nancy will not deny that the world is one in some way, but this oneness of the world follows the logic of singularity, according to which a singularity is not only always in relation with a plurality of singularities but is also always plural in its origin as well. The world is not the totalisation of what is, an overarching horizon or a super container that would unite everything into a whole:

> The unity of a world is not one: it is made of a diversity, including disparity and opposition. It is made of it, which is to say that it is not added to it and does not reduce it. The unity of a world is nothing other than its diversity, and its diversity is, in turn, a diversity of worlds. A world is a multiplicity of worlds, the world is a multiplicity of worlds, and its unity is the sharing out [*partage*] and the mutual exposure in this world of all its worlds. (CW, 109)

According to the logic of the singular plural, each world is a multiplicity of singularities exposed to each other and is itself exposed to other worlds, without any overarching, final Singularity totalising all these worlds. Despite this lack of final unification, the world has a stance: it holds together the multiplicity of expositions of this 'prodigious *press* of bodies'.

One thing about which Merleau-Ponty agrees is that the world is not a given, realised totality, whether this realisation or completeness is thought to be already in things or first brought about by an intellectual synthesis. The world is essentially incomplete. Yet, despite this openness and incompleteness, the world displays some sort of unity: the unity of a style. I can recognise an individual, a perceptual thing, a town, a composer, and so on, according to its style without possessing the formula of its being and despite its undergoing variations. The unity of the style is 'known' and 'recognised' through the body. It is my body which 'synchronises' with a city space or a landscape, recognises it through its style, and deploys this embodied knowledge, for example when I find my way back to a beloved café in a city I haven't visited in many years and despite all the new constructions. Interestingly enough, Nancy will also appeal to style to define the kind of unicity that singularities possess. Speaking of the city of Sarajevo more specifically, but also of languages, cultures and forms of 'identity' more generally, Nancy speaks of all singularities or ipseities as an indefinite mêlée of traits and characteristics. As mêlée, a singularity presents a certain identifiable tone or style, but one that can never be contained in any exhaustive and fixed set of features and that, as a result, remains ultimately unidentifiable, inimitable (BSP, 152–3). Yet again Nancy also emphasises dislocation and difference and the double movement of entanglement and disentanglement – always a kind of struggle *against* – over the unification and identification of singularities.

The difference between Merleau-Ponty and Nancy in terms of unity and multiplicity, integration and dislocation, is quite subtle then. It is more a question of emphasis or priority than a marked opposition. Or maybe it is a question of their respective worries: Merleau-Ponty is worried that the body and the world only be understood as a collection of parts. Hence he is seeking for a kind of relation, synthesis or whole, all the while trying to avoid positing a given unity, be it transcendental, ideal or metaphysical. Nancy, working in the wake of the deconstruction of the Subject, is worried about the myriad ways in which some sort of unitary Subject reconstitutes itself in anti- or post-metaphysical discourses. This worry is at the basis of his early works, including his book on Descartes, but comes to the fore most clearly in his work on community: how can we think a plurality that does not rebuild a kind of interiority at a lower or higher level? What Nancy emphasises then is resistance to synthesis or unification, even if one must in the end say that the subject or the world finds in this resistance its 'stance', that is, a certain kind of unity.

There is one consequence of Nancy's emphasis on the dislocation of the body 'proper' that we have avoided addressing so far and which marks a more radical departure not only from Descartes, but also from phenomenology more generally: the radical blurring of the line between the living, sensing body (*Leib*) and the extended substance (*Körper*). Let us quote the 36th of Nancy's 'Indices on the Body' again:

> Corpus: a body is a collection of pieces, bits, members, zones, states, functions. Heads, hands and cartilage, burnings, smoothnesses, spurts, sleep, digestion, goose-bumps, excitation, breathing, digesting, reproducing, mending, saliva, synovia, twists, cramps, and beauty spots. It's a collection of collections, a *corpus corporum*, whose unity remains a question for itself. (C, 155)

We find in Nancy's works many such enumerations, many such corpuses. What is notable in all of these is that they contain what could be considered category mistakes. They mix together nouns and verbs, anatomical parts and first-person activities and experiences. In short, they confuse the body I experience in the first person with the body conceived from the third-person perspective, for example the body of medicine or physiology. Of course, if Nancy confuses, or collects, *Leiben* and *Körper* in one disparate corpus, it is not because he overlooks Merleau-Ponty's analyses, which should have cleared up this confusion once and for all. Rather, it is because Nancy's bodies, unlike Merleau-Ponty's lived body or body proper, are neither 'living' nor 'proper'. Nancy is wary of the philosophies of the body proper (*corps propre*) because what they are always looking for under the form of the body-subject (*corps-sujet*) is in the end 'Property itself', a substance that belongs only to itself (C, 5). For Nancy, all thoughts of the body proper are merely 'laborious efforts at reappropriating what we used to consider, impatiently, as "objectified" or "reified," [but] all such thoughts about the body proper are comparably contorted: in the end, they only expel the thing we desired' (C, 5). That is, they find room in their philosophies for the body only insofar as this body is not considered as object, as extension.

Against the body proper, then, Nancy will have no problem affirming that the body or corpus 'is always an "object," a body ob-jected precisely *against the claim of being a body-subject*, or an embodied subject [*sujet-en-corps*]' (C, 29, trans. mod.).[10] This affirmation should not be too striking given Nancy's reading of Descartes. For Nancy, the body proper can only be a reconstruction after the fact, an objection to the body that is ob-jected in the uttering of ego: 'Either the body is still just the "extending of itself," and it's too early for the "proper," or it's already caught in this contrariety, and it's too late. *But corpus is never properly me*' (C, 29, trans. mod.). To continue the dialogue between Merleau-Ponty and Nancy, then, it is necessary to move away from the focus on my own body and take up the question of the status of things or objects, exemplarily the stone, which has, for Nancy – and perplexingly enough – all the characteristics of bodies we have discussed in this first part of this study.

Notes

1. Nancy, *The Inoperative Community*, 76.
2. Perpich, 'Corpus Meum: Disintegrating Bodies and the Ideal of Integrity', *Hypatia* 20, no. 3 (2005): 83.
3. On the reference to Gabriel Marcel, see SC, 81–99.
4. I use these two adjectives purposefully here as an allusion to Nancy's 'Strange Foreign Bodies', which is the title both of a section of *Corpus* and of a stand-alone text found in *Corpus II*. Of course, it would be possible to provide a more generous reading of the *Phenomenology* that highlights the proximity with the later work. Indeed, Merleau-Ponty also uses the term 'co-existence' to speak of the communion or communication that sensing is. Whether this co-existence helps us bring Merleau-Ponty closer to Nancy would depend on the valence we give to the co-, to the sharing of existence: union or parting. On communication and how *co-naissance* does not imply co-incidence, see Landes, 'Le sujet de la sensation et le sujet résonant. Communion et renvoi chez Merleau-Ponty et Nancy', *Chiasmi International* 19 (2017): 143–62.
5. The note is cited in EC, 129, n. 3. The parenthetical references are to the chapter on the sociology of the body-image in Schilder's *L'image du corps*. See Schilder, *The Image and Appearance of the Human Body*, 227, where he writes: 'It is true that there is a continual interchange between our own body-image and the body-image of others. What we have seen in others we may find out in ourselves. What we have found out in ourselves we may see in others.' Merleau-Ponty also discusses Schilder in the third Nature lecture; see N, esp. 278–81.
6. Nancy, 'Extraordinary Sense', *The Senses and Society* 8, no.1 (2013): 12–13. Merleau-

Ponty, of course, will also come to understand sense as *écart*. This convergence forms the starting point of the last chapter of this study. For now, it is enough to note that even if Merleau-Ponty recognises the necessity of the plurality, that is, the difference or divergence between sensations and between the senses, these senses still exhibit a 'common dimension'. See Barbaras, *The Being of the Phenomenon*, 199–200.
7. Nancy, *The Muses*, 23.
8. Nancy, *The Muses*, 23.
9. The question that will occupy us later is whether this conclusion still applies to the Merleau-Ponty of *The Visible and the Invisible*, where the emphasis lies more and more on the 'imminence' (VI, 142), and hence the 'failure' or 'miscarriage' (VI, 9), of any coincidence.
10. Hence I think it is necessary to nuance Ian James's claim that *both* Merleau-Ponty and Nancy, when using the term 'body', do not refer to the body as an object. See James, *The Fragmentary Demand*, 131. I also disagree that Nancy's thinking 'cannot be understood without reference to' phenomenology (66). Indeed, I think that bringing Nancy too close to phenomenological concerns with the lived body actually risks obfuscating the originality of his thinking of the body. Like James, I think that Nancy's starting point is that of a primary fragmentation or dislocation. Yet, in my view and as the next part of this study will show, this starting point undermines any attempt to assimilate Nancy's body with the lived body or body-subject of Merleau-Pontian phenomenology.

Part II
THING

Whereas in the first part of this study we focused on Merleau-Ponty's and Nancy's understanding of the body – assuming that we were in both cases speaking of my own body, or the lived body of first-person experience – the blurring of the distinction between *Leib* and *Körper* – *meum corpus* and *alia corpora* – found in Nancy raises the question of the status of objects or things in Merleau-Ponty's and Nancy's respective philosophies. Hence, in the second part of this study, we take up the comparison between Merleau-Ponty and Nancy from the other end, so to speak, starting from the notion of object or thing. Whereas the conversation partner of both Merleau-Ponty and Nancy in the first part was Descartes, here I will stage a more direct dialogue with recent thinkers of objects or things: object-oriented ontologists, new materialists, speculative realists.

I start with a discussion of things in Merleau-Ponty's *Phenomenology of Perception*. While it is clear that for Merleau-Ponty the things I encounter are not bodies, at least not in the same sense as my own body, what is their mode of being? Or more specifically is their mode of being reducible to their mode of appearing? By raising the question of the status of things in the *Phenomenology*, we can begin to understand where exactly the accusation of correlationism takes hold but also how the terms of the debate are already displaced in the *Phenomenology*. Still, at this point, the status of things, or more precisely the status of their transcendence, can leave us dissatisfied. Indeed, the *Phenomenology*, and phenomenology in general, cannot ask about the natural world qua underside of the phenomenal world. The next chapter explores the transformation of Merleau-Ponty's thinking of things right after the publication of the *Phenomenology* as he engages with Sartre's essay 'Man and Things'. There we start to notice a movement away from phenomenology toward the ontology that will occupy us in the last part of this study, an ontology that can account for the wildness of things. In this section, my focus is on the strategic role played by anthropomorphism in Merleau-Ponty's description of 'inhuman' things.

This leads us, in the next chapter, to Nancy's meditations on the stone. Though these are doubtless one of the most puzzling parts of his corpus, I think that it is fair to say that their purpose is to turn our attention radically away from our own experience, our own living bodies, toward what Nancy calls the sense of world. We can only understand Nancy's claims that the stone exists, is free and makes sense once we have radically recast the concepts of existence, freedom and sense away from their phenomenological, and especially Heideggerian, acceptations. Of course, as we will see in the third part of this study, Nancy's ontology is deeply influenced by Heidegger, and its terminology remains, at least on the surface, predominantly Heideggerian. Nevertheless, the emphasis placed on Nancy's

Heideggerian heritage often obscures the radical transformation of the concepts of existence, freedom and sense Nancy operates. Only when we include the stone in our discussion of existence, freedom and sense are we in a position to take the measure of the radicality of Nancy's departure from phenomenology and the strangeness of his materialism, and situate his thinking more precisely in relation to the 'cautious' or strategic anthropomorphism we find at work in Merleau-Ponty.

Chapter 4

Things in the *Phenomenology of Perception*: The Paradox of an In-Itself-for-Us

Merleau-Ponty opens the first part of the *Phenomenology*, which will acquaint us with the body proper or one's own body, with a description of the paradox at work in perception: the paradox of an in-itself-for-us. Perception is always situated and perspectival but perception is also always perception of the thing, and not of a perspective as a sign of the thing. It is this paradox that objective thought forgets by taking the terminus of perception, the object, as the reason for and the explanation of the experience through which it appeared.

What we must attempt to understand then is 'how vision can come about from somewhere without thereby being locked within its perspective' (PP, 69). The answer will be found in the inner and outer horizons of the perceived, which are correlates of the imminent power of exploration of my gaze. My gaze enters into the object and inhabits it. Exploring it, I experience 'all things according to the sides these other things turn toward this object', but these other things are also 'places open to my gaze' and as such 'I already perceive the central object of my present vision from different angles' (PP, 71). The house, then, as the terminus of my perception, is not the house seen from nowhere. Such an object would be a thought or idea and not something perceived. Rather it is the house seen from everywhere (PP, 71). But this formulation is also not quite accurate. Indeed, as Merleau-Ponty writes,

> if the synthesis could be actual, if my experience formed a closed system, if the thing and the world could be defined once and for all, if spatio-temporal horizons could (even ideally) be made explicit and if the world could be conceived from nowhere, then nothing would exist. I would survey the world from above, and far from all places and times suddenly becoming real, they would in fact cease to be real because I would not inhabit any of them and I

would be nowhere engaged. If I am always and everywhere, then I am never and nowhere. (PP, 347)

While I do reach the thing with my gaze, this thing never achieves in my vision the 'perfect density' of an object. This seems to be a flaw of perception that is due to my being able to occupy only one perspective at the time. An absolute object would require 'an infinity of different perspectives condensed into a strict coexistence'. An absolute object would be given 'as if through a single act of vision comprising a thousand gazes' (PP, 72). But such a gaze would not require exploration, and the thing would not *show* itself since nothing of it would be hidden. Trying to give the object perfect density, I thought it was necessary to leave behind the perspective I inhabited in order to gather all perspectives all at once. Yet what happened instead is that the perceived lost all density and depth.

The mistake of objective thought then is not that it follows perception to its end, the object, but rather that it gives in to its own obsession with being: objective thought finds being in objects and objective relations and forgets the birth of the object in perceptual (perspectival, situated, incomplete) experience, which it treats as mere appearances: 'Obsessed with being, and forgetting the perspectivism of my experience, I henceforth treat being as an object'; I exceed 'perceptual experience and the synthesis of horizon', which extends into anonymity and leaves the object 'incomplete and open' (PP, 72–3). We must remember that 'it is my inherence in a point of view that at once makes possible the finitude of my perception and its opening to the total world as the horizon of all perception' (PP, 317). Similarly to Nancy, finitude for Merleau-Ponty is not a flaw or lack to be bemoaned or overcome; rather it is constitutive of what it means to be an embodied perceiver perceiving things. There would be no world, and nothing to call 'real', if we were not situated in the world we open on to as perceivers. Finitude then is part and parcel of the experience of reality; rather than a limitation on my experience, it is my 'way of inserting myself into the world' (PP, 345). Far from undermining any claim to reality, then, the perspectival nature of my experience of the world is the guarantor of the reality of what is experienced.

1. The order of the phenomena: Between being and appearance

The question, then, is not whether appearance and being are the same – whether what is is the same as what appears – or whether they are different – whether what appears dissimulates what is or what is lies behind what appears. The first position is that of a philosophy of immanence: 'if I think I see or sense, then I see or sense beyond all doubt, whatever may be true of the external object' (PP, 308). The reduction to the sphere of immanence, to the sphere of *Erlebnisse*, renders the distinction between appearance and reality inoperative. What appears is real and what is real appears, there is no reality beyond what appears and there is no appearance that distorts reality. The distinction between perception and illusion, then, can only be a distinction within their way of appearing: 'If the entire being of my perception and the entire being of my illusion is contained within their manner of appearing, then the truth that defines the one and the falsity that defines the other must also appear to me' (PP, 308). Perception is and appears as true; illusion is and appears as false. There cannot be a false perception or a true illusion.

This is the position speculative realism attributes to phenomenology. Because it is stuck 'within', it has no way of comparing reality as it is in-itself and reality as it appears 'within' consciousness. It is condemned to take what appears at face value. By articulating the demand for transcendence, speculative realism separates appearance and being to assert that reality is disconnected from appearance. But as Merleau-Ponty clearly sees, 'once this break [between appearance and reality] is made, it cannot be repaired. The most clear appearance can from then on be deceptive, and this time it is the phenomenon of truth that becomes impossible' (PP, 308). While a philosophy of immanence cannot explain the ambiguous nature of perception, a philosophy of transcendence cannot explain the experience of truth.

In his usual fashion, Merleau-Ponty will demonstrate the reciprocity between these two positions by showing how they are grounded in the same presupposition: that sense must be absolute or not be at all (PP, 309). At the level of the phenomenon, however, one does not need to follow a philosophy of immanence in affirming the identity between being and appearing, nor a philosophy of transcendence in denying that identity. One does not need to say either 'that *everything has a sense* or that *everything is non-sense*, but merely that *there is sense*' (PP, 309). It is this order of phenomena that Merleau-Ponty wants us to learn to recognise, an order in which we are neither a being nor a constituting consciousness, but 'are mixed up with the world and with others in an inextricable confusion' (PP, 481). That there is 'consciousness of something', that 'something appears', takes place without the need to *posit* consciousness on one side and the world or the object on the other and then choose which is prior. Something appears prior to any question or doubt as to what it is that will determine it as truth or falsity, as perception or illusion.

To say that the order of phenomena is first is to say that consciousness is not directly in touch with being (or with its own being) but is united to being 'through the thickness of the world' (PP, 311). This thickness is not a third thing that would stand between consciousness and being and hide the latter.[1] It is rather the world not as thing but as promise of something more that sustains my explorations. To perceive is 'to put [one's] confidence in the world' or 'to believe in a world' (PP, 311). This confident belief that connects consciousness to the world is what Merleau-Ponty expresses when he says, in the Preface to the *Phenomenology*: 'we must not wonder if we truly perceive a world; rather, we must say: the world is what we perceive' (PP, lxxx), or more paradoxically even, at the beginning of the section on perceptual faith in *The Visible and the Invisible*: 'We see the things themselves, the world is what we see' (VI, 3). This latter formulation brings together the choice between the priority of objectivity or subjectivity, of transcendence or immanence. If we see the things themselves, this means that perception brings us to what is objective, what exists in itself beyond consciousness. If the world is what we see, this means that whatever perception gives access to, whatever enters consciousness, must count as world no matter what exists beyond consciousness. Putting these two affirmations together is the role of perceptual faith. This faith, Merleau-Ponty continues, is strange because 'if we seek to articulate it into theses or statements, if we ask ourselves what is this *we*, what *seeing* is, and what *thing* or *world* is, we enter into a labyrinth of difficulties and contradictions' (VI, 3). In other words:

> The world is what I perceive, but as soon as we examine and express its absolute proximity, it also becomes, inexplicably, irremediable distance. The 'natural' man holds on to both ends of the chain, thinks at *the same time* that his perception enters into the things and that it is formed this side of his body. Yet coexist as the two convictions do without difficulty in the exercise of life, once reduced to theses and to propositions they destroy one another and leave us in confusion. (VI, 8)

Of course, perceptual faith, this belief in the world, does not amount to the certainty of any or each particular thing in the world. This is why phenomenology dismisses the Cartesian doubt about the existence of the world as confused: while I can doubt this or that thing in the world, and even all the things I believe are in the world, I cannot doubt the world if by that we mean that upon which I open as perceiver. Doubting the world would amount to doubting the 'opening' that I am. No perceived is ever necessary, since it can always be unfolded some more – this is the function of internal and external horizons: there is always more to be perceived – but this does not mean that each perceived is merely possible or probable: 'Possibility and probability presuppose the prior experience of error, and they correspond to the situation of doubt. The perceived is and remains, despite all critical training, beneath the level of doubt and demonstration' (PP, 359; see also 309). The perceived is not of the order of truth but of reality; it is not of the order of necessity but of facticity (PP, 360). Each perceived can eventually be 'crossed out' (PP, 360), but when it is, it is replaced by another perceived: 'it wasn't a rock, it was the reflection of the sun in a puddle.' What can never be crossed out is the world of perception: 'Of course, each thing can, *après coup*, appear uncertain, but at least it is certain for us that there are things, that is, that there is a world. To wonder if the world is real is to fail to understand what one is saying, since the world is not a sum of things that one could always cast into doubt, but precisely the inexhaustible reservoir from which things are drawn' (PP, 360; see also VI, 28).

We can now see why neither the idealist nor the realist understanding of 'things' adequately captures the 'nature' of things in the *Phenomenology of Perception*, which also amounts to showing that Merleau-Ponty is, but also isn't quite, a correlationist. In short, the reason is that transcendence for Merleau-Ponty is a function of my body or my bodily grip on the world: 'my experience opens onto things and transcends itself in them because it always accomplishes itself within the framework of a certain arrangement [*montage*] with regard to the world that is the definition of my body' (PP, 317). The example Merleau-Ponty gives is that of a thing being large when my gaze cannot encompass it. He explains: 'Thus, it is certainly true that every perception of a thing, of a form, or of a size as real, or that every perceptual constancy sends us back to the positing of a world and a system of experiences in which my body and the phenomenon would be rigorously connected' (PP, 317). This seems to subjectivise reality, even if we emphasise that for Merleau-Ponty the real thing is an intersensorial thing that speaks to all of my senses. Because the thing speaks to all of my senses, there is a depth of the object 'that no sensory sampling [*prélèvement*] will ever exhaust' (PP, 224, trans. mod.). I can withdraw from the experience of the thing and isolate one sensory layer: I close my eyes in the concert hall and focus on the sound (PP, 230–1) or I abstract from the lighting and the surrounding objects and focus on the colour of the 'white' sheets of paper (PP, 234–5). I harvest (*prélève*) these 'sensations' on the intersensorial object. But on what ground does Merleau-Ponty claim that this sensory harvesting or sampling can never be complete and hence that the thing cannot be reduced to its appearance? Is the incompletion contingent on the finitude of the subject or does it belong to the thing as such? This is the crucial question.

In order to understand how Merleau-Ponty can claim the inexhaustibility of the thing as a matter of necessity, we need to ask about the kind of unity the intersensorial thing possesses. Contrary to Husserl, the thing is 'not a substrate, an empty X, or a subject of inherence' on to which properties would be tacked, but rather 'that unique accent that is found in each [thing], that unique manner of existing of which its properties are a secondary expression' (PP, 333). Each property expresses the unique manner in which this thing *west*, exists. This means that in order to provide a complete definition of an attribute ('blue') we would need to define the entire subject of this attribute: 'it is impossible to describe fully the color of a carpet without saying that it is a carpet, or a woolen carpet, and without implying in this color a certain tactile value, a certain weight, and a certain resistance to sound' (PP, 337). The style of the thing as its manner of being is also what Merleau-Ponty calls the thing's sense. The sense of the thing is not behind the various appearances of the thing, but is found right at the thing itself. It inhabits the thing like the 'soul inhabits the body' (PP, 333). Sense for Merleau-Ponty, like for Nancy, is not to be reduced to signification: while I can signify the thing through a name by abstracting from certain qualities and reducing the appearance to a name or an ideal essence ('blue carpet'), the sense of the thing lies in its total appearance, where each sensuous property affects all the others. In other words, the thing is a unity that is more than the sum of its parts, a total Gestalt.

2. Answering the accusation of correlationism

Yet if we pay attention to the way Merleau-Ponty speaks of this sense, style or soul of thing, we see where the accusation of correlationism takes hold. It is worth quoting a passage at length:

> The sense of the ashtray (or at least its total and individual sense, such as is presented in perception) is not a certain ideal of the ashtray that coordinates the sensory appearances and that would only be accessible to the understanding. Rather, it animates the ashtray, and it is quite evidently embodied in it. This is why we say that in perception the thing is given to us 'in person,' or 'in flesh and blood.' Prior to other persons, the thing accomplishes this miracle of expression: an interior that is revealed on the outside, a signification that descends into the world and begins to exist there and that can only be fully understood by attempting to see it there, in its place. Thus, the thing is the correlate of my body and, more generally, of my existence of which my body is merely the stabilized structure. The thing is constituted in the hold my body has upon it; it is not at first a signification for the understanding, but rather a structure available for inspection by the body. And if we want to describe the real such as it appears to us in perceptual experience, we find it burdened with anthropological predicates. Given that relations

among things or among the aspects of things are always mediated by our body, all of nature is the setting of our own life and our interlocutor in a sort of dialogue. (PP, 333–4, trans. mod.)

Here Merleau-Ponty states very clearly that the thing is constituted (*elle se constitue*, which can also means that it constitutes itself) through its very interaction with my body so that the thing as it appears to perception is always burdened or loaded (*chargée*) with anthropological predicates. Hence, it seems that perception does not reach the 'real' but only a pseudo-real covered with anthropological predicates, because of what Merleau-Ponty calls 'the coupling of our body and things' (PP, 334). In this coupling, we should not say that the thing gives itself (in the sense that it imposes itself on me), but rather that it is 'inwardly taken up' by my body, *re*constituted by it (PP, 341), like a text is taken up in reading and interpretation. What is for me is only in accordance with my body and its power.

The accusation of correlationism seems to be even more pointed if we bring into account Merleau-Ponty's infamous statement about Laplace's nebula: 'Nothing will ever lead me to understand what a nebula, which could not be seen by anyone, might be' (PP, 338). Here Merleau-Ponty is discussing what Meillassoux calls the problem of ancestrality: how can a philosophy of experience – even if it is not explicitly a philosophy of consciousness as Husserl's – speak intelligibly about events or phenomena that precede human beings, and hence the possibility of experience (see AF, 9–10)? For Meillassoux, the phenomenologist will need to transform the meaning of ancestral statements: statements about the accretion of the universe and the Laplacian nebula are not about the universe as it existed prior to the possibility of its being experienced but rather about what is now experienced or thought about the universe, what can be calculated and proven, and so on (see AF, 13–15). If the phenomenologist reduces everything to the experiences I can have of it, then she cannot account for things that are in principle unexperienceable, such as the Laplacian nebula, without first turning them into a correlate of experience: the nebula that existed at the accretion of the universe becomes the nebula of my statements about it. In a sense, Merleau-Ponty is making such a move when he states that 'Laplace's nebula is not behind us, at our origin, but rather out in front of us in the cultural world' (PP, 456). The nebula is not a thing in itself but a perceptual object the meaning of which is culturally dependent. The point is not merely that the meaning of the word 'nebula' is socially constructed so that there was nothing *called* a nebula prior to humans who created the word, but rather that for a nebula to make sense at all, it must be something *in relation to which* a perceiver can in principle be situated.

Hence, the nebula is a perceptual and cultural object not because 'the world is constituted by consciousness, but rather [because] consciousness always finds itself already at work in the world' (PP, 456). Rather than reducing all things to their meaning for consciousness, Merleau-Ponty emphasises our a priori embeddedness in the world we are trying to make sense of. Of course the mathematical expression of the nebula, which for Meillassoux would reach the 'real' nebula rather than the one that is correlated to me, does not seem to require our embeddedness in the world or our body's position relative to it. But for Merleau-Ponty it is a mistake to assume that one expression (the mathematical) reaches the true or real thing while others would be merely subjective. All forms of expression are ways of taking up what is given – or to be more precise we should say, since even perception is a form of expression, that all forms of expression are ways of responding to the solicitation of the world and hence participate in the giving of the thing. Even the most abstract and 'objective' ones are grounded upon perceptual experience and the dialogue between body and world, without being restricted to it.

This would of course not satisfy the speculative realist. While it is true that Merleau-Ponty does not reduce things to their meaning as it is constituted by consciousness, a thing is, for him, always the correlate of the body: it is through my body that I reach things. Yet, if we return to the passage where Merleau-Ponty insists on correlation, dialogue, coupling, and continue our reading, we find Merleau-Ponty stating very clearly that the preceding discussion of the thing was one-sided and partial (PP, 336). For Merleau-Ponty it is also the case that the thing I perceive is 'presented as a thing in itself even to the person who perceives it' (PP, 336). This is why Merleau-Ponty can say that perception 'poses the problem of a genuine in-itself-for-us' (PP, 336), a category that undoes the Cartesian (and Sartrian) ontology upon which the problem of ancestral statements is based. Merleau-Ponty's question is, then, 'how might we simultaneously understand that the thing is the correlate of my knowing body and that it denies that it is?' (PP, 339, trans. mod.).[2]

The in-itself of perception has to be able to be given to us, without this givenness destroying its independence, its quality as in-itself. Phenomenologically, this experience is not mysterious. Yet the categories of objective thought, which start by severing the ties that unite body and world, cannot make sense of this experience. The experience Merleau-Ponty is concerned with is of course perception, but at this point he differentiates between everyday perception, what in 'Eye and Mind' he calls profane vision, 'which bears on things just enough to find in them their familiar presence', and a perception that would 'rediscover what of the non-human [*inhumain*] is hidden within them' (PP, 336). We said above that in our encounter with things, things seem to adapt themselves to the powers of our body. Yet here, 'if we suspend our everyday dealings', we realise that 'the thing is unaware of us'. The thing is 'hostile and foreign, it is no longer our interlocutor, but rather a resolutely silent Other [*Autre*], a Self that escapes us as much as the intimacy of an external consciousness' (PP, 336). It is always possible to see human artefacts as having been 'placed into the world' intentionally – they are fabricated, part of an artificial world; things on the contrary 'are rooted in a background of non-human nature [*nature inhumaine*]' (PP, 338). Because of this, they lend themselves 'to an infinite exploration' and are 'truly inexhaustible' (PP, 338). Another way of saying this is that they have depth. Merleau-Ponty uses the example of a painting: the painting has sense and gives us to see but it doesn't lend itself to my infinite exploration: if I look at it sideways or from the back, there is nothing more to see; if I tear it to pieces I am left with pieces of canvas. A stone by contrast can be explored from all and any perspective; if I shatter it to pieces, I have fragments of stone that can also be explored, and so on.

Unlike the philosophies of consciousness, Merleau-Ponty does not reduce transcendence to a way of being given (as one could claim Husserl does). By returning to the body, and to the body's ties to the natural world, Merleau-Ponty is able to point to a more resistant form of transcendence, to something strange or inhuman within experience itself. Yet this strangeness or inhumanity of the thing seems to come from our body and our body's attachment to the natural world: 'Although lived by us, the thing is no less transcendent to our life, because the human body, along with its habits that outline a human environment around itself, is crossed by a movement toward the world itself' (PP, 341). This 'world itself' is the natural world upon which all anthropological worlds are constructed and presented.[3] Now my habitual body projects around itself human worlds, but as body it remains anchored in the natural world: 'My body, which assures my insertion within the human world through my habitus, only in fact does so by first projecting me into a natural world that always shines through from beneath the others – just as the canvas shines through from beneath the painting – and gives the human world an air of fragility' (PP, 307). The thing then is not reducible to its anthropological predicates because I am in the world through a body that is never fully mine, i.e. that is never constituted by and hence laid out in front of consciousness. Here, the resistance of the perceived is not merely a function of the perspectival nature of experience, of the fact that since I am in the world, inserted in it, I necessarily open on to it from a certain point of view. Rather, the inhumanity of the perceived is a function of the 'inhumanity' of my body. I do not possess the secret of the thing because I do not possess the secret of my body and its latent knowledge (PP, 241–2). As Merleau-Ponty writes:

> This is what I express by saying that I perceive with my body or with my senses, my body and my senses being precisely this habitual knowledge of the world, this implicit or sedimented science. If my consciousness constituted the world that it perceives at this moment, there would be no distance between it and that world, and between them no interval would be possible, my consciousness would penetrate the world all the way to its most secret articulations, intentionality would transport us to the heart of the object, and in the same stroke the perceived would not have the thickness of a present and consciousness would become neither lost nor ensnared in the perceived. On the contrary, we are conscious of an inexhaustible object and we get bogged down in it because, between it and us, there is this latent knowledge that our gaze uses, of which we merely presume that the rational development is possible, and that always remains prior to perception. (PP, 247)

There is an intentional life of the body that does not concern my personal life but rather 'the life of my eyes, hands, and ears, which are so many natural selves' (PP, 224) that operates with a latent knowledge I do not possess. The 'thickness' of the perceived, its inexhaustibility, is a function of this nature that traverses me in the natural or anonymous life of my senses.[4]

3. The limit of the answer in the *Phenomenology* and the move to ontology

Still, in the *Phenomenology of Perception*, 'Nature' occupies an ambiguous and unstable place in relation to experience. Is nature an elusive thing *beyond or behind* what is given in our experience? Or is it rather something that is necessarily part of my experience insofar as it is needed in order to be able to make sense of our experience at all? Nature in the broadest sense is the ultimate background or context of all possible experiences. It is this 'immense individual from which my experiences are drawn, and who remains on the horizon of my life' (PP, 343). This nature (or natural world) is the ultimate correlate of my experiential life as well as what I am inserted into and what I inhere in insofar as I am a natural being. Nature, however, also names a restricted part of the natural world, one that is opposed to all the anthropological or cultural worlds that are instituted upon it. As such, nature in this restricted sense is a layer of nature in its wider sense, one that is purified of all human artifice. This nature is non-human but only with regard to a certain experiential perspective, namely that of my pre-personal, general bodily intentionality. Between these two senses of nature, Merleau-Ponty is reaching for something like an outside: nature as something that resists or refuses to appear within experience and more precisely that appears within experience only as this resistance, refusal or withdrawal.[5]

In the *Phenomenology*, Merleau-Ponty uses the concept of Nature to do two different things: to explain the thickness or inexhaustibility of the perceived, and to explain the teleology of consciousness (see PP, 307). In the same way that 'the pre-logical unity of the body schema' guides the perceptual synthesis of all these natural selves that are my senses, the unique natural world is supposed to guide the teleology of consciousness. This nature guarantees that all my experiences and all the anthropological worlds are gathered in a unified whole that form the ultimate horizon of my life. Nature as the horizon of my life remains at the limit of my experience, grounding and guaranteeing the unity of my experiential life. Yet this limit is not the paradoxical experience of an outside. Rather it is the experience of a horizon, of a unity that always remains an idea in the Kantian sense insofar as experience is never finished and hence the possibility of additions and corrections always remains open. This does not explain the thickness of the perceived, however. In order to do so, Merleau-Ponty relies on another experience of nature, one which he positions as outside of my personal life, hence outside of the possibility of questioning and doubt, but one which is still very much experienced insofar as I am a body, a natural self. Radical resistance or refusal has become the resistance of one part of me (unreflected life of the body) with regard to another part of me (reflective consciousness).[6] The thickness of the perceived is referred back to a fact about experiential life, not any more the finitude of consciousness incapable of infinite synthesis, but the pre-personal, pre-reflective knowledge that inhabits my body. This fact (my body) is the starting point of a phenomenology of perception, one that cannot be questioned, since it is always from within the dialogue between body and world that any question or doubt arises.

Merleau-Ponty will grapple with the limits of phenomenology more explicitly when he will seek to question this belonging-together of body and world, their being applied to one another. In the *Phenomenology*, Merleau-Ponty has dialecticised the notion of subject and object into one single system of which they are correlates. But phenomenology cannot account for the being of the dialectical relation itself. Because the body–world (natural selves–natural world) correlate is posited as the ultimate fact out of which all intelligibility arises, and hence as that which itself cannot be questioned intelligibly, there can be no investigation of the natural world or natural being as the underside of the phenomenal world, of a kind of pre-world upon which the perceived world rests qua correlate of existence. The nature that is our partner in dialogue has meaning, but outside of this dialogue nature has no meaning of its own.[7] This is the reason why the last word of the *Phenomenology of Perception* is contingency. Radical reflection illuminates everything but the origin of the intentional relation itself, which sinks into the darkness of pure contingency. Beyond this correlation, again, as Merleau-Ponty says, 'there is nothing more to understand' (PP, 383). Or, as Gary Madison puts it:

> If then the ground of reflection, as it itself discovers it, is our bodily being in the world which appears to reflection as a contingent and unmotivated fact, reflection is forced to recognize that it itself exists and that consequently truth exists only on the basis of a radical contingency, that the absolute is unthinkable, and that all meaning maintains itself on the ground of non-meaning.[8]

The problem with phenomenology and its ultimate assertion of the contingency of the correlation, beyond which we cannot go, is that it remains unable to explain the thingliness of the thing, that is, the thing insofar as it always resists the sense that it gives to me, in any other way than by reference to the finite or contingent structure of my means of access to it: my body. The problem is neither that the intentional relation is a one-way relation from consciousness to world, nor that what is given is always an essence (an idea, Cubeness). As we have seen, Merleau-Ponty's phenomenology overcomes these two prejudices of traditional phenomenology. Instead, the problem lies in the fact that the intentional relation – even when dialecticised and incarnate – is still conceived as absolute: as having no limits, or better as having a limit it cannot think and hence that doesn't make a difference. As Ted Toadvine puts it, phenomenology 'cannot express resistance or contingency', the 'wildness' of things,[9] or it can do so only in Husserl's convoluted way – which is similar to the convolution Meillassoux finds in relation to the fossils: the in-itself is for us, non-sense is a sense. Such convolution points to phenomenology's inability to think an outside, a non-sense, that is also not already a kind of inside, a kind of sense. This is the crux of the new realist criticism, and it applies to Merleau-Ponty insofar as he oscillates between integrating nature into experience as a primordial layer of experience, one that still refers to a certain form of subjectivity (lived body, tacit cogito) and hence can be described by phenomenology, and positing nature as an outside that is the mysterious, unintelligible source of experience but of which phenomenology cannot speak.

As he moves toward his later ontology, Merleau-Ponty will undertake an examination of the logic of the outside, questioning phenomenology's own mode of access to what lies in principle outside of experience: 'the back side of things that we have not constituted', what is also called 'Nature' (S, 180). In this transition, the Nature lectures form a crucial step since they allow Merleau-Ponty to move away from a naturalistic Cartesian conception of nature toward an ontology of sense where sense is made right at nature itself. The very reality of Nature includes its reference to perceptibility (to sense or Gestalt) so that the perceived is referred to a natural being without necessitating the passage through subjectivity. Rather than relating the perceived to the natural world through the experience of the body (and the senses as so many 'natural selves'), Merleau-Ponty will find the sense of the perceived, or necessity of a reference to sense, within nature itself, but a nature now understood as containing its own *percipii* – a certain negativity or generativity.[10] If nature is the originary productivity or generativity underneath all of our creations or institutions, then we can make sense of the question of the emergence both of the self-sensing body and of consciousness as an event within nature. Consciousness – logos – need not be produced by another, transcendent dimension, but is rather another dimension, fold or complication of nature itself.[11]

Phenomenology will, in a sense, 'overcome' its own limits in an ontology of nature that forms the first 'leaf' of Being. It will do so not by positing a pure exteriority and asking that we leave ourselves behind to reach it, as the new realists ask us to do, but rather by meditating its own shadow. Merleau-Ponty's thinking then will become a thinking of what cannot be given: the latency that gives to figures all their depth and dimensionality, their visibility or their shadows, and that phenomenology cannot grasp because it 'obliges whatever is not nothing to present itself to consciousness', to appear in an act, in one *Erlebnis* (VI, 244). As Merleau-Ponty writes,

> the ultimate task of phenomenology as philosophy of consciousness is to understand its relationship to non-phenomenology. What resists phenomenology within us ... cannot remain outside phenomenology and should have its place within it. The philosopher must bear [her] shadow, which is not simply the factual absence of a future light. (S, 178)[12]

Or in the words of Madison again:

> As the shadow of consciousness and its own latency, Being is the absence of light and what consciousness can never illuminate, since it is the very source of its own light. Consciousness cannot think Being except by thinking its own blindness, what it cannot see because it is that which makes it see.[13]

When we turn more explicitly toward Merleau-Ponty's ontology in Chapter 8, our question will be to what extent Being (or the Flesh) is a plural principle that allows for a plurality of bodies, experiences and worlds that remain incompossible. This is also the question of whether the source of the inexhaustibility of the thing and of the incompletion of the world is due to the contingent form of my own embodiment as my point of access to things and the world, or whether it is due to a principle of inexhaustibility that is 'older than my operations or my acts' (VI, 123). This is also the question of the possibility of 'wild things', things that are not fitted to my operations and my acts, of a sense that is not a sense 'for me'. As a first step toward the discussion of wild things, let us first look at the transformation of the notion of 'things' in Merleau-Ponty's work in the few years following the publication of the *Phenomenology*. There we will see that Merleau-Ponty approaches the 'inhumanity' of things through a strategic anthropomorphism that resonates with some new realist approaches. We will also find the seeds of the later ontology.

Notes

1. Here we find a key insight that will become central in Merleau-Ponty's ontology: distance not as an objective quantity to be traversed but as an ontological thickness that is not the opposite of proximity but its condition of possibility. Hence, Merleau-Ponty will speak of Being as 'Being of the far-offs (*être des lointains*)' (VI, 248). See also Barbaras, *The Being of the Phenomenon*, chapter 12, esp. 210–11.
2. *Elle le nie* does not mean, as both Landes and Smith seems to think, that the thing denies or rejects my body but rather that the thing denies *that it is a correlate of my body*.
3. In this sense, the method in the *Phenomenology* is still progressive: it is a question of returning to a primordial ground and reconstructing a higher level of experiences as founded modalities of being-in-the-world. When experience is conceived as expression through and through, however, the soil of expression becomes an infinite depth, an origin that remains withdrawn or in excess of what is expressed and as such indefinitely relaunches the work of expression. Such a conception of the 'soil' or 'origin' also transforms Merleau-Ponty's conception of teleology. See Barbaras, *The Being of the Phenomenon*, chapters 3 and 4, esp. 59–67.
4. For a discussion of the limits of anonymity when it comes to thinking the ontological rather than phenomenal transcendence of the world, see Barbaras, *The Being of the Phenomenon*, 33–40.
5. On these three senses of 'nature', see Toadvine, 'Naturalism, Estrangement, and Resistance: On the Lived Sense of Nature', in Kuperus and Oele (eds), *Ontologies of Nature*, esp. 195.
6. To complicate matters even further, the 'unreflected life', as we have already discussed, is understood as 'tacit cogito', a minimal reflexivity or contact of self to self. It is as if the *natural* self as tacit cogito had already broken with nature and introduced a minimal space of interiority within nature that is then used to explain personal, reflective life. On this tension between nature and the tacit cogito as the ground of reflection in the *Phenomenology*, see Toadvine, *Merleau-Ponty's Philosophy of Nature*, chapter 2.
7. Hence, there would be a remnant of naturalism in the *Phenomenology*. According to Jocelyn Benoist, in the later works, Merleau-Ponty would abandon the 'truth of naturalism' – that there is something below meaning that is not yet meaning – by including meaning and intentionality in first nature. This would lead to complete loss of exterior-

ity and resistance. See Benoist, 'The Truth of Naturalism', in Alloa, Chouraqui and Kaushik (eds), *Merleau-Ponty and Contemporary Philosophy*, 111–20.
8. See Madison, *The Phenomenology of Merleau-Ponty*, 162. The inability to think the Absolute is of course Meillassoux's core issue with correlationism.
9. Toadvine, 'Chiasm and Chiaroscuro', *Chiasmi International* 3 (2001): 228, 230.
10. The growing importance of Heidegger in Merleau-Ponty's development of this negativity is discussed in Chapter 7.
11. On the importance of the Nature lectures for Merleau-Ponty's ontology, see Barbaras, 'Merleau-Ponty and Nature', *Research in Phenomenology* 31, no. 1 (2001): 22–38. See also Vanzago, 'Nature, Negativity, Event', *Chiasmi International* 11 (2009): 171–83, and of course Toadvine's *Merleau-Ponty's Philosophy of Nature*.
12. Barbaras explains this passage by saying that here sense is not opposed to fact and phenomenology is not opposed to ontology. Rather than a phenomenology that would give us the sense of facts or an ontology that would give us brute facts foreign to sense, we are seeking the fact of sense so as to 'catch sense in the act, at its very Birthplace'. See Barbaras, *The Being of the Phenomenon*, 78. Here the influence of Derrida's introduction to Husserl's 'Origin of Geometry' on Barbaras is undeniable. Barbaras's entire study is exemplary in its attempt at demonstrating how Merleau-Ponty's philosophy tries to situate itself (not always successfully) between or beyond the alternatives of realism and idealism. See esp. chapters 5 and 6.
13. Madison, *The Phenomenology of Merleau-Ponty*, 196.

Chapter 5

Things after the *Phenomenology*: Merleau-Ponty's Cautious Anthropomorphism

Following the publication of the *Phenomenology*, Merleau-Ponty returns to the question of things again but this time outside of the context of a phenomenology of perception per se. In the 1948 conference 'L'homme et l'objet' and in the *Causeries*,[1] also from 1948, responding to Sartre's 1947 article 'Man and Things', Merleau-Ponty takes up some of Sartre's own references (Ponge, Bachelard, surrealism) in order to challenge Sartre's ontology of the object. We said earlier that Merleau-Ponty is starting to sketch a movement out of phenomenology toward an ontology that can account for the wildness of things. What interests me particularly in the texts from this period is the role that anthropomorphism plays in this move. We know that in *The Visible and the Invisible*, speaking of the flesh of the visible, Merleau-Ponty is quick to point out that he in no way means to 'do anthropology' or to 'describe a world covered over with all our own projections, leaving aside what it can be under the human mask' (VI, 136). Yet it would be difficult to deny that Merleau-Ponty often speaks in ways that sound anthropomorphic, and such a tendency is especially marked in the texts from 1948. For example, in the *Causeries*, he speaks of things as 'clothed [*revêtues*] in human characteristics' (WP, 49), as 'a combination [*mélange*] of mind and body' (WP, 43), and as 'symboli[sing] for us a particular way of behaving [*conduite*]' (WP, 48, trans. mod.). But even in *The Visible and the Invisible*, Merleau-Ponty speaks again of the necessity for my gaze to 'clothe [things] with its own flesh' (VI, 131). How is this not supposed to lead us to believe that we are only doing anthropology and addressing things only insofar as they are 'covered over with all our own projections'?

Rather than attempting to defend Merleau-Ponty against the charge of anthropomorphism, I want to highlight the role it plays in his thinking. By focusing on his engagement with Sartre's essay and reading carefully the texts from 1948 in which we find the most direct and most puzzling anthropomorphic statements, I think we come to see that, when Merleau-Ponty emphasises the necessity to 'clothe' things with our own flesh, it is not to reduce them to objects that can be experienced or grasped by us, but rather to ensure their own resistance or adversity, and even, paradoxically, their inhumanity, against a Cartesian-Sartrian ontology of the object. Merleau-Ponty's anthropomorphic statements, then, must be read in the context of the polemic against the Cartesian-Sartrian ontology of the object, which is carried out indirectly through a reading of Ponge, as well as others (Bachelard, surrealism). In this way, Merleau-Ponty's thinking of things resonates with and to a certain degree anticipates more recent thinkers, such as Steven Shaviro and Jeffrey Cohen, who have adopted 'a cautious anthropomorphism' as a strategy to dislodge the human from the centre of the universe and give things back their inhuman vitality and agency.[2]

1. Sartre's things

As we all know, for Sartre, 'man' as lack of being is essentially 'desire to be'. The ontological description of the being of the human being we find in *Being and Nothingness* is supplemented by an existential psychoanalysis, the goal of which is to unearth the fundamental choice of the human being, or how its desire to be deploys itself. And since what the human being seeks in its 'choice of being' is *being*, and since each thing – or more precisely each quality of things (watery, slimy, smooth, hard) – functions as an objective symbol of being, this psychoanalysis takes the form of a psychoanalysis of things. This psychoanalysis of things should be 'rigorously objective', that is, without reference to our affective dispositions, and primordially our sexual desire. For Sartre psychoanalysis discovers that 'deeply engaged in the matter of things there are other potentialities which remain entirely transcendent even though they correspond to a still more fundamental choice of human reality, a choice of being' (BN, 602). These material potentialities are not merely psychological projections of our desires but rather objective qualities – objective in the sense that they are transcendent, even if they are only revealed through the for-itself – that come to 'function as a symbol of being-in-itself' (BN, 604). For Sartre, then 'a psychoanalysis of things and of their matter ought above all to be concerned with establishing the way in which each thing is the objective symbol of being and of the relation of human reality to this being' (BN, 602–3). It is in this context of a psychoanalysis of things that we find Sartre's famous description of the honey, a description Merleau-Ponty will often refer to alongside that of the lemon and the pebble.[3]

The sliminess of the honey symbolises not the fear of death or nothingness but rather the fear of being absorbed into the in-itself (BN, 609). The slimy resists my desire for assimilation or possession. When I try to grasp it and hold it in my hands, it yields all the while sticking to me. Rather than letting itself be possessed, it possesses me (BN, 609). The attempt to possess the slimy reveals the priority of the In-itself over the foundationless For-itself. In this sense, the slimy is related to the experience of nausea, where consciousness *s'empâte* or *s'englue*, thickens, and loses its nihilating power to cut into being, which lets the world appear as a differentiated totality of 'thises'. Nausea befalls us when the coat of veneer that consciousness put on Being has melted and the world returns to the undifferentiated mass of the In-itself. This is how Roquentin, the protagonist of the novel *Nausea*, describes his experience: 'the diversity of things, their individuality, were only an appearance, a veneer. This veneer had melted, leaving soft, monstrous masses, all in disorder – naked, in a frightful, obscene nakedness.'[4] The oppressiveness of the contact with the world arises because Roquentin is unable to differentiate himself from the world around him ('I am not the whole of being') and to differentiate between singular beings ('It is this and not that'). Because there is no differentiation and no articulation between the existents, there remains only the oppressive paralysis or stiffness of Being. Indeed, nausea is what reveals the general sense of bodily existence to my consciousness. It is the taste of contingency as such, unqualified, insipid, without colour (BN, 444–5).[5] In nausea, consciousness apprehends itself, others, and the world in the pure contingency of bodily presence.

What nausea helps us understand is how the human being negotiates its desire to be in order to avoid getting entangled in things, overtaken by them. It is here that we should locate the role of the stone in Sartre's psychoanalysis of things. While the slimy represents the possible assimilation or absorption of the for-itself in the in-itself, the stone, as a 'digested indigestible', represents, as Sartre writes, 'the dream of a non-destructive assimilation' (BN, 579). The problem with desire is that as desire to assimilate – read: consume, devour, ingest – it necessarily destroys its object. Hence, 'the For-itself dreams of an object which may be entirely assimilated by *me*, which would be me, without dissolving into me but still keeping the structure of the *in-itself*' (BN, 579). This object would be possessed by me but in such a way that my possession would leave no trace on it. This kind of possession, Sartre continues, 'is deeply symbolized in the quality of "smooth" or "polished." What is smooth can be taken and felt but remains no less impenetrable, does not give way in the least beneath the appropriative caress – it is like water' (BN, 579).

According to Saint Aubert, the stone is the element Sartre chooses for his psychoanalysis of things because the stone is a false element. In *Being and Nothingness*, our fundamental desire to be manifests itself as the desire to be God, that is, the 'in-itself-for-itself, consciousness become substance, substance become the cause of itself' (BN, 575).[6] In 'Man and Things', this desire for the substantialisation of consciousness is symbolised by the stone. What we desire is 'to be entirely consciousness and, at the same time, entirely stone' (MT, 449). If Sartre shows interest in Francis Ponge's collection of poems *Le parti pris des choses*, it is because he finds in it exactly such a (failed) attempt at 'symbolically fulfilling our shared desire *to exist after the manner of the "in-itself"*' (MT, 449). Ponge's project, as the title of the collection shows, is to take the side of things, to come to terms with the existence of things by coming around to their terms (MT, 396). To do so, Ponge effects a dehumanisation of the world. He strips things of the practical significations that human beings have projected on to them to render them docile: 'any kind of object will appear as a thing as soon as we have taken care to divest it [*déshabiller*] of the all too human significations initially bestowed upon it' (MT, 400). Of course, the attempt at describing things without the human, to surprise them in their solitary and inhuman existence, remains an ideal limit. There is always a relation to the human being since, as Ponge himself recognises, 'it is not things that speak among themselves, but human beings who speak among themselves about things' (Ponge cited in MT, 400). If we cannot get rid of the human, then the second best option is to dehumanise the human being itself as much as possible. If Ponge 'ascribes human behaviour to mineral objects', and hence is guilty of a certain anthropomorphism, Sartre tells is, it is 'in order to mineralize human beings' (MT, 447–8):

> Look at the stone, it is alive. Look at life, it is stone. Anthropomorphic comparisons abound, but at the same time as they cast – a relatively dubious – light on things, their effect is mainly to degrade [*degrader*] the human, to 'tangle it up' [*empêtrer*], as our author has it. (MT, 441, trans. mod.)

Even words themselves are naturalised and turn to stone. It is true that Ponge compares words to the slime secreted by the human-mollusc, but this secretion builds a hard shell that protects the soft body of the human mollusc and allows it to glide on things without being assaulted by them. It is in this sense that Ponge, as we said above, 'symbolically fulfill[s] our shared desire *to exist after the manner of the "in-itself"*' (MT, 449).

Ultimately, for Sartre, however, Ponge's approach remains naïve. In asserting the pre-eminence of the object over the subject, his position ends up being that of scientific materialism. His 'universe of pure observation', which seeks to 'describe things as they are by taking them up from within', ends up being the 'universe of science' (MT, 444). Ponge, Sartre claims, 'came to things not, as he claimed, with naive wonderment, but with a materialist bias' (MT, 447). After having 'locked up everything in the world, including himself insofar as he is a thing', Ponge should realise that 'all that remains is his contemplative consciousness which, precisely because it is consciousness *of* the world, finds itself necessarily *outside of* the world: a naked, almost impersonal consciousness' (MT, 450–1). Instead, Ponge opts for a theoretical materialism that reduces human beings to mannequins. While the inhumanity of things should throw us back upon ourselves and make us recover our consciousness in its meaning-given activity, in Ponge's poem 'there is constant mention of man's relationships with the thing in question, but these are stripped of all human meaning' (MT, 437). What he forgets is himself: he tries to close the world and enclose himself within it, yet 'he still ends up on the outside, staring at things, all alone' (MT, 450). What Ponge should do as a good phenomenologist, however, is content himself with describing what he sees, which includes *human* significations. If he did so, Sartre claims, 'The sense of things and their "ways of behaving" would shine all the more brightly' (MT, 451, trans. mod.).

Galen Johnson in a recent contribution states that the problem with Sartre's reading of Ponge is that he lacks a distinction between object and thing.[7] To be fair, Sartre does differentiate between the in-itself (or being) and objects (or 'thises'), and in 'Man and Things' he also mentions Ponge's distinction between objects – what is overlaid with human signification – and things. Yet it is true that Sartre imposes his own ontology on to Ponge's universe and hence can only interpret the priority given to things as a reduction to mechanistic materialism: a world without consciousness or meaning. In Sartre's ontology, things are objects, and as such, they cannot be active. As we have seen, when things start to exist underneath my hands, when things take the initiative, then my consciousness is compromised and threatens to be reduced to mere passivity: it becomes thick, sticky, and I feel nauseated.

In Sartre's ontology, objects are without their own adversity or aggressivity. They are strictly localised and have clearly delimited boundaries that give them stability and ensure that they remain in their place. As a result, I can walk all around the object, vary my point of view upon it at will and come to possess it. My relation with objects then is one of detached contemplation, exemplified by the Cartesian *inspectio mentis*. Yet as we recalled from Descartes's Second Meditation, it is only after having stripped the piece of wax of all its human qualities – the sensible qualities that speak to the human body as sensing body – that the mind can contemplate the true object. Hence contemplation comes at a price: the object does not speak to our body any more. It is true that Sartre agrees with Bachelard, who 'rightly reproaches phenomenology for not sufficiently taking into account what he calls the "coefficient of adversity" in objects' (BN, 324). For Sartre, however, it is the project of my freedom that reveals 'realities provided with a coefficient of adversity and utilizable instrumentality' (BN, 509). For example, 'It is because I am there and because I have made of myself what I am that the rock develops in relation to my body a coefficient of adversity' (BN, 489). Adversity is a function of my freedom and hence of the revelation of being. It is the necessary resistance that allows me to feel my freedom or to feel myself exist as freedom – how else would freedom, which is nothing, feels itself existing? As we will see, by engaging with Sartre's ontology and with his reading of Ponge, Merleau-Ponty is led to a different notion of things and a different understanding of their aggressivity or adversity.

2. Merleau-Ponty's things

In the conference 'Man and Object' as well as in the third of the *Causeries*, Merleau-Ponty will propose a different reading of Ponge's materialism by putting it in relation with Bachelard's psychoanalysis of things as well as Breton's surrealism.[8] Unlike the Cartesian ontology Sartre inherits, for Merleau-Ponty, things are never 'simply neutral *objects* which stand before us for our contemplation' (WP, 48).[9] Rather, 'each one of them symbolises or recalls a particular way of behaving, provoking in us reactions which are either favourable or unfavourable' (WP, 48). Things are, as Ponge says, 'complexes'. A complex, Merleau-Ponty writes in relation to Lacan, 'is a stereotypical attitude regarding certain situations. In some way, the complex is the most stable element of behavior, being a collection of behavioral traits which are always reproduced in analogous situations' (CPP, 84). To speak of a thing as a complex is to acknowledge that it possesses a certain style of behaviour that is recognisable in each of its qualities. It is to acknowledge the fact that 'the tenacious physical personality of the object' is inseparable from 'its moral personality, and this personality reveals all of itself through each of its qualities' (CPP, 172).

It is in this context that Merleau-Ponty mentions Sartre's analysis of the honey and the lemon as well as Ponge's pebble. Each quality of the object manifests its 'personality'. For example, the viscosity of the honey describes 'a particular relation between the thing and us, a particular behavior it suggests or imposes upon us, a particular way it has of seducing, attracting, or fascinating the free subject who is confronted with it' (WP, 47, trans. mod.). Even Ponge's pebble has such a personality. Merleau-Ponty then is not so much concerned with opposing the cold, smooth carapace of the pebble to the nauseating sticky slime of the honey. His point is that each quality 'symbolises an entire pattern of human behavior', which 'can only be understood in the light of the dialogue [*le débat*] between me as an embodied subject and the external object which bears this quality' (WP, 47; see CPP, 421). In speaking of a dialogue or debate between the embodied subject and the external object, Merleau-Ponty seems to imply that subject and object stand opposed to one another, facing each other. But this would miss the point. Ponge's pebble, Sartre had already noticed, is not an object that lies there in the 'outside' world, but something that inhabits him and resonates within him.

Each thing, Merleau-Ponty writes, 'speaks to our body and to the way we live. They are clothed in human characteristics (whether docile, soft, hostile or resistant) and conversely they dwell within us as emblems of forms of life [*conduites*] we either love or hate. Man [*L'homme*] is invested in the things of the world and these are invested in him' (WP, 49, trans. mod.). The objects to which we 'become uniquely attached' are not indifferent to us. They are, in Breton's words, 'catalysts of desire': 'the place where human desire manifests itself, or "crystallises"' (WP, 50). The question is: how are we supposed to understand this investment or attachment? And what role does the anthropomorphisation of things play in such attachment? This question is important beyond the context of the 1948 texts we are focusing on here. Indeed, in the discussion of sexuality in Freud found in 'Man and Adversity', which is also the context in which the notion of *chair* first appears, Merleau-Ponty speaks of sexuality, and corporeality more generally, as a universal 'power of investment'. Sexuality is neither a physiological function nor an intellectual act, but the carnal opening of an existence on to another body that matters. It is 'our way – carnal because we are flesh – of living our relationships with others' (S, 230, trans. mod.). While in the 1948 texts Merleau-Ponty is focused on sensible things rather than on the Other, it is the same power of investment that allows us to enter into a dialogue or debate with these things. So the question of whether we should understand our investment (in things or in others) as the projection of our own ways of being on to them, as a bad narcissism if one wants, leads into the question of how to interpret the flesh in the later works. I will allude to this issue at the end of this section but for now, it suffices to point out that what is at stake is a certain resistance or adversity that would be irreducible, despite or thanks to a certain investment or 'projection'.

Now there is some evidence that speaks to Merleau-Ponty's anthropomorphisation of objects as the projection of our own ways of being on to it, a projection that allows for recognition and return to self. In the conference 'Man and Object', speaking again of our attachment to objects in the context of Breton's surrealism, Merleau-Ponty speaks of an object found at the flea market, for example a 'mask or a spoon', which is 'a "marvelous precipitate of the human face," heavy with reminiscence' (MO, 94). What Merleau-Ponty seems to be saying is that we become attracted to a specific spoon found at the flea market because it looks human, because it reminds us of a human face, for example that of a friend. This would explain why Merleau-Ponty continues by saying that 'Objects are our own possibilities projected in space and as a result they always have the ability to refer consciousness back to itself' (MO, 94). The object would be merely a means of reminding me of a given internal possibility. It would refer me back to myself, for example to my memory of my lost friends. While this interpretation is undoubtedly warranted, it might elide too quickly the role desire plays in this encounter. Indeed, the phrase 'marvelous precipitate of the human face', which Merleau-Ponty borrows from Breton's *Mad Love*, reads in the original 'marvelous precipitate of desire'.[10] This becomes clearer if we place these affirmations again in the context of the critique of the Cartesian-Sartrian ontology of the object.

Whereas the ontology of the object assumes that if we remain at a distance, indifferent to what we perceive, we will be able to reach the thing itself, for Merleau-Ponty, it is the spectator's point of view that removes the adversity of things and misses their 'agency', that is, the way in which they attack us, encroach upon us, fascinate us, and interrogate us. If things can be our active partners in dialogue, if they can initiate a debate, it is because we are not active meaning-giving consciousness and they are not powerless objects. They are, like us, a passive-active 'combination of mind and body' (WP, 43). This needs not be interpreted in an occultist way.[11] To attribute an inside or a soul to things is only to say that they are not fully laid out in front of me, but have a hidden depth that resists my grasp and has the power to tear me from myself and make me dive into them. This power of the thing is a function of the fact that the 'inside' is not strictly 'contained' within a well-defined limit – which was, let us remember, the role of the smooth carapace of the stone – but rather passes into the outside.[12] Things burst their envelopes and bleed in front of me.

This is something Merleau-Ponty observes in his ontological study of modern painting. In modern painting

> we encounter objects ... that do not pass quickly before our eyes in the guise of objects we 'know well' but, on the contrary, hold our gaze, ask questions of it, convey to it in a bizarre fashion the very secret of their substance, the very mode of their material existence and which, so to speak, stand 'bleeding' in front of us. (WP, 69)[13]

By contrast, in classical painting, each object occupies a strictly delimited space. Classical perspective forces the painter to circumscribe his vision and make compromises between the various objects that compete in front of his eyes. He has to renounce the simultaneity of incommensurable objects (the tree and the moon) and decide upon a common measure (the coin) that will be transferred into the single dimension of the paper.[14] By adjudicating the rivalry of objects in lived perception in favour of a common measure, classical painting leaves nothing to be sought or desired. Of course, classical painting is also a form of expression, which means that it is one way in which the painter takes up the question of vision. Yet unlike modern painting it takes up this question by seeking to provide a univocal answer. Modern painting on the other hand paints the *question* of vision itself. It paints objects that overflow their contour and encroach upon one another and that also encroach upon us, attacking or hurting us and so arousing our desire.[15]

Merleau-Ponty will define desire as the exchange between the inside and the outside – both mine and that of others and of things – and will link this work of desire to expression (see VI, 144). There is expression – something to be seen, said, painted, and so on – because being is not merely what it is, or because the outside – the visible, the given – has an inside that attracts us and demands to be taken up by us: it demands that I make myself the outside of the inside and the inside of the outside. In 'Eye and Mind', the exchange between inside and outside will be explicitly used to define painting: the painting is the inside of the outside – that is, not merely the visible layer of things but also their depth or their inside, which is their visibility or our vision of it – and the outside of the inside – that is, this vision made into a visible outside, a picture (see PoP, 164).

The desiring relation between body and thing as combinations of outside–inside or body–soul will become crucial in Merleau-Ponty's development of the chiasmatic structure of the flesh in his later ontology. Reading Freud's sexual-aggressive through Melanie Klein's universal power of incorporation (projection-introjection) (see TFL, 129–30), Merleau-Ponty will claim that the encounter with the other is never devoid of aggressivity, resistance or adversity, which would be impossible if I were merely projecting my own desire on to the other in order to then assimilate him all the more smoothly. Adversity here is also not the adversity of another with which I stand in a dialectical relation, so that I come to know myself through the other who resists. It is rather the adversity of the other who has, like me, another side. In the later ontology, the flesh will become the principle of this adversity: a certain 'unconscious', an opacity, thickness or resistance that is inserted between me and myself, me and the other, or me and the thing, and that radically undermines the givenness or guarantee of a common world or a common sense.

We see now that if it is necessary that we lend things our flesh in order to make them flesh, it is so that things can speak to us and be our partners in dialogue rather than neutral objects of an intellectual contemplation. Anthropomorphism then is a guarantee of the thing's irreducibility to a mere intellectual idea. By making things flesh we allow them to be given 'in the flesh', an expression which, Merleau-Ponty tells us, we must take literally (S, 167). To be given 'in the flesh' means to be given not only with this graininess that interrupts my exploration but also with this depth that arouses my desire. As Saint Aubert writes: '*Leibhaftigkeit* is truly not a one-way donation but the encounter between two resistances, two forces – that of adversity and desire.'[16] In the 'givenness in the flesh', the inaccessibility and inexhaustibility of the thing are given as such, which amounts to saying that a certain depth or inside of the outside – what will become the invisible of the visible – is 'given' right at the object itself.

The adversity of things, then, is indeed a function of my engagement with them – it demands the gift of my flesh – but unlike Sartre it does not result from my freely chosen project. Of course, it is only insofar as I lend the world my body, insofar as I clothe things with my flesh, that things can be given in the flesh. But this anthropomorphism needs not be interpreted as projection of subjective human characteristics. To flesh out this non-human-centric interpretation of Merleau-Ponty's anthropomorphism, I want to turn to those 'new' realists or materialists who advocate a cautious anthropomorphism. Borrowing this notion of 'cautious anthropomorphism' from Steven Shaviro and Jeffrey Cohen, we can understand why, in criticising the Sartrian ontology of the object, Merleau-Ponty resorts to anthropomorphic language. Such a strategy allows Merleau-Ponty, not unlike Jeffrey Cohen, to maintain both ontological distance and affinity between human and things, between humanity and nature.

3. Anthropomorphism as defamiliarisation

When describing his 'cautious anthropomorphism', Steven Shaviro says that he attributes feelings to stones 'precisely in order to get away from the pernicious dualism that would insist that human beings alone (or at most, human beings together with some animals) have feelings, while everything else does not'.[17] If we are unable to discern activity, vitality or agency in stones, it is because we apply to stones our familiar ways and look for something that resembles *human* vitality or activity. When we attribute a capacity for thought or feeling to everything that exists (animals, plants, minerals, artefacts, etc.), this attribution must come with a dislocation of our understanding of thinking and feeling in its conscious and intentional mode. Without such a dislocating we would be guilty of a reckless anthropomorphism that, in the words of Meillassoux, 'consists in the illusion of seeing in every reality (even inorganic reality) subjective traits the experience of which is in fact entirely human, merely varying their degree (an equally human act of imagination)'.[18] A 'cautious anthropomorphism' then does anthropomorphise stones but not so that stones may become more knowable – as if stones had feelings *like us* – but to make both the stone and what we mean by feelings unfamiliar. Such a dislocating of our familiar categories is also necessary if we want to avoid smuggling anthropocentrism back into our philosophy, something Shaviro thinks Meillassoux is guilty of.[19] If thought is limited to its rationalist or intentionalist definition, then of course only humans think, and attributing thought to other entities seems to be an undue projection of our subjective mode of being on to the rest of what exists. In rejecting this anthropomorphism wholesale, Meillassoux is led to assert that all there is to thought is what thought is for us. Thought is exceptional to human beings. We could say that for Meillassoux humans are still in some way at the centre; it is just that the centre is bad and the Real has to be sought as far away from the centre as possible. Meillassoux's philosophy would seek to evade the gravitational pull of the human centre and find an escape from thought in thought.[20] Object-oriented ontology, on the other hand, and Harman in particular, rejects anthropocentrism. Its ontology is flat – all objects are *equally objects* and there is no privileged object – which as such undoes the privilege of the human as the centre of the world and the agent of meaningful encounters. But this also opens the door to a certain 'reckless' anthropomorphism: when Harman speaks, for example, of the sincerity of objects, he seems to attribute human predicates to all other beings. This is still 'man' making the world in 'his' own image.

In the context of the confrontation between Sartre and Merleau-Ponty, the most interesting application of a cautious anthropomorphism is found in Jeffrey Cohen's book *Stone: An Ecology of the Inhuman*. Though Cohen's goal is not explicitly to confront the ontology of the object head-on, he does see human exceptionalism as nothing but the other side of what he calls 'lithic or elemental indifference',[21] because what is indifferent can be easily thought to exist only for our use (see SEI, 19, 23). Cohen is interested in the liveliness, dynamism or agency of the stone, then, because '[i]nhuman agency undermines our fantasies of sovereign relation to the environment' (SEI, 9). There is undoubtedly a kind of anthropocentrism in Cohen's book – it is about how stone 'appears' to us, how it enters the circuit of our existence – but this anthropocentrism is strategic. By looking at the human-lithic 'enmeshment', Cohen's goal is to show us how the stone is not 'mere thingness, a figure of recalcitrance, even silence' (SEI, 16), but is an 'active partner in the shaping of worlds' (SEI, 14). Here we see the similarities with Merleau-Ponty's dialogue or debate between body and things.

One is justified, however, in asking whether speaking of stones as active partners in the shaping of worlds does enough to overcome human exceptionalism. Indeed, this manner of speaking raises two related issues, issues we also encountered in our discussion of Sartre and Merleau-Ponty. First, are stones only of interest insofar as they help shape the human world? This would mean that stone only becomes meaningful once it enters the circuit of my existence, for example as an obstacle to be surmounted or a material to produce tools. Stone itself would be meaningless or indifferent, not worth speaking of. Here we recognise the Sartrian view Merleau-Ponty is writing against. Second, are we not anthropomorphising stones when we see them as our 'partner', thereby removing their alien character? While Cohen does often speak of companionship or collaboration between us and things in the world, including the stone, this should not be equated with the 'domestication of an element' (SEI, 61). Companionship does not imply commensurability, assimilation or harmonisation. Rather the experience of 'collaborating' with a stone, for example by touching it, should be disorientating and displace my human frame and scale. It should make me realise 'that stone's time is not ours, that the world is not for us, *even as material continuity becomes palpable*' (SEI, 83, my emphasis). For Cohen, then, it is 'as much about the liveliness or agency of the inhuman as about the petric in the human and the living more generally. The lithic in the living and the lively in the stone' (SEI, 20). Like Ponge, for Cohen, a transformed understanding of stones comes with a transformed understanding of the human as well as an understanding that we are all 'fellow travellers'.

There is in the encounter with stone, then, withdrawal and remoteness, what Meillassoux seeks, namely 'the legitimate feeling of being on foreign territory – of being entirely elsewhere' (AF, 7). At the same time, there is always also a certain intimacy, a geophilia, 'a pull, a movement, and a conjoint creativity that breaches ontological distance' (SEI, 19). Geophilia – alliance, continuity, companionship, kindredness – is as important as withdrawal or remoteness because it acts as an antidote against our tendency to accentuate the foreignness and strangeness of the stone in a way that leaves us *untouched*.[22] The foreignness of the stone, the realisation that its time is not ours and that its materiality is not for us, is experienced because of what Cohen calls a 'trans-ontological affinity'. This affinity breaches the ontological distance between human and stone, which are on the classical ontological scale the farthest away, but it does so without reducing human and stone to 'the same', for example by saying that they are both 'objects'. Cohen's 'trans-ontological affinity', then, is more in line with Merleau-Ponty's ontology of the flesh than with Harman's 'object-oriented ontology' since it does not require that we eliminate the ontological distance between human and stone in order to allow for human to become stone and stone to become human in an encounter that is radically disorientating.

In Sartre, such ontological disorientation happens in nausea. As we saw, in the limit-experience of nausea, consciousness is on the brink of touching or being-touched by the In-itself, but because of the sharp ontological divide between For-itself and In-itself, this experience is not interpreted as revealing the fundamental ontological ambiguity or affinity between the two. Rather it reveals the In-itself as a threat to freedom. Object-oriented ontology, for its part, undermines the ontological divide between subject and object. Yet by asserting that everything is an object in the same way, it robs us of the possibility of a genuinely disorientating experience, one that would be ontologically transformative. Such ontological transformation as can happen in the encounter with stone would not just be a transformation of our ontology (at the philosophical level) but also, and primordially, a transformation of our mode of being that is triggered by our relationship with, or our being touched by, something that is ontologically other or foreign, here emblematically the stone.

Cohen's approach is instructive here insofar as his emphasis on the trans-ontological affinity between the human and the rest of the world, including the stone – in Merleau-Ponty's vocabulary, the fact that we are 'of' the world – is expressly set against both indifference and assimilation, which are both characteristics of the object. If the encounter with the stone is transformative, if it can tear us away from our human-centred ways and captivate us – which is, let us remember Merleau-Ponty's non-subjectivist, non-egoistic definition of narcissism: not see oneself in the outside, but 'to be seduced, captivated, alienated' by it (VI, 139) – then the stone must in some way be enmeshed in our own lives and speak to us.

Merleau-Ponty's anthropomorphic claims can be read along the lines of a 'cautious anthropomorphism' that seeks to defamiliarise and dehumanise our own experience of ourselves and of the world. At the same time, the rapprochement with Cohen can alert us to the places where Merleau-Ponty does overemphasise, in the dialogue or debate between body and world, commensurability, fittedness and continuity at the risk of losing sight of what remains withdrawn, distant and inhuman in this encounter.[23] When we turn more explicitly to Merleau-Ponty's later ontology, we will need to remember, sometimes against Merleau-Ponty's explicit wording, that the flesh as general *Ineinander*, as *homou en panta*, is not a unifying element but a regime of non-dialectical adversity and desire.

Notes

1. A summary of the conference by Jean-Louis Dumas was published under the title 'Lectures' in *La Nef* 5, no. 45 (1948): 150–1. The text of the lecture remains unpublished. An English translation of the summary is available in *Chiasmi International* 20 (2019): 93–5. The *Causeries* are translated as *The World of Perception*.
2. Simon P. James makes a similar argument in the context of environmental philosophy. Merleau-Ponty's philosophy would decentre the human in favour not of a metaphysical realism but rather of a transhumanism that undermines the 'broadly subject-centred conception of the world presupposed by realists and anti-realists alike'. See 'Merleau-Ponty, Metaphysical Realism and the Natural World', *International Journal of Philosophical Studies* 15, no. 4 (2007): 516.
3. In the conference 'Man and Object' and in the *Causeries*, as we have already said, but also in the lectures on child psychology at the Sorbonne: 'Structure and Conflicts in Child Consciousness' (1949–50) and 'Method in Child Psychology' (1951–2), published in *Child Psychology and Pedagogy: The Sorbonne Lectures 1949–1952*.
4. Sartre, *Nausea*, 127.
5. Bodily existence can be apprehended by consciousness in other ways, for example in physical pain. Pure 'lived' pain would be pain that is neither apprehended as part of a disease nor surpassed into a project of not being pain. It would be pain that is not pain-consciousness (BN, 438).
6. Such an attempt, as we learn in *Being and Nothingness*, is bound to fail, and as long as our desire to be manifests as the impossible desire to be the In-Itself-For-Itself, or the Consciousness-Stone, then 'man is useless passion' (BN, 615). This is something that Saint Aubert does not sufficiently acknowledge in his reading of 'Man and Things'.
7. See Johnson, 'Merleau-Ponty, Ponge, and Valéry on Speaking Things: Phenomenology and Poetry', in Ghosh (ed.), *Philosophy and Poetry: Continental Perspectives*, 175–94.
8. The first references to Bachelard in the unpublished notes, Saint Aubert tells us, appear in the conference 'L'homme et l'objet' and the *Causeries* of 1948 and the Mexico conferences of 1949. See LEEE, 255. According to Saint Aubert, the presence of Bachelard wanes in 1953 before coming back in the 1957 course on Nature.
9. Though Merleau-Ponty differentiates between things and objects theoretically, this difference is not always maintained in language. The distinction doesn't seem to be at work in 'L'homme et l'objet', perhaps because the title for the cycle of conferences was 'L'Objet et la Poésie' or because Sartre had already used the title 'L'homme et les choses', forcing Merleau-Ponty to speak of objects. In the *Causeries*, the distinction is maintained most of the time yet it is not always carried over in the translation. For example, in the third lecture, *les choses sensibles* is translated as 'sensible objects' and *l'unité de la chose* as 'the unity of the object'.
10. Since we do not have access to the text of the conference but only to Dumas's summary, it is impossible to say whether the error is Merleau-Ponty's or Dumas's. On the relation between Merleau-Ponty and Breton's surrealism as well as on the 'found object' as 'marvelous precipitate of desire', see Johnson, 'Art after the Sublime in Merleau-Ponty and André Breton', in Alloa, Chouraqui and Kauschik (eds), *Merleau-Ponty and Contemporary Philosophy*, 221–51, esp. 234–7.
11. Though it can be the basis for an animist or panpsychist reading of Merleau-Ponty. For example David Abram uses Merleau-Ponty's thought to propose an animist metaphysics: 'Prior to all our verbal reflections, at the level of our spontaneous, sensorial engagement with the world around us, we are all animists,' he writes in *The*

Spell of the Sensuous, 43. See also Jennifer McWeeny, 'The Panpsychism Question in Merleau-Ponty's Ontology', in Alloa, Chouraqui and Kaushik (eds), *Merleau-Ponty and Contemporary Philosophy*, 121–44. McWeeny will argue in favour of a panpsychist conception of the flesh, where inanimate things also possess both sensibility and sentience.
12. In other words, it is not an object but an element in the Bachelardian sense. On Merleau-Ponty's appropriation of Bachelard's notion of element, see the second part of LEEE, esp. 266–7.
13. See LEEE, 215–16 for all the references.
14. See Merleau-Ponty, *The Prose of the World*, 52.
15. On encroachment, see LEEE, chapter 1. See also EC, chapter 7, especially §2, §4. Saint Aubert shows the importance of the figure of *empiètement*, developed after the War, for understanding the ontology of the flesh. Contra Michel Haar and Bernard Sichère, as well as Barbaras (see *The Being of the Phenomenon*, 135–6), Saint Aubert shows how the figure of the flesh as a general *Ineinander* is not absent of conflict and desire, and that the conflictual nature of encroaching and promiscuity that was emphasised after the War remains prominent as Merleau-Ponty's discourse becomes more ontological. We return to encroachment in the last chapter of this study in the context of Merleau-Ponty's ontology.
16. Saint Aubert, 'Au croisement du réel et de l'imaginaire: les « ultra-choses » chez Merleau-Ponty', in Dufourcq (ed.), *Est-ce réel? Phénoménologies de l'imaginaire*, 253, my translation. Here we could pursue the comparison with Sartre's description of the caress. We would find a notion of flesh as pure passivity without depth and of desire as the encounter of an activity (the movement of the caress) with a passivity (the flesh of the other) rather than the intertwinement of passivity/activity.
17. Shaviro, *The Universe of Things*, 61. See also Bennett, *Vibrant Matter*, 99: 'A touch of anthropomorphism, then, can catalyze a sensibility that finds a world filled not with ontologically distinct categories of beings (subjects and objects) but with variously composed materialities that form confederations.'
18. 'Iteration, Reiteration, Repetition: A Speculative Analysis of the Meaningless Sign', talk pronounced at the Freie University in Berlin in June 2012.
19. See Shaviro, *The Universe of Things*, 125.
20. To use Jeffrey Cohen's terminology, we could say that Meillassoux's philosophy goes too far in that rather than being disanthropocentric, it ends up being squarely misanthropic. See SEI, 25, 63, among others.
21. Of course, 'elemental' here is not used in its Bachelardian sense.
22. Hence, Cohen is critical of Meillassoux's insistence on the divide between deep time and more recent history because it separates the world 'into solitary segments, silencing conversations across a gap of our own devising' (SEI, 85). Meillassoux forgets our enmeshment, our embeddedness, our worldedness, and thinks of the muteless, lifeless stone as that which we have left behind. Cohen writes: 'I find that this outdoors [the past where both humanity and life are absent], though, is always knotted within and that the separation between matter and life Meillassoux assumes does not hold' (SEI, 289–90, n. 31).
23. This overemphasis is often also taken up by those who, like David Abram, seek in Merleau-Ponty's thinking a foundation for an ecological ethics. See, among many other statements of the kind: 'The friendship between my hand and this stone enacts an ancient and irrefutable eros, the kindredness of matter with itself', in *Becoming Animal: An Earthly Cosmology*, 29. Ted Toadvine has already pointed out that 'the "kinship" of perceptual reciprocity described by Abram excludes the singular and the senseless'. See 'Limits of the Flesh: The Role of Reflection in David Abram's Ecophenomenology', *Environmental Ethics* 27, no. 2 (2005): 169.

Chapter 6

Nancy's Materialism and the Stone

Turning to Nancy's conception of things, and more specifically focusing on his statement about the stone, we will see how Nancy also uses a strategy similar to Shaviro's and Cohen's cautious anthropomorphism. Indeed, in his statements about the stone, Nancy attributes to stone properties normally restricted to human beings – most remarkably freedom – but not before dehumanising or de-subjectivising these properties. Because Nancy is working against the Heideggerian paradigm here, he will also attribute to the stone everything that Heidegger refuses it – existence, touch, sense, worldliness – in such a way that radically challenges and displaces Heidegger's still humanist or human-centred understanding of these terms.[1] At the same time, Nancy will do so in a way that is – let us claim in a preliminary way, even though these terms will have to be clarified – more materialist and less vitalist than Merleau-Ponty's. In the end, we will see how Nancy departs from phenomenology by radically detaching sense-making from any form of intentional givenness, even the givenness to a living sentient body.

1. The freedom of the stone and the creation of the world

The first set of statements about the stone is found in a fragment at the end of *The Experience of Freedom*. In the book, Nancy has operated a radical de-subjectivisation of freedom, which will lead him to affirm, in the fragment that interests us, not only the 'freedom of the world', but the freedom of each thing, including the stone (EF, 158–60). Traditionally, freedom is supposed to be the property of a subject or the structure of subjectivity itself. To be free means not to be subjected to any external determination.

In this sense, I can be free only if I absolve myself from any contact with what is other and find the reason or determination of my existence within myself. The free being is the self-founding entity absolved from any relation with exteriority. Thought in this way, freedom becomes a ground. For example, in Kant, freedom becomes uncaused causality, the ability to be the absolute origin of a causal chain; similarly, in Sartre, it becomes the ability to be the origin of one's own life-project, one's own meaning. For Nancy, on the contrary, to be free does not mean to be self-determined but to be absolutely without 'why'. Freedom means that existence is 'abandoned' without being abandoned by anything that would precede it (for example, God or Being) nor abandoned to anything other than its own existence. Freedom is the unfounded factuality of an existence that surprises itself in existing. It is the deliverance from foundation and the releasing into existence (EF, 92–5, 114–15). At this point, there is no difference between existence and the existent; the existent's 'reality' is nothing other than the putting into play of its own existence (CW, 71–3, 102–3).

Once we understand how Nancy recasts the thought of freedom, we are in a better position to understand its essential link to the thought of the limit we discussed in Chapter 2, or to what Nancy also calls finitude. If Nancy insists on the finitude of what exists, this must not be taken to mean that each entity is encircled within a limit that separates or absolves it from all other entities since the limit, as we have already seen, is also the place of exposure. The limit does not cut us off from the world, but is rather 'both inherent to the singular and exterior to it: it ex-poses it. It is immediately and conjointly the strict shape of its "inside [*dedans*]" and the drawing of its "outside [*dehors*]".'[2] In other words, finitude is not a limitation imposed on a being by the fact that there happens to be other things outside of it that press against it. Rather, it consists in the fact that any being must be exposed to an exteriority or an otherness in order to be what it is:

> *Finitude* does not mean that we are non-infinite – like small, insignificant beings within a grand, universal, and continuous being – but it means that we are *infinitely* finite, infinitely exposed to our existence as a nonessence, infinitely exposed to the otherness of our own 'being' (or that being is in us exposed to its own otherness). We begin and we end without beginning and ending: without having a beginning and an end that is *ours*, but having (or being) them only as others, and through others. (BP, 155)

Accordingly, finitude denotes that which exists at its limits or is affected by its end, not as something external imposed on it, but as something that is originary (SW, 31–2). Since the finite being does not cease to be exposed at its limits, its exposition is endlessly repeated and therefore never finished once and for all. Hence, finitude is the true infinite: 'the good infinite or the actual infinite – it is infinity in the actuality of the act itself insofar as it is the act of exceeding itself' (C II, 15). The finite being has no proper beginning or end; at no point can it be properly complete or finished, yet this incompletion is not a lack: in every instant, each finite being is fully exposed, without holding anything back, without leaving anything to be actualised later. Yet, this being fully offered of the finite being should not be confused with a standing in full presence, since it always remains in the movement of coming to presence. As Nancy says:

> The *coming* is infinite: it does not get finished with coming; it is finite: it is offered up in the instant. But that which takes place 'in the instant' – in this distancing of time 'within' itself – is neither the stasis nor the stance of the present instant, but its instability, the inconclusiveness of its coming – and of the 'going' that corresponds to that coming. The coming into presence of being takes place precisely as nonarrival of presence. (SW, 35; see EF, 159)

To be finite is to never cease to 'arrive' to the world and hence to never cease to be exposed to 'all there is'.

The question that occupies us here is: what does it mean to extend the claim of free existence not only to all living beings but also to the stone? In a fragment at the end of *The Experience of Freedom*, where he directly confronts Heidegger's distinction, in *Being and Time*, between the facticity of Dasein and the factuality of the stone, Nancy asks whether he must claim that all beings are free and replies candidly: 'Yes, if I knew how to understand this.' And he adds: 'But at least I know that it would have to be understood' (EF, 159). The task then is to ask what the 'there is' of the world and the 'there is' of each existent in its singularity, including this stone, mean as freedom. In the same fragment, Nancy is clear that such a thought does not amount to a subjectivism, as if the freedom of this tree or this stone were merely a way in which they appear to me.[3] Rather it is 'a question of the material reality of the being-in-the-world of the finite existent' (EF, 192, n. 2). Here we see how the question of freedom, and the claim that the stone is free, leads to Nancy's conception of the world, and especially his redeployment of the Christian creation *ex nihilo* as a 'materialist' doctrine.

Nancy links the freedom of the world to what he often refers to as the 'end of the world', that is, the deconstruction of any *cosmos* or *mundus*, any clear, pre-given order. While this deconstruction can be experienced as the 'loss of sense', it represents for Nancy a transformation in the meaning of sense. Rather than the world *having* a sense bestowed upon it from the outside (be it God or the transcendental Subject), the world itself is sense (SW, 8). For Heidegger too world is sense insofar as it is the space or clearing of intelligibility that allows entities to be encountered meaningfully.

Hence, there is no sense outside of the world, that is, there is no sense, no intelligibility or significance, unless a Dasein exists. Dasein's world is the intelligibility of the 'environment' of the stone, its 'light'. Speaking of world and worlding (or world-forming) independently of the human being is only possible if we radically challenge the Heideggerian understanding of world and its relation to sense.

For Nancy, the world is not merely the wherein of factical human existence; it is not a coherent milieu of significance already laid out in advance, but the space of sense: the sharing of singularities exposed to one another: stone, ground, dog, grass, star, and me, and you. It is in order to think this 'world' that Nancy redeploys and displaces the Christian motive of creation *ex nihilo*. That the world is created out of nothing does not mean that it is produced out of some pre-existing nothing by an especially powerful artisan; rather it implies that it has no presupposition or precondition, no ground, no reason, no origin, no end: '*Ex nihilo*, which is to say: . . . nothing but that which is [*rien que cela qui est*], nothing but that which grows [*rien que cela qui croît*] (*creo, cresco*), lacking any growth principle' (D, 24; see BSP, 83). This is the connection between freedom and world: the rose and the stone are free in the sense that one grows and the other rolls without 'why', but this absence of ground does not enclose them within themselves. If this were the case, the rose or the stone would find in this absence of ground all the reason of the world. Rather, the stone or the rose is without ground because it grows or rolls outside of itself, 'with the reseda, the eglantine, and the thistle – as well as with crystals, seahorses, humans, and their inventions' (BSP, 86). To speak of the creation of the world is therefore to see the world as the free dissemination of being (EF, 13). The *ex nihilo* of creation is not a religious doctrine, but signifies the groundlessness of the world, the ever-renewed coming-to-presence of the world: singularities, each time other, each time with others, coming and going without coming from or going anywhere. It is the expression of a 'radical materialism', a materialism 'without roots' (CW, 51).

2. The existence of the stone and its feeling hard

Let us try to specify Nancy's materialism a little bit more by looking at the second set of affirmations regarding the stone, those found in *The Sense of the World* and 'A Finite Thinking'. For Nancy, the stone is neither an essence for the understanding alone nor a pure in-itself waiting there to be taken up in the circuit of human existence. If the stone makes sense, if there is sense for and with the stone, it is because the stone ex-ists and as such is already exposed to itself and to others. To say that the stone exists, for Nancy, is to say that its being has the structure of differance and spacing described earlier, that it is even if only minimally *to* or *toward* (itself). It should be clear by now that ascribing existence as the movement of being to or toward (itself) to the stone is not a matter of 'endowing the stone with an interiority' (SW, 61) and of improperly anthropomorphising 'the Real'. Nancy is not proposing an animism or panpsychism because he has decoupled existence as being-to not only from intentional consciousness, but more generally from the interiority or unity of sentient life. At the same time, we could argue that Nancy is proposing a kind of animism or panpsychism, provided we remember his definition of soul: 'The soul is the body's difference from itself, the relation to the outside that the body is for itself' (C, 126). The soul here is not a principle of animation, life, unity, interiority but rather of the body's diaresis and exposure.[4]

The stone that lies out there then is already ex-tended, ex-posed:

> *Extensa* doesn't designate the quality of breadth, of surface magnitude: what is extended is what is precisely not 'one' and what is 'one' is precisely what is not extended, the *point*, say, which is what occurs at no point in space and is the negation of space. Extension is not in relation but is in exposure: everything about the extended thing is only ever exposed, put forth, turned outward without there being an inside, nowhere turned back in upon itself and hence devoid of 'self'. (FT, 312, trans. mod.)

The stone is a body in Nancy's sense: not the contact of self to self that characterises the lived body of phenomenology and its tacit cogito, but rather exteriority, *partes extra partes*. It is only as body in the Nancean sense, that is, as extension or as a spacing that gives place to existence, that this stone can exist in its minerality and hence that 'its hardness [can] *feel* hard': *se faire sentir dure* (FT, 322, n. 14). The stone makes its hardness be felt, or more literally, the stone's hardness make itself feel hard. For both Merleau-Ponty and Nancy, it is clear that we cannot understand such a 'making oneself *feel* hard' as the encounter between the stone and a consciousness: a constituting consciousness would only ever encounter the signification or essence 'stone' and never the concretion of the stone. We have already seen that for Merleau-Ponty, a constituting consciousness 'would penetrate the world' and 'transport us to the heart of the object' so that the perceived would have not thickness (PP, 247). Though this criticism of constituting consciousness is addressed at (a certain) Husserl, Nancy finds the same inability to address the stone in its concreteness and discreteness in Heidegger. By reducing sense to givenness and to access, Heidegger's stone remains abstract and misses the 'concreteness of the stone [*le concret-de-pierre*], which does not come about only when the stone is encountered, thrown, or manipulated by or for a subject' (SW, 62). In other words, Heidegger 'fails to weigh precisely the weight of the stone that rolls or surges forth onto the earth, the weight of *the contact* of the stone with the other surface, and through it with the world as the network of all surfaces' (SW, 61). We know that for Heidegger the stone does not touch the earth because the stone is not opened to and cannot make sense of the ground as such.[5] Dasein can say that the stone is on the ground because by meaningfully relating to the stone and the ground and to their relation 'as such', it can let one be open to the other. For Nancy, the problem with Heidegger's recasting of intentionality as the 'gift' of 'there is' is that this gift is still only conceived in finalised terms: the gift – the 'there is' of beings – must be destined for a being capable of receiving it as such.

The problem with phenomenology, including in its Heideggerian vein, according to Nancy, is that by focusing on intentionality, it ends up electing an intentional power as the sole locus of sense and interpreting all things as meaningful only *for* this intentional power, that is, insofar as they become intentional correlates. Merleau-Ponty's great achievement within the phenomenological movement is to have moved this locus of sense away from transcendental consciousness back into the lived body itself and to have emphasised the dialectical relation between subject and object rather than conceiving of the subject as imposing its meaning on an inert object. Yet, Merleau-Ponty is still too much of a phenomenologist for Nancy in that he thinks access, meaningfulness or sense in terms of commensurability. Body and thing, hand and stone, solicit and respond to each other, adapt themselves to each other. The stone that I pick up enters into the circuit of existence, my gesture responds and adapts itself to its weight. Phenomenology thinks access in terms of appropriation. But Nancy wonders: 'Is it not necessary that there should be nonaccess, impenetrability, in order for there to be also access, penetration?' (SW, 60). For phenomenology, access is the a priori of being-in-the-world. Yet Nancy's ontology challenges this a priori, in the form of a series of questions or suggestions:

> Why could the world not also *a priori* consist in being-among, being-between, and being-against? In remoteness and contact without 'access'? Or on the threshold of access? (And this *a priori* would be identically the *a posteriori* of the material world, the indefinite grouping from one threshold to the next of one thing with another, each on the edge of the other, at the entrance yet not entering, before and against the singular signature exposed on the threshold.) (SW, 59–60, trans. mod.)

For Nancy, the sense of the world and of each being within the world is not its appearing 'as such' and Heidegger's being-in-the-world as a gift *for* . . . hides another, more primordial gift: the spaciousness of the world, the distribution or spacing of places receiving a stone, a shadow or a tree.

Sense, then, is what happens on the edge or threshold, in-between singularities, in the encounter with an exteriority or an alterity that resists assimilation, the alterity of another 'singularity', to which there is access precisely only in the mode of non-access.

The stone is not exposed by the human or for the human but it exposes itself to (itself and others). The stone's weight or its feeling hard, then, is neither a function of a living, sensing body that has the capacity to adapt itself to the weight of the stone, to respond to the pressure it exerts on the hand, nor is it a function of an existent who can let it be what it is as such. Hardness does not first accrue to the stone when it is encountered by a sentient body or a Dasein that can relate meaningfully to this hardness. Rather, it is because the stone is not a mass closed in upon itself (a point without extension) but is stretched out and exposed at its limits that it can be encountered in its exteriority, that is, in its resistance and impenetrability. Furthermore, it is because I am also stone, and have 'the consistency and, in part, the mineral nature of a stone' (SW, 61), that I can touch and be touched, according to the Nancean modality: not access to the 'as such' but the contact-separation of surfaces, in an approach that remains on the threshold, 'at the entrance yet not entering' (SW, 60).

That I am able to encounter the stone only insofar as I am also always already stone (and not insofar as I am a living or thinking being) is also an insight that will become more and more central to Merleau-Ponty's later ontology of the flesh. Already in the *Phenomenology*, it is only because I am of the world upon which I open as sensing body that there can be sensation: I see as visible, I touch as touchable, and so on. In the later work, Merleau-Ponty will draw the ontological consequence of this fact and say that vision and visible are 'caught up in the fabric of one sole Being' (VI, 110), that my body and the world are made of the same flesh (VI, 148).[6] We find this insight taken up in many contemporary works of the material turn influenced by Merleau-Ponty.[7] For example, in *Bodily Natures*, Stacy Alaimo argues for 'more robust and complex conceptions of the materiality of human bodies and the more-than-human world' and proposes to achieve such a conception by exploring 'the interconnections, interchanges, and transits between human bodies and nonhuman natures'.[8] Like many others, she seeks to undo the divide between the human and its environment, the human and the more-than-human world, by showing how, through their bodies, human beings are always embedded or 'intermeshed' in the world that seems to stand in front of them. It is not just that the human body is always in contact with the non-human (nature) but that human corporeality is a 'trans-corporeality'. 'Nature', if we want to keep this word, is within (as well as outside of) the human. Thinkers like Alaimo take inspiration from Merleau-Ponty to develop a theory that recognises that the human 'is always the very stuff of the messy, contingent, emergent mix of the material world' by claiming that 'my body and the natural things are continuous with each other. . . . The fiber of culture and nature compose one *continuous* fabric.'[9] Thus, even if the body is always open so that its interactions with other bodies always alter it, the question is to what extent these interactions allow for the intrusion of the most strange and foreign, for example the stone, into the living, organic body or to what extent this intrusion is thought in terms of assimilation or homogenisation. Indeed, it is quite different to point out the minerality inside and outside my body, to say that I am also stone and lizard, as Nancy does, and to appeal to a flesh as the ontological fabric out of which body and things are cut out. We will come back to these differences in the last chapter of this study. For now, let us try to specify Nancy's materialism by bringing it in conversation with some new realist and materialist thinkers.

3. Materialism, materiality, matter

For Nancy, sense does not accrue to a senseless in-itself, 'for the differance of the toward-itself, in accordance with which there is opening of sense, is inscribed *right at* [à même] the "in itself"' (SW, 61). The 'in-itself' is already to-itself or toward-itself, and as this spacing it is liable to sense. As Nancy writes in a short text titled 'Toute chose se trouve': 'In an athematic mode, however, this pebble distinguishes itself. It finds itself distinct and situated. Such is its materiality, like that of an odour, a desire, or an atom of carbon.'[10] Earlier in the same paragraph, Nancy had mentioned, as an example of things that turn up in their distinction: a flower, a sound, a smartphone. How are we to understand the 'distinction' of the thing that turns up? Earlier we mentioned the fact that for Nancy bodies are not in space but rather space is in bodies so that bodies are extended places of existence, not merely in the mode of an expanse or spread but as a stretching and a tension. As such bodies weigh against one another, not because they are dense and massive but because weight is 'the raising of their masses to the surface. Unceasingly, mass is raised to the surface; it bubbles up to the surface' (C, 93). How are we supposed to understand this tension, this tensed existence, when it comes to the stone?

In a short intellectual biography titled 'Biography of an Inquiry', where he recounts how he came to see the necessity of undoing the modern divide between subject and object and see all beings as 'actants', Bruno Latour recounts his encounter with a stone and the epistemological shift that ensues. The encounter with the stone was preceded by discussions with Isabelle Stengers in which she remained sceptical that they had really succeeded in pulling themselves 'away from the text, the social, the symbolic' and where she shared with Latour a quote from Whitehead 'about the risk taken by rocks – yes, rocks – in order to keep on existing'.[11] Here is how Latour describes what happened next:

> In August of that year, stretched out in the sun on an island across from Gothenburg, in Sweden, I couldn't stop running my fingers over the rough red surface of the rocks as if to find out whether Whitehead could have been right. . . . There exists a completely autonomous mode of existence that is very inadequately encompassed by the notions of nature, material world, exteriority, object. This world shares one crucial feature with all the others: the risk taken in order to keep on existing. Thus the hiatus that I had detected very early on . . . was here as well, here in the first place, in the apparent continuity of being-here.[12]

In his recounting of this specific encounter with a rock, Latour puts the emphasis not on the rock itself but rather on the epistemological shift that results from his encounter with the rock. As such, the rock only functions as an external prompt for Latour's thoughts, which remain at the centre. Yet, we could say that the result of this encounter is an even more radical decentring of Latour's way of thinking than had been the case before. Material or inert beings – whose mode of being seems to be continuous, effortless persistence – also contain a hiatus or what Nancy would call a spacing. If they endure or persist, it is by insisting and repeating themselves across this hiatus, the same way that an intentional course of action 'is constantly interrupted by a minuscule *hiatus* that requires, from moment to moment, an inventive act of repossession by the actor equipped with his own micromethods'.[13] We could express the same thought by saying that the essence of the stone's existence is *conatus*.[14] Though the influence of Spinoza on Nancy is often palpable, there are only a few mentions of Spinoza throughout Nancy's corpus.[15] One of these most important mentions of Spinoza's *conatus* for us is found in a short section, titled 'The Sense of Being', from *The Sense of the World*. There Nancy writes, referring to Spinoza,[16] that *conatus* means 'at least this: that sense does not add itself to being, does not supervene upon being, but is the opening of its very supervenience, of being-toward-the-world' (SW, 28).

We should be careful, however, not to understand this effort or risk taken by each existent in order to keep existing as if it would isolate each existence and pit them against each other. In *Being Singular Plural*, Nancy speaks of being-with as a form of *conatus*, as 'the effort and desire to maintain oneself as "with" and, as a consequence, to maintain something which, in itself, is not a stable and permanent substance, but rather a sharing and a crossing through [*partage et passage*]' (BSP, 87). Even though the context is here a discussion of language and of *speaking*-with, the point is that the *conatus* of each being is not an effort to maintain itself in existence at the expense of others; it does not lead each being to enclose itself upon itself, but rather opens each being to itself and to others – thanks to a hiatus (Latour) or spacing (Nancy). A good translation of *conatus*, Nancy will thus claim, is the French *engagement*: engagement, implication, commitment (BSP, 183). If the essence of Being is *conatus*, then to be means to be engaged or implicated by one's own being, to put one's existence into play. This engagement is not solipsistic because being is sharing out or communication (BSP, 93). Even the stone, in its effort to keep existing, communicates. This does not mean that the stone would speak or emit significations, but only that it addresses itself to others in its own way, namely through its distinctive material presence, its weight. It is through this 'address' that the stone comes to the world, touches and is touched.

Using the traditional dichotomy, we could say that sense, for Nancy, is material rather than intelligible.[17] Yet we can already anticipate how this requires a new thought of materiality that does not reduce it to an indifferent substrate or an inaccessible, senseless 'in-itself'. There are only bodies but sense itself is not a body. Despite this, sense is not beyond the world of bodies. This seeming contradiction can be easily dissolved if we remember Heidegger's mantra: 'Being is not a being' without being any 'thing' beyond beings. What is not corporeal in the world of bodies is the 'with' of these bodies, their exposure to one another, or their *rapport*. In 'The "There Is" of Sexual Relation', a play on Lacan's famous claim that there is no sexual relation, Nancy explains that a *rapport* or a relation is 'nothing that is [*rien d'étant*], it takes place between beings [*les étants*]. It is – insofar as it is, or according to the mode of being which is precisely not beingness [*étantité*], let's say presence, being given, being posited there) – it is of the order of what the Stoics called the incorporeal' (C II, 6–7). As incorporeal, the relation is 'the *distinguishing oneself* in which the distinct comes into its own, and it does so only in relation to others, which are also distinct' (C II, 7). We are by now familiar with this logic. The *rapport* is the between, but again it does not constitute a connective tissue or a bridge. On the contrary,

> it must open the *between two* by means of which there are two. But what is between two is not either one of the two: it is the void – or space, or time . . . or sense – which relates without gathering, or gathers without uniting, or unites without accomplishing, or accomplishes without bringing to its end. (C II, 8, trans. mod.)

There are only material bodies, then, and they make up, through their articulations, the inorganic body of sense (SW, 61–2). If Nancy calls this body of sense inorganic, it is first because sense is a function of the spacing – or, as Derrida would say, the technical supplement – of each body within itself and amongst each other, rather than of the *living* unity and property of an organism. And it is inorganic also because 'the body of sense' is not organised into a functional whole.

Nancy, then, calls his ontology 'materialist' not because it would be about matter as 'a substance or a subject (or anti-subject)' but because it is about 'what of oneself is shared out, what is only distinct from itself, *partes extra partes*, originally impenetrable to the fusional and sublimating penetration of a "spirit" or "mind," understood as a dimensionless, indivisible [*sans partage*] point beyond the world' (BSP, 83–4). Nancy's philosophy is a materialism, then, because it starts from a plurality of origins and their resistance to synthesis or fusion, and insists that there is all there is, singularly: the ever-renewed coming-to-presence of singularities, each time other, each time with others.

In order to understand Nancy's materialism, we can appeal to the distinction between materiality and materials made by Tim Ingold in the second essay of his book *Being Alive*. Of course, Nancy doesn't use such a distinction and rarely, if ever, speaks of materials (in French, it would be *les matières* or *les matériaux*[18]), and he would probably ultimately disagree with Ingold's description of the world of materials, which is more influenced by the later Merleau-Ponty than by Derrida. Still, there is something about his approach that is enlightening when it comes to Nancy. According to Ingold, materiality is a theoretical abstraction that has very little to do with the materials a sculptor or hiker encounters, for example. Anthropologists and philosophers alike have a tendency to produce an understanding of 'materiality' without ever engaging materials and their properties: 'What academic perversion leads us to speak not of materials and their properties but of the materiality of objects?' he asks (BA, 20). His answer: 'the excessive polarisation of mind and matter that has led generations of theorists to suppose that the material substance of the world presents itself to humanity as a blank slate, a tabula rasa, for the inscription of ideational forms' (BA, 21). Moving from materiality to materials should allow us, according to Ingold, to undermine the mind/matter divide, as well as the subsequent divide between brute materiality (or the 'material nature' of the world) and materiality as it is taken up in human projects. If we think of a stone as a constituent of the material world (rather than of the world of materials), 'a stone is indeed both a lump of matter that can be analysed for its physical properties and an object whose significance is drawn from its incorporation into the context of human affairs. The concept of materiality, as we have seen, reproduces this duality, rather than challenging it' (BA, 31). What is missing is the *concret-de-pierre* Nancy also couldn't find in Heidegger.

To counter to tendency of 'theory' to produce an abstract understanding of materiality without engaging with materials, Ingold opens his essay by addressing the reader in the second person and instructing her to fetch a stone:

> Before you begin to read this chapter, please go outside and find a largish stone, though not so big that it cannot be easily lifted and carried indoors. Bring it in, and immerse it in a pail of water or under a running tap. Then place it before you on your desk – perhaps on a tray or plate so as not to spoil your desktop. Take a good look at it. If you like, you can look at it again from time to time as you read the chapter. At the end, I shall refer to what you may have observed. (BA, 19)

In the middle of the essay, we are instructed to stop reading and touch the stone on our desk: 'To be sure, your finger has come up against a hard material – stone. It is cold to the touch, and perhaps still damp. But has touching this particular stone put you in touch with *the materiality of the world*?' (BA, 23). Or again a bit later: 'I can touch the rock, whether of a cave wall or of the ground underfoot, and can thereby gain a feel for what rock is like as a material. But I cannot touch the materiality of the rock' (BA, 24). The point is that as long as we are focused on accessing or grasping 'materiality', we miss what is really going on – the encounter between fingers and rock – and posit something immaterial – a mind or a thought – on the hither side of materiality. Indeed, to say that I touch materiality is to say that whatever does the touching is not materiality. Following James Gibson, Ingold argues, then, that the world is not made of immaterial thoughts and material objects, but of surfaces that are nothing but interfaces between one kind of material and another (stone, fleshy fingers). Rather than assuming a separation between materiality and immateriality, we would be better served by looking for surfaces separating various materials (BA, 23).

At the end of the essay we are asked to return to the stone. Noticing how, like one of David Nash's sculptures but at a greater speed, it has changed, we realise that

> Stoniness, then, is not in the stone's 'nature', in its materiality. Nor is it merely in the mind of the observer or practitioner. Rather, it emerges through the stone's involvement in its total surroundings – including you, the observer – and from the manifold ways in which it is engaged in the currents of the lifeworld. (BA, 32)

As Nancy said: 'it must be said that it is difficult to reduce "the stone in the stone" to a "pure" immanence. . . . The stone isn't an essence . . . an essence for the understanding alone' (FT, 322, n. 14). The 'stoniness' of the stone is to be found neither in the stone's nature nor in its representation in the human mind. It is only to be found in the manifold ways in which a stone is involved in its surroundings. This involvement is what Nancy describes as touching and as sense.

Despite these resonances, Nancy would probably find Ingold's 'world of materials' problematic for at least two reasons, both of which can be extracted from the following statement by Ingold: 'Far from being the inanimate stuff typically envisioned by modern thought, materials in this original sense are the active constituents of a world-in-formation. Wherever life is going on, they are relentlessly on the move – flowing, scraping, mixing and mutating' (BA, 28). The first problem is that the world of materials seems to be an elemental world of fluxes underneath the world of fixed, substantial things, from which these things are generated and back into which they dissolve or disintegrate. This seems both to reintroduce some dualism and to undermine the emphasis on the limits separating surfaces that touch.[19] Appealing to Nash's sculptures, Ingold writes: 'For beneath the skin of the form the substance remains alive, reconfiguring the surface as it matures' (BA, 27). If materials allow us to undo the mind/matter divide, they do so by appealing to another dualism, that between the elemental, wild world (materials and their properties) and the prosaic world of stable things (objects and their attributes).[20] Here the influence of James Gibson, but also of Merleau-Ponty, is evident. Underneath the stable things of profane vision, there is something more fundamental, whether we call it materials, elements or even 'brute or wild being'.[21]

Second, and despite a certain emphasis on the stone, there is still an implicit primacy of life in Ingold's proposal (after all, the title of the book in which this essay is collected is *Being Alive*). When we move from the material world to the world of materials, we bring things to life. We do so not by 'adding to them a sprinkling of agency but [by] restoring them to the generative fluxes of the world of materials in which they came into being and continue to subsist' (BA, 29). This is not a form of animism because it is not a question of putting life into things – Nancy would say of endowing things with interiority and agency – but rather of seeing how 'things are in life' (BA, 29). Things are alive because they are constantly swept up in currents of materials that undermine their boundaries or limits, limits upon which, according to Nancy, they are exposed and make sense. Furthermore, these currents of materials are called 'life', which seems to give a certain ascendance, if not priority, to organic life.[22] Let us recall that Nancy's ontology is an ontology of *bodies* (rather than a philosophy of *the body*), and that these bodies build, by means of their spacings and limits, the *inorganic* body of sense.

To turn the tables on Nancy, Ingold could accuse Nancy of falling prey to the kind of abstraction he decries, reducing all singularities in their distinction to some indefinite substrate or blank materiality, losing as a result the concreteness of the stone. Indeed, a thing, Nancy writes, 'is anything whatever [*n'importe quoi*]' (BP, 174); a thing, *some* thing (*quelque chose*), is always whatever, any thing whatsoever (*une chose quelconque, n'importe quelle chose*). But Nancy clarifies right away that the indetermination or anonymity of this 'whatever' does not mean that this 'whatever' forms an indeterminate 'background' (*fond*); rather, 'the *whatever* is the difference'.[23]

Here we can respond to a criticism raised by Harman against Nancy's thought of singularities as 'whatever'. According to Harman, Nancy's ontology would run the risk of reducing singularities 'to their currently accessible features, thereby allowing them no excess beyond their presentation here and now'.[24] It would fall prey to a form of reductionism Harman calls 'overmining'. Rather than undermining objects by locating their true being in some underlying matter or particles, overmining

> happens whenever a philosophy tells us that an object is nothing more than how it appears to the observer; or an arbitrary bundling of immediately perceived qualities; or when it tells us that there are only 'events,' not underlying substances; or that objects are real only insofar as they perceive or affect other things. In all these cases, objects are treated as a useless hypothesis, a false depth lying beneath the immediate givens of consciousness or the concrete events of the world.[25]

Of course, Nancy does not reduce existence to what appears to consciousness, but because singularities have no depth or no hidden interior of their own, 'no individual character outside their mutual touching and weighing', they are reducible to a series of relational events.[26] If the singular character of each thing is completely determined by its relations, then singularities are merely effects of relations rather than entities in their own right. Because nothing determinate would exist prior to or independently of relations, nothing would exist but relations. For Harman, such a 'continuum of relational structure without individual zones' is essentially a monism.[27] As a result, Nancy's ontology would ultimately not be an ontology of the plurality of singularities, or, in Harman's vocabulary, of determinate objects, but an ontology of an indeterminate in-itself. Having removed what exists from its reliance on an indeterminate material substance as well as a transcendent principle, Nancy's creation of the world sought to affirm the plurality of what exists. Yet by defining what exists in terms of relational events, it goes too far and leaves us with a big mixture of relations without independent *relata*, without determinate parts.[28]

This lack of determinacy, Harman thinks, comes to the fore when Nancy speaks of the thing as 'whatever', of *quelque chose*, something, or of *n'importe quoi*, anything at all, as *quelconque*, as anything whatsoever (see BP, 173–4). Hence when Nancy writes that '*some* thing is free to be a stone, a tree, a ball, Pierre, a nail, salt, Jacques, a number, a trace, a lioness, a marguerite' (BP, 186), Harman takes this to mean that 'there is no Pierre, no salt, and no lioness before they touch one another. The in-itself is a unified *whatever*.'[29] The thing would be 'whatever' – read: an undifferentiated in-itself – before it enters in relation with other things and through these relations gets determined as this or that. But such a unified in-itself is exactly what Nancy's thinking of freedom has undermined. To say that the thing is free to be salt, Pierre or a lioness is not to say that it is some undifferentiated mass or glob, but rather to say that the coming to presence of some thing is 'unfettered by any attachment to or foundation in a substance or a negation of substance' (BP, 177). The indeterminacy of the *some* of something, or of the *whatever* of anything whatsoever, is 'not a privation, nor is it a poverty', but 'its most characteristic affirmation, with the compaction, the concretion, wherein the thing "reifies" itself, properly speaking' (BP, 174). Indeed, *quelconque*, from the Latin *qualis* and *cumque*, does mean a certain indeterminacy with regard to the *quality* or kind, the 'what' of the thing, but for Nancy this indeterminateness is also the material concretion of the thing as existent. As Nancy writes, '"Whatever" is the indeterminateness of being in what is posited and exposed within the strict, determined concretion of a singular thing, and the indeterminateness of its singular existence' (BP, 174). The whateverness of the thing is both its 'conceptual' indeterminacy (its lack of essential determinations) and its concretion (its determinacy: *this* tree).

For Harman, singular beings can only be rescued from ontological overmining or undermining if they are withdrawn from their relations, that is, if they are 'deep'. Now it is true that for Nancy things are not 'deep' if by that we mean that they have a hidden interior in which they would conceal their ownmost truth, locked away from any interactions or encounters. Yet the fact that each singularity is essentially 'with' all others does not mean that it is nothing outside of its relation. Harman seems to equivocate between two different claims: there is nothing prior to relations, and there is nothing but relations. While the first claim is true of Nancy's ontology, the second is not. There is nothing prior to relations – not even a substrate we could call prime matter or even 'the nothing' – because existence for Nancy denotes not the presence of the thing by itself or in itself, but the coming of what is *to* itself and others. What is primordial, then, are neither self-identical things (in Harman's vocabulary: determinate non-relational objects) nor relations within an indeterminate, undifferentiated glob, but rather the spacing or opening of the to-itself. Let us quote again the crucial passage about selfhood and relation from the essay 'A Finite Thinking':

> Thought rigorously, it is not a matter of 'other' or of 'relation.' Rather, it is a matter of a diaresis or a dissection of the 'self' that precedes not only every relation to something other but also every identity of the self. In this diaresis, the other *is* already the same, but this 'being' isn't confusion, still less a fusion: it is the being-other of the self inasmuch as neither 'self' nor 'other,' nor some relation between them, can be given to them as an origin. (FT, 7, trans. mod.)

As this quote makes clear, Nancy's ontology is not one of pure relations without *relata*, yet each *relatum* is not constituted by an inside that would remain unaffected by its relations. Rather the 'inside' of each self is always felt on the outside or through some exteriority. If it is indeed the case that there is no singularity in-itself, no singularity that would have its own identity within itself prior to its exposition to and contact with other singularities, we must also remember that exposition, contact and weight all imply an interruption or a resistance, and hence a certain identity or ipseity of the singular beings. The 'inside' is an effect, not an illusion. This is how we should read Nancy's claim that the question of the 'with' ultimately means 'never any identities, always identifications' (BSP, 66, trans. mod.).

4. Thinking and things

We made a detour through Ingold's 'world of materials' to highlight a feature of Nancy's materialism: it is not a philosophy that starts from an abstract concept of matter. Rather, it is one that starts from the essential plurality of bodies and their impenetrability. It is here that Ingold's exercise with the stone is enlightening. What does it mean to start from the material in the stone? Isn't philosophy condemned to reduce 'the stone in the stone' to an essence for the understanding alone? Isn't the alternative one where we confine ourselves to describing the various and varying properties of material objects? Or even one where we abandon thinking altogether to engross ourselves in the currents of materials? If we recall, a similar objection was presented to Merleau-Ponty's 'doctrine of perception': it can only be lived and not theorised, and hence cannot act as starting point for a new philosophy. We will see in the third part of this study how Merleau-Ponty replied to this critique. For now, the question is: is it possible to develop a materialist philosophy that neither treats matter as an abstraction, nor calls for a dismissal of thinking in order to engross itself in materials?

The first step toward escaping this either/or is to work through the relation between the material world, what Nancy calls the world of bodies, and thought. The assumption underlying the choice between materiality or philosophy, stone or thought, is that stone and thought are essentially different, that there can be nothing of the stone in thought or of the thought in stone. But this assumption is only true on a certain conception of both stone (senseless matter, pure in-itself) and thought (transparent idea, pure for-itself). We know that Merleau-Ponty worked tirelessly to undermine this dichotomy. Nancy also undermines this dichotomy, not only by attributing sense-making to stones, as we saw above, but also by showing how thinking is always a material event.

We find Nancy's most direct engagement with the difference between thinking and thing in two very difficult texts: 'The Weight of a Thought', collected in *The Gravity of Thought*, and 'The Heart of Things', collected in *The Birth to Presence*.[30] Part of what Nancy attempts to show in these two texts is that thought – like language – is always material event. Of course, this should not be understood along the lines of those who want to naturalise phenomenology by showing how phenomenology can be married with cognitive science and neuroscience. By saying that thinking is material, Nancy does not mean that it is a merely physical event happening in the brain, even though he does mention the brain and the nerves (but also arms and hands, belly and legs) in the Preface to the new French edition of *Le poids d'une pensée*. Rather, he means that thought is always *this* or *that* thought, a singular thought rather than thinking in general, and so is a thing among other things. Remember that materialism for Nancy is linked to the plurality of origins in their impenetrability. Thought finds its place in this 'materialism' because it shares the same characteristics as other things: a singularity, impenetrable, and exposed to itself and others. As a result, the thing is not foreign to thought and neither is thought foreign to the thing.

What the 'material' thing and 'immaterial' thought have in common is weight. There is, Nancy claims, a 'weighty/weighing property of thought', which is 'identical to a thoughtful property of the weighty thing' (GT, 76). This weighing of the thing against other things, including that thing that is thought, and the weighing of the thing in thought is what Nancy calls, in 'The Weight of a Thought', sense.[31] To understand Nancy's claim, it is useful to remind ourselves not only that *pesée* in French is linked to *pensée* – a point Nancy underlines at the beginning of the essay – but also that the verb *peser* in French, like the English 'to weigh', has a double meaning. On the one hand, weighing refers to the action of ascertaining or measuring the weight of something, for example by holding it in one's hand or putting it on a scale, or of figuratively assessing the value of something. On the other hand, weighing means having weight, exerting a pressure by virtue of one's heaviness. While we can easily see how things weigh in the second sense and how thought weighs in the first sense, it is a matter of remembering that thought also weighs in the second sense:

> We certainly do experience the weight of thought. Sometimes the heaviness, sometimes the gravity of a 'thought' ('idea,' 'image,' 'judgment,' 'volition,' 'representation,' etc.) affects us with a perceptible pressure or inclination, a palpable curve – and even, with the impact of a fall (if only the falling of one's head into one's hands). (GT, 76)

The point is that the thing can weigh upon thought because thought is itself a material event, and hence weighty in the second sense. Furthermore, it is because of this encounter, this pressure between the two weighty things, that there is weighing in the first sense, that thought weighs, ponders or thinks. What thought thinks here is the weight of things or their sense. But this sense, which is the 'content' of thought, is not immaterial if by this we mean transparent, clear or luminous. On the contrary, '*what* we think, the content of our thoughts is material, physical, tangible, sensible in all senses, experienceable as well as experienced and tested [*éprouvable et éprouvé*] – and very often also straining and challenging [*éprouvant*]'.[32] We have a tendency to speak of the activity of thinking as an abstract, immaterial process and we forget that the formations and transformations of even the most abstract concepts and ideas, as well as 'each of their uses and errancies [or meanderings, *errances*] constitute a concrete experience, eminently *concrete*: that is, an experience in which one grows with the thing itself, one espouses its coming, its pace [*son allure*, also its look], its manner, its accent, its consistence and its resistance'.[33]

Thought, according to the Cartesian paradigm, should dissolve all obscurities and present its object fully and completely. For Nancy, on the contrary, true thinking does not dissolve the materiality of the thing into a purely intelligible concept, but lets that which is outside of thought weigh on thought. This 'experience' of thought, Nancy writes, 'remains a *limit-experience*, like any experience worthy of the name. It does take place, but not as the appropriation of what it represents; this is why I also have no access to the weight of thought, nor to the thought of weight' (GT, 76). This means that thought cannot fold back upon itself and appropriate for itself the weighty character of the thought that thinks the thing. It is exactly this weighty character of thought/thing, of bodies against each other and against thought, that phenomenology in general (which thinks Being as sense and sense as intentional access), and Heidegger's concept of world as significance in particular, obscure.

To say that philosophy must turn or return to 'the thing themselves', then, is to state the obvious (BP, 169). There is no thinking worthy of the name that is not a turn or return to the thing. The question for Nancy is how to think this turn to the thing that thought is. Nancy phrases this question in the following way: 'One can think nothing without thinking this inappropriable property of the thing, and without thinking it as the heart of thought itself. "To think the thing" or "to think things": to what else could thought be devoted?' (BP, 170). Of course thought thinks things, but what it thinks or ponders (that is: what it weighs, or what weighs upon it) is the inappropriable property of things.[34]

According to Nancy, philosophy as appropriative thinking remains unable to acknowledge this inappropriable property of things. The problem with philosophical thinking is not that it deals in abstractions and concepts. Concepts, like philosophy itself, are things among things – which again, does not mean that they are inert and senseless. Rather, the problem is that philosophy thinks it can appropriate the thing, makes the thing *its* thing, and in so doing it forgets what always remains inappropriable (see BP, 177). 'At the heart of thought', Nancy writes, 'there is *some thing* that defies all appropriation by thought' (BP, 169). It is here that thought stumbles, but also here that it thinks:

> The heart of things: where thought stumbles or bangs itself [*se cogne*], where it knocks [*cogne*]. Hard thought: that does not mean 'difficult.' On the contrary, it is always too simple. Simple hardness of stone that thought endures in order to simply be thought, that is, to be 'the stone *itself*' [« *la pierre même* »]. (BP, 182–3, trans. mod.)[35]

The inappropriable 'property' of the thing is neither the thing itself in its determination and essence nor in its materials. Rather it is the 'this' or the 'some' of the thing, the *quelque* of *quelque chose*. Or, what amounts to the same thing: it is the 'there' of 'there is' some thing there, the *y* of *il y a*. What resists thought but also makes it that there is this thing called thought is the 'there is' of things – *la pierre* même.[36] That some thing happens, comes to presence: this is what cannot be 'dissolved' in thought.

A thinking of things that does 'justice to the *some* of the thing' (BP, 177), then, is not content merely with being 'open' and 'welcoming' in its appropriation of the thing. Such an open, welcoming thought still ends up reducing the thing to being merely the thing *of* thought. What is needed is a depropriation of all appropriation that forces thought to 'submit to this: that thought itself is nothing but some thought, any thought. Some thing or other among so many other things [*Une chose quelconque parmi tant des choses quelconques*]' (BP, 178–9, trans. mod.). It is clear here that we do not have to do with two different regimes: things on the one side and their representation or signification in thought on the other. At the heart of thought but also at the heart of the thing there is the '*il y a*', the 'there is' of *some* thing, including of this thing that thought is. This is neither immediacy nor mediation but an *'immanence without immediacy'*, in which the thing is not posited as or for another but rather remains in itself (*in-manere*) and lies there suspended in its position, ex-posed (see BP, 182).

The problem of mediation and immediacy, if we recall, was at the core of the critiques addressed to the project of the *Phenomenology*. The unreflected life of the body, if it is immediate, falls outside of the purview of philosophical thinking. There is nothing to say about it, no truth to be sought in it. If we want to speak of this immediate life, make assertions about it, then we must start by positing it as such, thereby transforming it into an object of reflection. In the *Phenomenology*, Merleau-Ponty tried, unsuccessfully as he came to understand, to open a path between these two options. Against an idealistic interpretation of phenomenology, he sought to ground reflective thinking as *pensée de survol* back into the factical life-world, opening factical life to expression and truth. Yet, the relation between language, especially philosophical language and its truth-claims, and the foundation or ground that exceeds it remained undeveloped. As we have already discussed, Merleau-Ponty's project remained caught up in a bad ambiguity and in the end assumed rather than explained the passage from immediacy to reflection, from the silent world of perception to the linguistic meanings of a phenomenology of perception. As Renaud Barbaras has argued, the problem with the *Phenomenology* is that it couches the discovery of the perceptual field in a dualism of reflection and the unreflected, and in doing so opposes reason to a pre-reflective irrational, the cogito to the natural world, and essence to fact. As a result, the unreflected cannot be grasped as the *birth* of reason (a reason that is *of* the world in both senses). What is needed is a genuine understanding of the unreflected or the pre-reflective as 'zero of . . .' (VI, 257), 'which exists only as the beginning (on the side of the unreflective) or as the conservation (on the side of reflection) of what it negates. . . . Consciousness will have to be grasped as a moment of the world rather than as its opposite.'[37]

Putting Merleau-Ponty and Nancy in conversation with some new realist and materialist thinkers, we have seen how each undoes the divide that pits object and subject, matter and sense, against each other. As such, each also undermines anthropocentrism and human exceptionalism in a way that resists both eliminative materialism and vitalism or panpsychism.

The first path away from anthropocentrism and human exceptionalism corresponds to the way Sartre interprets Ponge: Ponge would reduce thought to the immediate material world of things and in the end be left with the materialist universe of science, a universe without thought or where thinking has been petrified. Such a position, for Sartre, is plagued with an obvious contradiction: Ponge forgets himself and his own experience of thinking in order to enclose himself within the world, yet 'he still ends up on the outside, staring at things, all alone' (MT, 450). The attempt to deny human transcendence is bound to fail so the question is how to account for human transcendence without rejecting the human outside of the world and breaking his ties with Being.

The second path is the one that passes through anthropomorphism in order to attribute some form of 'sense' to the things themselves. If there is already some sense in things then there is ontological continuity from the stone all the way to the human and the passage from one to the other is less mysterious. As we have seen, both Merleau-Ponty and Nancy, in their own way, take on a path that resembles this one, affirming a sort of ontological continuity. Yet it is misleading to speak of continuity here. As we saw in his reply to Harman, by opening the thing to thought and thought to thing, Nancy does not dissolve their difference. Rather he brings each to its limits, where it opens on to and touches its other. Merleau-Ponty, criticising idealism and the *pensée de survol*, is looking to grasp the emergence of thought as an event – or in Merleau-Ponty's vocabulary, an institution – that takes up the unreflected and transforms it, without dissolving it. For both, thinking in general, and philosophical thinking in particular, is a finite thinking, to borrow a phrase by Nancy: a thinking that feels itself indebted, always coming too late, emerging from Being and turning back upon it but always remaining attached to it through its moorings. Thinking this emergence from the ground up, so to speak, from the first opening of sense in the most simple differentiation or distinction up to the level of abstract thinking, requires, as Merleau-Ponty came to realise, a new ontology, one that develops a new kind of Being (*genre d'être*) between being and non-being, between the in-itself and the for-itself. It is to this ontology that we turn in the last part of this study.

Notes

1. By calling Heidegger's view in *Being and Time* and *Fundamental Concepts of Metaphysics* 'humanist', I do not mean to dismiss Heidegger's critique of humanism in the 'Letter on Humanism'. Yet, if the problem with humanism is that it 'does not set the *humanitas* of the human being high enough', this seems only to up the ante, even if the new, higher humanism understands the 'essence' of the human as its being claimed by Being, coming into its own when it lets itself be appropriated by this claim or this event. This decentres the human and undermines its priority *in some way*, but it does keep intact the privilege accorded to the human being thanks to its relation to Being. See Heidegger, *Pathmarks*, 251.
2. Nancy, 'Rives, bords, limites (de la singularité)/Banks, Edges, Limits (of Singularity)', *Angelaki: Journal of the Theoretical Humanities* 9, no. 2 (2004): 46.
3. Freedom for Nancy, then, has nothing to do with a freedom of the will, a freedom to give oneself determinations, but it is also not the 'fact of appearing', of standing 'in the

open and in appearing' as Heidegger would say. Derrida still operates, even if critically, with Heidegger's understanding of freedom and attributes it to Nancy, which gives rise to a host of misunderstandings. See Derrida, *For Strasbourg: Conversations of Friendship and Philosophy*, 76. See also my essay 'World's Apart: Conversations between Jacques Derrida and Jean-Luc Nancy', *Derrida Today* 9, no. 2 (2016): 157–76.

4. Ian James suggests that there is a 'possibility of some kind of panpsychism at work in Nancy's account of things', even if Nancy 'never mentions panpsychism as such'. See 'The Touch of Things: A Review of *The Universe of Things: On Speculative Realism* by Steven Shaviro', *Cultural Critique* 97 (2017): 226, n. 8. James must have missed Nancy's explicit disavowal of panpsychism in *The Sense of the World*, a fact that is noted by Sam Mickey in 'Touching without Touching: Objects of Post-Deconstructive Realism and Object-Oriented Ontology', *Open Philosophy* 1 (2018): 295.
5. See Heidegger, *Fundamental Concepts of Metaphysics*, §47 and *Being and Time*, H. 55.
6. On the chiasmatic relation between stone and flesh in Nancy with reference to Merleau-Ponty, see Carbone, 'Flesh: Towards the History of a Misunderstanding', *Chiasmi International* 4 (2002): 49–62.
7. These authors have a tendency to assimilate Merleau-Ponty's notion of the flesh with matter or nature. As Toadvine rightly points out in his critical engagement with David Abram's work, 'flesh is not simply a world of things, but a multidimensional constituting activity operative at all levels of meaning, from sensible to symbolic, and it is itself no more "corporeal" than "mental."' See 'Limits of the Flesh: The Role of Reflection in David Abram's Ecophenomenology', *Environmental Ethics* 27, no. 2 (2005): 170.
8. Alaimo, *Bodily Natures*, 2.
9. Alaimo, *Bodily Natures*, 11. The second part of the quote is from Edward Casey's *Getting Back into Place*.
10. Nancy, 'Everything Finds Itself', *Oxford Literary Review* 39, no. 1 (2017): 2.
11. Latour, 'Biography of an Inquiry: On a Book about Modes of Existence', *Social Studies of Science* 43, no. 2 (2013): 297. Latour says it must have been the passage about Cleopatra's Needle in Alfred North Whitehead, *The Concept of Nature*. The passage he has in mind is probably the following: 'If we define the Needle in a sufficiently abstract manner we can say that it never changes. But a physicist who looks on that part of the life of nature as a dance of electrons, will tell you that daily it has lost some molecules and gained others, and even the plain man can see that it gets dirtier and is occasionally washed. Thus the question of change in the Needle is a mere matter of definition. The more abstract your definition, the more permanent the Needle' (167). This passage is also discussed in Shaviro, *Without Criteria: Kant, Whitehead, Deleuze, and Aesthetics*, 16–21. Latour's recounting of the story is also discussed in Cohen, *Stone*, 42–3.
12. Latour, 'Biography of an Inquiry', 297–8.
13. Latour, 'Biography of an Inquiry', 292.
14. Jane Bennett, who is influenced by Latour, relies heavily on Spinoza (as well as Deleuze) to develop her vitalist or vibrant materialism. Indeed, she opens *Vibrant Matter* with Spinoza's definition of *conatus*, also cited by Nancy. See *Vibrant Matter*, 2–4; see also 21–3.
15. Nancy's most direct engagement with Spinoza consists in the marginalia in Alfonso Cariolato's book *Le geste de Dieu. Sur un lieu de l'Éthique de Spinoza*. For the role of Spinoza in Nancy's thinking of the body, see the section called 'Spinoza: The liberator of the body' in Daniele Rugo's *Jean-Luc Nancy and the Thinking of Otherness*, 24–31.
16. See Spinoza's *Ethics*, Third Part, Prop VI: 'The effort [*conatus*] by which each thing tries to stay in existence [*in suo esse perseverare conatur*] is nothing but the actual essence [*actualem essentiam*] of the thing.'
17. For an engagement with Nancy that also emphasises the materiality of sense, see James, *The Technique of Thought*, chapter 2, esp. 60–4. Though James does understand sense as material and matter as a principle of differentiation, his reading somewhat underplays the differance *at the heart* of things. The thing as an 'instance of material

differentiation' is constituted not only by its relation (contact and separation), but also by an opening or spacing in its self or as itself.
18. In the short text mentioned above we can find the following sentence: 'all matters [*matières*] refer to their materiality' ('Everything Finds Itself', 3), but the distinction between materials and materiality is not conceptualised. What it seems to indicate though is that if, as we saw earlier, materiality is for Nancy the sheer 'finding oneself there', then this means that there is never an indifferent, generic materiality, but always a specific material's way of being material, of 'relating to its materiality'.
19. Ingold does speak, following Gibson, of the medium as that which affords movement and perception, but for Gibson, the medium is not what is between surfaces but rather the surface is between substance (more or less solid stuff) and medium. Surfaces are 'where most of the action is' (Gibson cited in BA, 22). Furthermore, both surface and medium are material, while the limit upon which touch and sense happen for Nancy isn't.
20. Ingold does not use the term 'elemental world' but I don't believe it distorts what he has in mind when he speaks of a world of materials. It also helps bring the resonances with Merleau-Ponty to the fore.
21. I am not pretending that these are equivalent, but there are undeniable structural similarities.
22. David Abram also speaks of a deeper or 'wider Life': '*everything* is animate, *everything* moves' and there are only 'different ways of being alive'. See *Becoming Animal*, 269. That Nancy's meditations on things do not appeal to (an organic or metaphoric) life is clear from the following passage in 'The Heart of Things': 'here at the heart of things, one must not seek the living beat of a universal animation. This is not death, either, but rather the immobile, impassive gravity of the "there is" of things' (BP, 169–70). This should warn us against too quick an association between Nancy and the new materialist thinkers in the vitalist tradition.
23. This sentence does not appear in the English translation. It reads: 'Il n'y a donc pas un "fond" du "quelconque": le *quelconque* est la différence.' See Nancy, *Une pensée finie*, 206.
24. Harman, 'On Interface: Nancy's Weights and Masses', in Gratton and Morin (eds), *Jean-Luc Nancy and Plural Thinking*, 99.
25. Harman, 'Road to Objects', *Continent* 1, no. 3 (2011): 172.
26. Harman, 'On Interface', 100.
27. Harman, 'I Am Also of the Opinion that Materialism Must Be Destroyed', *Environment and Planning D: Society and Space* 28, no. 5 (2010): 787.
28. Ian James first addresses Harman's critique of Nancy in 'Lucidity and Tact', in James and Wilson (eds), *Lucidity: Essays in Honour of Alison Finch*, 9–19, and then again in his review of Shaviro's *Universe of Things*. As James shows in the latter, the central debate in Continental philosophy is not between correlationist and 'realist' or 'materialist' philosophies but rather between philosophies of relations and 'isolationist' philosophies of substance. It is within the latter debate that the originality of Nancy's ontology can be located. Ultimately for James this also aligns Nancy with the ontic structural realism of Ladyman and Ross, a claim he develops later in chapter 2 of his *Technique of Thought*. On the contrary, Sam Mickey argues that Nancy's philosophy is in need of the corrective provided by Harman's object-oriented ontology because for Nancy 'determinate qualities emerge only in contact' and 'the indeterminate whatever at the heart of things still fails to account for the specific qualities that are characteristic of real beings'. See Mickey, 'Touching without Touching', 296.
29. Harman, 'On Interface', 100–1.
30. The difficulty of the former is compounded in translation since Nancy plays on many idiomatic French expressions: the *y* of *il y a*, the *ci* of *ci-gît*, the *quelque* of *quelque chose*, and so on.
31. In chapter 5 of *Vision's Invisibles*, Véronique Fóti argues that because Merleau-Ponty

grants perception a 'quasi-transcendental position' in his philosophy, he is not able to 'embrace fully a "transcendental aesthetics" of weight in Nancy's sense'. See Fóti, 'The Gravity and (In)visibility of Flesh', in *Vision's Invisibles: Philosophical Explorations*, 75. It should be recalled, however, that Merleau-Ponty thinks vision as 'auscultation and palpation in depth' (VI, 128).

32. Nancy, *Le poids d'une pensée, l'approche*, 8. *Éprouver* means to feel or to experience and is synonymous with *ressentir*, as in *éprouver de la joie*. But it also means to put to the test to see whether something or someone has the qualities one expects. For example, one can put someone to the test, *mettre à l'épreuve*, so that she can *prove* her faith or valour, and hence be tested and tried, that is, considered reliable, *éprouvé*.
33. Nancy, *Le poids*, 7–8.
34. See also: 'The watchword of all modern thought is: "to the things themselves!" But in this "to" one must discern all the heaviness, the whole heavy fall of thought that is necessary in order to let what exceeds sense weigh in sense, what opens sense *to* the thing *to* which it is a matter of giving its sense, or, in truth, of letting its sense be given or delivered: what constitutes sense by exceeding all sense. The existence of the slightest pebble already overflows; however light it may be, it already weighs this excessive weight [*ce poids de trop*]' (GT, 79, trans. mod.).
35. The last sentence is omitted from the English translation.
36. Which could be translated not only as 'the stone *itself*' but also as 'the *very* stone'. The latter translation would have the advantage of removing the emphasis on what sounds like identity and ipseity: itself, *elle-même*. For another discussion of the 'there is' of the thing in relation to the nothing, the whatsoever and the thing in itself, see Nancy, 'Fantastic Phenomenon', *Research in Phenomenology* 41 (2011): 228–37.
37. Barbaras, *The Being of the Phenomenon*, 17. This also leads to a transformation of the understanding of the teleology of consciousness.

Part III
BEING

In the final part of this study, we have reached the point where we can stage a more direct confrontation between Merleau-Ponty's carnal ontology and Nancy's ontology of the singular plural. Both Merleau-Ponty and Nancy are looking for a principle of non-dialectical difference that allows for the emergence of sense right at Being itself. In bringing the chiasmatic structure of the flesh in conversation with Nancy's understanding of being as differance and spacing in the final chapter of this study, the focus is on the role of differance or spacing within sensing and sense-making. Before we can engage in such a confrontation, however, it is necessary to address Merleau-Ponty's and Nancy's relation to Heidegger's thinking of Being. What Merleau-Ponty and Nancy find through their engagement with Heidegger – and especially with the later Heidegger's thinking of the truth of Being and his critique of metaphysics – are the tools to think Being beyond the dichotomy of presence and absence. Yet both also remain critical of Heidegger. Addressing these critiques will prevent us from overlooking the originality of Merleau-Ponty's and Nancy's positions, an originality that runs the risk of being covered over by their respective usage of Heideggerian tropes.

Chapter 7

Merleau-Ponty's and Nancy's Engagement with Heidegger

Both Nancy and Merleau-Ponty appropriate Heidegger's vocabulary in a way that might mislead us into believing that they are largely in agreement with Heidegger's later thinking of Being and situate their own philosophy within its orbit. Such hasty conclusion would miss what is original about each. In Merleau-Ponty's case, his appropriation of Heidegger's notion of *Wesen* is always mediated by his reading of Husserl and by his search for the opening of sense within the sensible itself. This leads him to understand Being as depth and as the *Ineinander* of beings and to critique Heidegger for proposing a direct ontology. In his own reappropriation of the later Heidegger's thinking of Being, Nancy, for his part, takes issue with Heidegger's understanding of the withdrawal of Being as something that calls for a guarding or sheltering. In Heidegger, Being would hide behind what is present and be kept in reserve as a kind of super-presence.

In their engagement with Heidegger, both Merleau-Ponty and Nancy seek to undo the metaphysical difference between *existentia* and *essentia* in favour of a thinking of existence or presence that is not pure positivity but includes a moment of negativity that is not the other of presence but its opening. The last chapter of this study will track this moment of negativity within the Merleau-Pontian chiasmatic structure of the flesh and Nancy's understanding of being as differance and spacing. Before this can be done, however, it is important to spell out where Merleau-Ponty and Nancy, each in their own way, depart from Heidegger's own thinking of Being.

1. Is Merleau-Ponty's late ontology Heideggerian?

The extent of the influence of Heidegger on Merleau-Ponty, and especially on his later ontology, is widely debated. In his study of Merleau-Ponty's 'ontological turn', *Vers une ontologie indirecte*, Saint Aubert provides a useful survey of the literature on the question. On the one hand, we find authors such as Rudolf Bernet who defend the position that *The Visible and the Invisible* is 'one grand meditation on the phenomenological sense of the Heideggerian concept of ontological truth'.[1] Yet, without contesting the fact that in the late 1950s and early 1960s Merleau-Ponty does appropriate some Heideggerian vocabulary, the proximity of his later philosophy with Heidegger's project has been contested from the very start, for example by Sartre, who claimed that while Merleau-Ponty understood Heidegger better in the last years of his life, he was not influenced by him. According to Sartre, 'Being is the only concern of the German philosophy. And in spite of a philosophy which they at times share, Merleau's principal concern remained man.'[2] Marc Richir goes even further and claims that Merleau-Ponty indirectly asks us to commit a parricide against Heidegger.[3] While there would be in Heidegger a purely ontological '*es gibt*' that would be the condition of possibility of the disclosure of beings, for Merleau-Ponty there is only an '*il y a*' by inherence.[4] The difference between Heidegger and Merleau-Ponty would lie in the priority given to Being in the appropriating event. Despite this difference, some commentators also identify an anti-anthropological turn or a decentring of the subject in Merleau-Ponty's later work, one that would have been influenced by Heidegger.[5]

In retracing Merleau-Ponty's engagement with Heidegger's works, Saint Aubert divides Merleau-Ponty's stereotypical attitudes toward Heidegger's philosophy into four types, each corresponding to a different period of his oeuvre. First, in the *Phenomenology of Perception* we find a favourable appreciation of Heidegger's philosophy but one that remains vague and betrays a superficial knowledge of Heidegger's writings. Second, from 1946 until 1958 we find frontal critiques of Heidegger's philosophy, especially of its emphasis on anonymous co-existence and the immanence of philosophy. These criticisms remain tied to the French context of Merleau-Ponty's own thinking. Third, in the 1958–9 lecture course 'La philosophie aujourd'hui' we find an exposition of Heidegger's texts that demonstrates a closer familiarity with the itinerary of Heidegger's thought, but without much critical analysis or personal uptake. Finally, in the last years of Merleau-Ponty's life, from 1959 to 1961, we find what Saint Aubert calls a 'lateral and silent relation', a 'community of writing that is primarily figurative' (VOI, 103).⁶ Saint Aubert concludes that Merleau-Ponty engaged with Heidegger's texts late in his life, when his own thinking was already formed, so that we cannot really speak of an influence of Heidegger's thinking on Merleau-Ponty. But while Merleau-Ponty's ontology did not get formed in an intimate conversation with Heidegger, this does not prevent the later Merleau-Ponty from listening closely to Heidegger's language and borrowing phrases from it. These phrases (starting with the capitalisation of *Être*) find their way into Merleau-Ponty's language because they resonate with him, yet they remain entangled in Merleau-Ponty's own project. Hence when we read the last Merleau-Ponty we hear echoes of Heidegger, but the proximity of their respective formulations should not lead us to overlook the distance between the two.

Following Saint Aubert's analysis, it is not surprising that, depending on which period of Merleau-Ponty's oeuvre we focus on, we arrive at a radically different assessment of the relationship of Merleau-Ponty's thought to Heidegger's. For example, in an article that takes up the question of the relation between phenomenology and ontology in Merleau-Ponty's thought, Patrick Bourgeois links the Heideggerian distinction between (ontic) intentionality and (ontological) transcendence to the Husserlian distinction between act intentionality and operative intentionality, which then allows him to argue that phenomenology already implied an ontology. Relying on passages in the *Phenomenology* where Merleau-Ponty equates the more profound sense of intentionality with 'what Heidegger calls "transcendence"' (PP, 441) or what 'others have called existence' (PP, 520, n. 57), Bourgeois assumes a proximity and even an agreement between Merleau-Ponty and Heidegger on the meaning of Being. Merleau-Ponty would already have, in his early works, 'intimated the primary and originary being as the "within which" of intentionality for his later, more explicit and further developed ontology'.⁷ The later ontology, then, would remain fully in line with Heidegger's fundamental ontology.

In an essay devoted to being-in-the-world with others, Christina Schües indirectly puts into question the assumption behind Bourgeois's position, namely that Merleau-Ponty merely took over Heidegger's notion of being-in-the-world. Though her focus is mainly on the *Phenomenology of Perception*, she also relies on some texts from the second, more critical period identified by Saint Aubert to show how Merleau-Ponty is critical of Heidegger's preference for 'the monocentric, authentic Dasein, which exists beyond any involvement in the daily world, [over] the concrete-factual self who would be characterized by an inter-connection of personal and anonymous traits and by an involvement in the world'.⁸ Unlike Heidegger, Merleau-Ponty would be more acutely aware of philosophy as an event, that is, as situated and contingent and as dependent upon an unreflected from which it arises. Though we might dispute Schües's reading of Heidegger, it allows us to understand why Merleau-Ponty criticises what he sees as Heidegger's sharp distinction between the ontological and the ontic, and between authenticity and inauthenticity. Merleau-Ponty is critical of Heidegger insofar as he finds in his thought a 'heroic solipsism which strives to extract itself from a world seen as a place of facticity and as an obstacle to be overcome'.[9]

Nancy shares Merleau-Ponty's worry about a certain 'heroism' of authenticity, which would become apparent when we follow the analyses of being-with as we move from the inauthentic and the authentic modes of existence, that is, as we move from the inauthentic they to the authentic people through anxiety and resoluteness. As Nancy shows, for Heidegger, in everyday, common (in the sense of banal) existence, there is only improper being-with, similar to the juxtaposition of things. We do take care of things 'together' but this 'togetherness' remains external since it is determined by what one takes care of. Anxiety tears me from this average everyday business by putting me in front of my own essential finitude, my own being-toward-death. Death is what individualises me since it is the only possibility I have to take over myself. Authentic being-toward-death – what Heidegger calls anticipatory resoluteness – is not shared in common. Here, the essential 'with' seems to be lost.[10] Yet Heidegger insists that anxiety does release me for proper being-with-others-among-things. It allows me to properly take over my own existence in a way that is both 'with' and 'in' – this is why Schües's diagnosis of Heidegger's thought as acosmic and monocentric is a bit of a shortcut. Yet the authentic 'with' is cast right away as communal-historical destiny. It is the community that bestows upon my existence its sense, integration and wholeness, and it does so by appropriating me to the common destiny or the destinal unity of a people.[11] As a result, individual existence is sacrificed to a higher instance. What is lost, or what is covered over in Heidegger's analysis of the 'with', is the way in which everyday existence is a being-with one another that is more than the mere juxtaposition of interchangeable units. Beyond Heidegger's two singulars – *das Man*, the they, and *das Volk*, the people – Nancy will propose to think of *les gens*, people in their singular plurality, a plurality of 'ones' that are not lost in the anonymity of indifferentiation, where one is *like* 'anyone' else, nor reabsorbed in a higher One that takes charge of their fate and sublates them in a higher destiny (BSP, 7). If there is an authentic or proper way of being-oneself, it is not to be found in a mode of existence detached from everyday existence but right at everyday existence itself, in the way in which everyday existence exposes each and every one to an opening of sense.[12]

That sense is 'made' right at our contingent existence itself and not to be found in an extraordinary or detached mode of existence is also a proposition defended by Merleau-Ponty in the *Phenomenology of Perception*. As Merleau-Ponty clearly states: 'we have the experience of a *participation in the world*; "being-in-the-truth" [*l'être-à-la-vérité*, also being-towards-the-truth] is not distinct from being in the world [*être au monde*]' (PP, 415).[13] While on Nancy's reading this proposition could also be attributed to Heidegger, Merleau-Ponty's being-in-the-world is not the same as Heidegger's since the former is always primordially embodied. Indeed, we recall that in *Being and Time* Dasein is analysed in its neutrality prior to its 'dispersion' in a body.[14] The primordiality of the 'neutral' understanding of being (*Seinsverständnis*) over the bodying-forth (*Leiben*) of the body is clearly still at work in the Zollikon seminars.[15] It is always from a 'disincarnate' understanding of the ecstatic nature of Dasein, of its standing-out in the clearing of being, that we can come back to what it means to live as body (*das Leiben*). What Heidegger cannot think then is the ecstatic nature of the flesh itself, that is, the way in which our access to Being springs forth from within bodily existence.

We can already anticipate how Merleau-Ponty's critical attitude toward the sharp distinction between the ontic and the ontological, and between the authentic and the inauthentic, will carry over into the later work. Rather than going from Dasein to Being, or more precisely from Dasein through authentic Dasein to Being, Merleau-Ponty will seek Being right at the *Ineinander* of beings and will also insist that philosophy cannot be separated from non-philosophy because when we ask the question of Being independently of beings, we detach thinking from its pre-reflective ground. Yet in order to clearly assess the tenor of Merleau-Ponty's critique of Heidegger in his later works, we must look more closely at the third and fourth periods identified by Saint Aubert, particularly the 1958–9 lecture course, the chapter of *The Visible and the Invisible* on interrogation and intuition (written in spring 1960), and some unpublished notes from this period. This will allow us to shift the focus to Merleau-Ponty's later ontology and its relation to Heidegger's own shift from the fundamental ontology of *Being and Time* to a thinking of the truth of Being.

2. Merleau-Ponty between Husserl's *Wesenschau* and Heidegger's *Wesen*

We might think that the shift in Merleau-Ponty's philosophy, insofar as it seems to be a shift from phenomenology to ontology, would be a move away from Husserl and toward Heidegger. In his article 'Was

Merleau-Ponty on the Way from Husserl to Heidegger?', Jacques Taminiaux explicitly addresses this question and, focusing on the discussions of Husserl and Heidegger in the 1958–9 lecture course 'La philosophie aujourd'hui', answers in the negative. The title of Taminiaux's article comes from a statement made by Heidegger himself in response to a letter from Arendt in which she mentions reading Merleau-Ponty and finding him 'much more interesting than Sartre'. Acknowledging that he does not know Merleau-Ponty's work very well, Heidegger nevertheless replies that 'Merleau-Ponty was on the way from Husserl to Heidegger' even though it is 'difficult for French men to get rid of their innate Cartesianism'.[16] To ask whether Merleau-Ponty moved away from Husserl toward Heidegger is to ask whether there is a shift from a concern with our belonging to the *Lebenswelt* to the thought of Being as *Ereignis*. Let us recall that in his attempt to situate his own thinking with regard to Merleau-Ponty's, Nancy makes a distinction between a French carnal universe of thought and a German metaphysical one. While the thinkers of the first strand would inherit a concern for our carnal being in the world from Husserl's later phenomenology, notably *Ideas II* and the *Crisis*, the thinkers of the second strand, to which Nancy claims to belong, would be focused on existence insofar as it is the 'place' where Being is at stake as opening and transcendence. As we have already pointed out, given the importance of sensibility and embodiment in Nancy's work, this categorisation is a bit simplistic. However, it remains true that Merleau-Ponty is primordially concerned with a concrete philosophy that 'restore[s] to each experience the ontological cipher which marks it internally' (S, 157) and that he finds in Husserl's description of the experience I have of my own body (*Leib*) the 'ontological rehabilitation of the sensible' (S, 167) he is looking for.

Yet, it is also an oversimplification to assert that what is preventing Merleau-Ponty from 'becoming Heidegger' is his Cartesianism. In this sense, as Taminiaux points out, Arendt is more astute in her reading of Merleau-Ponty when she insists, contra Heidegger, that Merleau-Ponty writes against Cartesianism, even if that need not mean, as we have seen, that he rejects Descartes *en bloc*. Merleau-Ponty's target in the later work is still objective thought, which leaves the order of phenomena and dreams of surveying things from above, of seeing them 'all naked'. He finds this dream at work in the Cartesian *inspectio mentis* as well as in the Husserlian *Wesenschau*. Both try to get at the thing itself by abstracting from all that is contingent, and first and foremost from our own body as the means we have of reaching the thing. As a result, they turn the thing into an idea, an essence detached from any factical instantiation. Merleau-Ponty will also find a similar procedure in what he calls Heidegger's direct ontology: an attempt at seeing Being frontally apart from the intertwinement of beings.

Merleau-Ponty, however, does not merely advocate a return to the factical against the ideal, and this is clearer in the later work as a response to the misunderstanding of his early project as we laid out earlier. Rather he proposes a reappropriation of the Husserlian *Wesenschau* and its procedure of imaginary variations that is inflected by Heidegger's understanding of the verbal sense of *Wesen* in order to emphasise the intertwinement of fact and idea, or existence and essence.

The notion of *Wesen* understood in its verbal sense underlies the opposition between whatness and thatness. As Merleau-Ponty writes in a note from February 1959: 'The Wesen of the table ≠ a being in itself, in which the elements would be arranged ≠ a being for itself, a Synopsis = that which "tablefies" in it, what makes the table be a table' (VI, 175). Still in this note, Merleau-Ponty specifies that what *west* or holds sway, for example the 'being-rose of the rose', 'answers to the question *was* as well as the question *dass*'. It is not 'the rose seen by a subject, it is not a being for itself of . . . the rose'. Rather, 'it is the roseness extending itself throughout the rose' (VI, 174). The *Wesen* 'suppresses that opposition of the fact and the essence which falsifies everything' and if the *Wesen* 'rose' 'gives rise to a "general idea"', if there is a 'species rose', 'this is not insignificant, but results from the being-rose considered in all its implications (natural generativity)' (VI, 174). Bringing together Husserl and Heidegger, Merleau-Ponty concludes that the *Wesen* is the *Ineinander* 'which nobody sees' but which is *urpräsentiert* as *nichturpräsentierbar* (VI, 174). The essence then is seen or experienced right at the thing itself, or more precisely between all of its variants. Take the intuition of a blue patch of colour, for example. Without the other colours around the patch of blue and the other shades of blue that haunt this one and against which it distinguishes itself, 'blueness' would be nothing. There is no 'blue as such' independently of the variations of blue. Hence it is a mistake, according to Merleau-Ponty, to think that there could be a total variation, one that would remove everything that is inessential at once and let me intuit the pure 'what' of this thing. As a result, facticity is not an impurity that ought to be eliminated but the fabric that gives our essences their solidity. Merleau-Ponty compares ideas to 'the nervure that bears the leaf from within' (VI, 119). The individual thing is already a 'general manner of being', what Merleau-Ponty also call a style, or a 'system of equivalences', which already puts the singular thing in lateral communication with other things. Here existence and essence cannot be separated because the essence as style is always attached to a geography and a history, a where and a when. If one cuts off the singular thing from these moorings in order to see the essence, all naked, one is left blind.

The emphasis on the verbal sense of *Wesen* also allows Merleau-Ponty to overcome the opposition between Dasein and *Sein* understood as the opposition between the negative and the positive, the subject and the object, existence and essence.[17] It allows him to overcome the classical identification of Being with the Object, and hence with full presence, and the correlative understanding of the human being as the nothing who posits Being, which we find in Husserl's transcendental phenomenology as well as in Sartre. In 'La philosophie aujourd'hui', Merleau-Ponty distances himself from commentators of Heidegger who have overemphasised the role of nothingness in his philosophy and of the human being as the place where this nothingness comes to pass. For Merleau-Ponty this would mean that Heidegger would be stuck within the same alternative as Sartre: positivity of beings, negativity of 'man' as the being who exists, for whom in its Being Being is in question. This negativism and the anthropology that it implies – since transcendence of entities toward Being is the essential characteristic of the human being – is the popular interpretation of Heidegger. Yet, as Merleau-Ponty is quick to point out, Dasein is the theme of Heidegger's research only insofar as Dasein is interrogation of Being and hence our access to Being, which is something 'positive' without being a positive being (see NC, 92–3). Rather than a radical change, we have, after *Being and Time*, a deepening of the kind of negativity exemplified by Dasein, a negativity that is also opening on to something positive that is other than the ontic, namely, *das Seyn* (NC, 94). Heidegger's philosophy turns away from the centrifugal relation of the human being to Being, which necessarily privileges the human being, toward this new domain, one that presents itself as withdrawal and reveals itself as *verborgen*. As Merleau-Ponty writes in the summary of the lecture course: 'Existence might very well, when compared to beings, to entities within the world, be thought of as non-Being, but it is not nothingness or nihilation' (TFL, 110, trans. mod.).[18] Rather, philosophy begins beyond the correlative pair object/nothingness in an opening to ... what is not nothing.

As we have just seen, Merleau-Ponty is sympathetic to Heidegger's turn away from the centrifugal movement from Dasein to Being that was emphasised in *Being and Time*, since it corresponds also to the development of his understanding of philosophy beyond negativism and positivism. Whether Merleau-Ponty's later philosophy of interrogation really effects an anti-anthropological turn – recall that Sartre claimed that 'man' remains Merleau-Ponty's 'principal concern' – is a question we started addressing in the previous section and one we will address again when we discuss how my flesh is a prototype of Being.[19] For now, let us spell out Merleau-Ponty's interrogative philosophy to see how it succeeds in developing a third *genre d'être* between Being and Nothing, something it does through a more thorough engagement with Heidegger (and Heidegger's critique of Sartre), but which also leads to a more scathing criticism of Heidegger's philosophy as a direct ontology.

3. Merleau-Ponty between the negativism of doubt and the positivism of essences

In the chapter of *The Visible and the Invisible* on intuition and interrogation, Merleau-Ponty opposes the negativism of doubt, which in asking whether there is something always has to lean on Being, to the positivism of the essence, which in order to ask 'what is Being?' always needs to pretend that the questioner is nothing or is nothing that *is*. Negativism turns out to be a hidden positivism, and positivism a hidden negativism. This oscillation between negativism and positivism, as we saw in our discussion of Descartes, has to be embraced as belonging to being itself and this is done in interrogation.[20]

If we ask 'why is there something rather than nothing?', the answer, the reason or ground, once provided, erases the question. Similarly, if we ask 'what is Being?' we are after a positive signification that will come to fill the void opened by the question. But if we put the question into question, if we ask 'whence the question?' and 'whence the response?', then the question 'cannot be effaced. Henceforth nothing can continue to be as if there had never been any question. The forgetting of the question would be possible only if the questioning were a simple absence of meaning, a withdrawal into the nothingness that is nothing [*le néant qui n'est rien*]' (VI, 120). This is the Heideggerian *nichtiges Nichts*, which is the counterpart of Being as pure presence, as object. If to question meant to withdraw into such a nothingness, the questioner and his question would not be anything at all and hence would not add anything to Being. But, Merleau-Ponty continues, 'he who questions is not nothing, he is – and this is something quite different – a being that questions himself; the negative in him is borne by an infrastructure of being, it is therefore not a nothing [*un rien*] that eliminates itself from the account' (VI, 120). The positivism of essence or ground demands that the thinker detach herself completely from what she is trying to ground, and hence become nothing. Yet the questioner is, and so is her question, so that they are part of what is in question in the 'question of Being'. Philosophy begins, then, not in asking 'what is Being?' or 'why is there something rather than nothing?' but 'where am I? what time is it?'. If these questions are not quelled by pointing out an objective place or time, it is not merely because my place and time keeps changing. This would make the inexhaustibility of the question and the impossibility of providing a complete answer contingent. Rather, it is because what is in question is 'this indestructible tie between us and hours and places, this perpetual taking of our bearings on the things, this continual installation among them, through which first it is necessary that I be at a time, at a place, whatever they be' (VI, 121).

If Merleau-Ponty states quite explicitly that his philosophy of interrogation is a repudiation of both the negativism of doubt and the positivism of essences, it is also not a call for a return to our immediate ties with Being in a mute fusion or coincidence:

> if coincidence is lost, this is no accident; if Being is hidden, this is itself a characteristic of Being, and no disclosure will make us comprehend it. A lost immediate, arduous to restore, will, if we do restore it, bear within itself the sediment of the critical procedures through which we will have found it anew; it will therefore not be the immediate. If it is to be the immediate, if it is to retain no trace of the operations through which we approach it, if it is Being itself, this means that there is no route from us to it and that it is inaccessible by principle. (VI, 122)

The affinity between philosophy as interrogation and the ontology of the sensible lies in this participation without fusion. Philosophy questions our ties to Being, turns back upon them, but without either severing the ties or merging with them. This is because my ties with Being are already interrogative. Interrogation is our ultimate tie to Being or, as Merleau-Ponty says, our 'ontological organ' (VI, 121).

We can see the influence of Husserl on Merleau-Ponty's reappropriation of Heidegger more clearly here. While Merleau-Ponty rejects a certain idealist reading of the *Wesenschau*, he finds in Husserl's philosophy a paradoxical conjunction between 'our belonging to the world of appearances and the withdrawal requested by questioning thought'[21] that underlies a philosophy of interrogation or of 'pure questioning' (TFL, 105). Heidegger's Being becomes the Husserlian *Ineinander* as the inherence of self to world and of world to self, of constituting to constituted and of constituted to constituting, which then becomes, in the last unpublished manuscripts, the enveloping-enveloped relation that is characteristic of the flesh. The Husserlian *Ineinander* names the intentional implication Husserl elaborates with regard to the *Einfühlung* of the other (*autrui*), which becomes co-extensive with Being and replaces 'the idea of transcendental immanence' (NC, 387).[22] We know Merleau-Ponty's interest for the fifth *Cartesian Meditation*, especially for the notions of coupling (*Paarung, accouplement*) and of 'intentional transgression' or 'intentional encroachment' (*intentionale Überschreitung*).[23] The relation between the ego and the alter ego is the model for the *Ineinander* since both egos are incompossible yet simultaneous (NC, 79). There is a way in which the theoretical contradiction of an alter ego as another constituting consciousness is surmounted, or rather undermined, in the lived experience of the body, this 'subject which experiences itself as constituted at the moment it functions as constituting' (S, 94). Similarly, in my vision, each thing claims an absolute presence which is incompossible with the presence of other things, and yet all things are there together (see S, 181). Here we also find the reason for Merleau-Ponty's interest in infantile transitivism. The child lives in a world where what is incompossible co-exists without contradiction, or at least without the kind of contradiction that leads to negation. What is *ineinander* entertains lateral relation of kinship and co-existence rather than frontal relation of identity and difference, position and negation. This is the *homou en panta* in the *intentionales Ineinander* of the whole, which demands the kind of philosophy of interconnection Merleau-Ponty is attempting to develop in the last years of his life (NC, 85).

With Heidegger, then, but always through Husserl, Merleau-Ponty is led to a new conception of Being, one that is not metaphysical.[24] *Seyn* is not a being and hence not something that can be posited as the object of a science, yet it is also not what Heidegger calls in the Postscript to 'What Is Metaphysics?' '*ein nichtiges Nichts*', a negative, negating or nihilating Nothing (NC, 102). *Seyn* undermines the ontological difference as the separation between the ontological and the ontic. Yet there is in Merleau-Ponty a slight displacement of the meaning of these terms, one influenced by the Cartesian-Sartrian context of his encounter with Heidegger's thought. Merleau-Ponty calls 'ontic' everything that has to do with Being in Cartesian ontology: Cartesian extension, the objective being of Laplacian science, substance, *causa sui*, and so on. 'Ontological' then names the carnal, pre-objective Being, where not everything is visible or graspable as another visible but where one encroaches upon the other and can only be presented as unpresentable, made visible as invisible, like depth. The ontic is the product of an artificial cutting into, an abstraction from, the ontological. Ontology then looks for 'these folds where visibility transgresses the status of pure visible (the ontic) and manifests the exchange with the invisible (the ontological)' (see VOI, 136–8).

In its Merleau-Pontian inflection, then, Being or *Seyn* holds sway or gives itself as and in the latency of beings. This latency is never given as an object but is the milieu, element or dimension in which things are given. This is, in Husserlian vocabulary, the *Urpräsentation* of the *Nichturpräsentierbar* or in Heideggerian vocabulary the *Unverborgenheit* of the *Verbogenen*. For Merleau-Ponty, however, unlike for Heidegger, the sensible is precisely 'that medium in which there can be being without it having to be posited; the sensible appearance of the sensible, the silent persuasion of the sensible is Being's unique way of manifesting itself without becoming positivity, without ceasing to be ambiguous and transcendent' (VI, 214). Sensibility – vision, touch – is our way of having something without possessing or appropriating it (see PoP, 162). It is 'the non-mediated presence which is not something positive, which is being of the far-offs (*être des lointains*)' (VI, 248).

In the 1958–9 lecture course, Merleau-Ponty claims that when Heidegger speaks of mystery or secret (*Geheimnis*) and of *Verborgenheit*, these formulations are not mystical, or rather that 'the mystical formulations are no different than the phenomenological ones' (NC, 119). This is because, as we have just said, Being does not hide as if this hiddenness were a secondary quality or movement. Rather, Being is withdrawal that shows itself (see NC, 118–20). The risk in thinking Being as mystery or secret is to fall back into positing some 'Being' that would be nothing in relation to beings (or beingness). Such a thinking would remain stuck within the alternative of the positive and the negative and not reach what Merleau-Ponty calls the 'dialectic of *Verborgenheit* and *Unverborgenheit*' (NC, 118) – a dialectic that, rather than working through negation, would think the intertwinement or chiasm of the two terms. Being, like depth, cannot be seen. It is not one of the visible, and if I try to find it by focusing on this thing and then on that thing, it constantly escapes and I can only come to the conclusion that it is *nothing*. This is the bad ambiguity: alternating between two positive possibilities in an attempt to grasp their co-belongingness or intertwinement. Rather we must think the way in which depth gives itself right at the things themselves but always indirectly, through the tension between things (VOI, 135). That it escapes when I try to grasp it directly is its mode of revealing itself.

4. Merleau-Ponty's indirect ontology

The analogy with depth allows us to understand what Merleau-Ponty means when he criticises Heidegger for proposing a direct ontology. At the end of the 1958–9 lecture course, Merleau-Ponty speaks of a malaise in Heidegger's later thinking because it still seeks a direct expression of Being all the while showing that there cannot be any such direct expression (NC, 147). Merleau-Ponty concludes: 'One should attempt the indirect expression, i.e. show [*faire voir*] Being through the *Winke* of life, of science, etc.' (NC, 148).

To understand what a 'direct ontology' is – and what Merleau-Ponty means when he calls his own ontology indirect – let us recall what Merleau-Ponty says of the difference between direct and indirect language. Language does not signify directly, which means that the meaning or sense of a word – or of a gesture, a painting, a sentence – is not found directly or frontally in the word as if I could point to it as something that is precisely here and not there. Or rather, if a word appears to mean directly in this way, it is only because it is used in a habitual way. All language is at its source and at bottom indirect: its meaning is not in any parts of the language but rather in the gaps between them, in the difference or divergence they introduce in habitual language, what Merleau-Ponty sometimes also calls spoken speech or empirical language in contrast to speaking speech or creative language. Language is indirect because it means or says something by weaving words – something positive – together upon a background of silence – something negative. Without the silence behind and between words, there would be no meaning and nothing would ever be said. We would only ever be able to repeat what has been said without any divergence.[25]

It is important not to misunderstand the indirect nature of language. It is not that a detour through words is needed in order to reach a meaning that would hide behind the words. Here we would have two positive things, one hidden behind the other, rather than that intertwinement of positive things that 'produces' their depth. Meaning is not somewhere else than in the words, yet it is not present in any of them or in their sum. As Merleau-Ponty writes: 'Like a weaver, the writer works on the wrong side of his material. He has to do only with language, and it is thus that he suddenly finds himself surrounded by meaning' (S, 45).

The accusation against Heidegger, then, is twofold. First, as we have just seen, Being cannot be grasped or expressed directly since as soon as we attempt to do so, all we can do is point out its dissimulation, which ends up being its only truth. The alternative is to grasp the signs of Being, its *Winke*, within what it is not, that is, within beings. Hence, Merleau-Ponty also criticises Heidegger for dismissing 'non-philosophy' as unworthy of thinking insofar as it cannot grant us any access to Being in any way. In refusing all the 'mirrors of Being' (TFL, 112), Heidegger would be more Cartesian than he is willing to admit (VOI, 118). A direct ontology that refuses such mirrors, that does not pass through experience – through the *Lebenswelt* and its expressions – ends in formalism and in silence. The *Winke* (life, science, painting, and so on) are not a detour through which we must pass into order to gain a view of Being because Being is not hidden behind them.

Of course, we can turn the tables on Merleau-Ponty and ask whether his ontology does not remain naïve from a Heideggerian point of view. An ontology can be naïve if it fails to reflect upon itself and its own starting point. An ontology that would answer the question of Being without accounting for the possibility of the question – and hence for the possibility of ontology – as a possibility of human existence would remain naïve.

Here the naivety comes from the fact that we are doing ontology from the outside, so to speak, as if our own Being were not implicated in the question we are seeking to answer. We have seen how Merleau-Ponty's philosophy of interrogation does not fall prey to this naivety. But according to Heidegger there is a second type of naivety, one that he attributes to ancient ontology in *Basic Problems of Phenomenology*. The Ancients didn't fail to reflect upon their ontological enterprise as a comportment of Dasein and hence didn't fail to return to Dasein. Yet they did so in a naïve way because they took as their starting point Dasein's 'everyday and natural self-understanding' so that their ontology remained oriented 'naively in conformity with this productive or perceptual-intuitive comportment'.[26] In this context, Merleau-Ponty's later ontology is certainly naïve but as Richir argues, this is not necessarily a fault. On the contrary, by dismissing the domain of everyday existence – the '*il y a* by inherence' – and by pushing philosophical questioning in the direction of the meaning of Being *as such* or the truth of Being – a purely ontological *es gibt* – Heidegger is led to a kind of abstraction or formalism that remains classical.[27] Merleau-Ponty, on the contrary, reclaims the naïve starting point of reflection which, rather than springing forth from nothingness (*le néant*), always feels itself 'as emerging from something, from an antecedent being' (N, 134).

5. Nancy and Heidegger's withdrawal of Being

In his engagement with Heidegger's later thinking of Being, Nancy takes up many of the same motives as Merleau-Ponty: the active sense of *Wesen* as undermining the existence/essence distinction, the necessity to rethink 'the Nothing' away from the dichotomy between being and nothingness or presence and absence, and the collapse of the ontological difference as difference between two realities. Since Nancy generally engages with Heidegger's texts more directly, his reading of Heidegger's texts can help us flesh out some of Merleau-Ponty's claims, especially the source of Merleau-Ponty's malaise.

In the simplest terms, Being means, for Nancy, *Setzung*, position or positioning. An essence does not exist or it exists only when it is positioned. This seems in line with the traditional understanding of essence and existence and the Kantian thesis according to which 'Being is not a real predicate', or as Heidegger formulates it positively in *Basic Problems of Phenomenology*, 'Being is absolute position of a thing'.[28] Yet, Nancy's understanding of 'positioning' is inflected by Heidegger's transitive understanding of the verb 'to be':

> Being is neither substance nor cause of the thing, rather, it is a being-the-thing in which the verb 'to be' has a transitive value of 'positioning,' but one in which the 'positioning' is based on and caused by nothing else but Dasein, being-there, being thrown down, given over, abandoned, offered up by existence.[29]

Existence – following the traditional notion: that there is such and such, rather than what there is as such – is 'abandoned being'. This expression has a double meaning. First, Being is abandoned or left behind as a cause or ground, or a condition of possibility that would precede what is and serve to explain why what is is. In other words, the answer to the fundamental question of metaphysics, 'why are there beings rather than nothing?', is not to be sought in the antecedence of Being. The answer already lies in the question: 'Since there is something, and not everything, it is because this thing is in abandonment, it is because everything is abandoned' (BP, 43).[30] This is the second sense of abandonment: the cause/ground of the thing withdraws, but rather than withdrawing behind the world, it withdraws into the thing itself. Nancy's notion of creation *ex nihilo* is another way of thematising this abandonment or withdrawal of the cause/ground of beings. As we have already explained in Chapter 6, that the world is 'created' does not mean that it is produced by a very powerful demiurge on the basis of a pre-existing nothing. Rather it allows us to think the world in its proper sense: 'nothing but that which grows [*rien que cela qui croît*] (*creo, cresco*), lacking any growth principle' (D, 24; see BSP, 16).

The abandonment of Being in the double sense in which Nancy uses the phrase is of course a 'translation' of Heidegger's *Seinsverlassenheit*. Yet, according to Nancy, Heidegger's *Seinsverlassenheit* still has the connotation of withdrawing, leaving behind in one's retreat, and holding to oneself, connotations from which Nancy will try to distance himself. Indeed, in *Der Spruch des Anaximander*, Heidegger characterises the way in which Being discloses itself in the unconcealment of what is as an *Ansichhalten*, a keeping to oneself.[31] On the contrary, what Nancy emphasises in the abandonment is an expenditure without reserve, and hence a certain availability and abundance of what is. While it is true that *abandonner* has the connotation of a withdrawing or leaving behind, and hence of a neglecting or not caring for, *être à l'abandon* also points to a certain freedom, availability and even overabundance: a garden *à l'abandon* is an overgrown garden (see BP, 36–7).

What we witness, then, from Heidegger to Nancy, is a subtle shift in the meaning of Being, and more specifically in the significance of the abandonment or withdrawal of Being. This slight shift in emphasis, which moves from '*es gibt*' to '*il y a*', from gift to freedom, from guarding and sheltering to opening and exposing, however, has radical consequences, as we saw in our discussion of the stone's existence in Chapter 6. The crux of the problem could be formulated in the following way: in the withdrawal or abandonment of Being, is Being kept in reserve, hidden and withdrawn, or is it rather the case that Being is nothing more than the thing itself in its sheer existence? Rightly or wrongly, Nancy sees Heidegger as holding on to the first option: Being withdraws and is effaced by the presencing of beings. The 'free gesture' of the disclosure of Being – the gesture that lets beings be encountered meaningfully in the world – is also at the same time a holding back that is responsible for the history of Being as errancy. Only beings are, so that when Being is thought, it is thought as an exemplary or supreme being. This forgetting or oblivion of Being is a consequence of the essential withdrawal of Being, the fact that Being, which is not a being, is only the 'letting-be' of beings.

For Nancy, Heidegger's thought of the concealing of Being is an ontodicy, a justification of evil (see EF, §12).[32] This is the case because evil is made possible by the withdrawal of Being but it does not ruin Being as such. Rather Being holds itself back, and in this way enables both *das Grimmige* and *das Heile*, fury and grace, by enabling good and evil. Thought in such a way, the withdrawal of Being holds within itself the possibility of a 'saving'. Being withdraws behind good and evil and remains the potential for both good and evil, even in the midst of fury. Even though evil does not necessarily lead to its reversal into the good, that is, even though the history of metaphysics is not necessarily the history of a redemption, evil is still justified. In 'The Question Concerning Technology', reading the two verses of Hölderlin's *Patmos*, 'But where *danger* is, *grows* / The *saving power* also', Heidegger shows how the saving power (*das Rettende*) is the reverse side of revealing (*Entbergen*) insofar as the latter happens or comes to pass 'from out of a granting [*Gewähren*] and as such a granting'.[33] As the translator points out, the verb *gewähren* is connected, for Heidegger, to both *wahren*: to watch over, keep safe or protect, and *währen*: to endure. Besides to grant, it can also be translated as to guarantee or vouchsafe.[34] The highest dignity of the human being lies in keeping watch over the unconcealment insofar as it is a granting, that is, insofar as it harbours a granting gesture that necessarily conceals itself in granting the unconcealment of what is.

In the *Letter on Humanism*, instead of using the terms *wahren* or *Wahrnis*, Heidegger speaks of a guarding (*hüten*) or shepherding (*hirten*) of the truth of Being.[35] What is so shepherded is not what is insofar as its appearance is granted to us, but the 'source' of the meaningful appearance of what is. Thought as the mystery, *das Geheimnis*, this source is not only responsible for the giving or sending, the opening up of a world, but it also holds open the inexhaustible possibility of other worlds. Thought as

Ereignis, as the 'event' that binds the human being to Being and vice versa, it is what throws the human being into a specific meaning-formation and calls forth the human being to sustain this meaning-formation. If the source is hidden, it is not because it stands behind something that blocks our access to it but because the bond between the human being and Being cannot be surveyed or mastered by the human being since it would require that the human being steps out of its bond with Being. At the same time, there is an 'experience' of the mystery that does not betray this mystery by making it present, but lets us experience it as holding in reserve possibilities of radical transformation of the human being–Being bond. Such is the experience of the history of Being in its epochal character, that is, as both a granting and a refusal, or as granting refusal. The sheltering or guarding of the mysterious source of the meaningfulness of beings requires that we hold on to the reciprocal bond between the human being and Being, that we become the grounder of the 'there' or the 'open' that is opened through this reciprocal bond. But what is guarded then is not a thing but an opening. As Nancy points out, an opening cannot be guarded by protecting it from or guaranteeing it against closure since such a move would turn the opening into something given, stable, fixed. The guard of the open can only happen through its opening without protection or guarantee (see FT, 184). There is nothing 'there' to be safeguarded.

What Nancy diagnoses in Heidegger is a subtle displacement in the understanding of Being from a letting/opening to a giving that has to be received and kept. In order to prevent this displacement, Nancy will insist on shifting the emphasis from a granting or giving of Being toward the freedom of this granting. In this way, the granting does not become subordinated to a *truth* of Being as concealing, refusal, mystery, a truth that would have to be retrieved, remembered and kept. A *free* giving is not a movement of concealing in the unconcealing of beings, a concealing of Being's own giving in the given beings. Such a giving gesture is not 'free' since it runs the risk of turning into the 'origin' or ground, albeit mysterious, of beings. Or at least it is not free of the metaphysical thought of freedom that questions what is with regard to its ground. In the shift of emphasis Nancy proposes, Being is not thought as '*es gibt*' but as '*il y a*': that there are beings there/here. While the '*es gibt*' is the formulation of a *Verlassenheit/Vergessenheit* that also calls for a guarding/sheltering or a reminiscing, the '*il y a*' is the formulation of freedom, of the abandonment of beings to the *y*, to the spacing of a place.[36]

Let us recall that for Merleau-Ponty, *il y a* is, contrary to what Heidegger says in the *Letter on Humanism*, a good rendition of *es gibt* precisely because *es gibt* does not mean '*donner*', 'to give' (NC, 113–14). For Nancy too, *es gibt* does not mean that Being gives the given. Being is neither the subject nor the author of the gift or of the given. Rather, we must hear the Heideggerian *es gibt* through Derrida's deconstruction of the gift in *Given Time*. Following Derrida the gift must not only be thought as without giver and without given (beyond subject and object) but also as without property or propriety. While Heidegger would succeed in thinking the former, he would fail to think the latter.[37]

Now, if in the releasement of beings into the clearing of Being, nothing is properly held back or 'withdrawn', this means, according to Nancy, that the ontological difference is annulled. We know that for Heidegger the ontological difference is the way in which *Seyn* comes to pass as the forgetting of Being. Metaphysics thinks Being always from out of beings and in view of beings, as that which is different from beings so that Being is the answer to the question: 'what are beings qua beings?' This way of questioning beings sets Being apart from beings and thinks it as their ground. Hence the ontological difference is invoked by metaphysics, but it is not thought as such since the focus is the relation of grounding between the two different elements. The ontological difference is overcome in a leap into *Ereignis*, where the difference is thought as *Unter-schied* and *Austrag*.[38] What is so thought is not Being as the different, but rather the inbetween that perdures and out of which Being and beings differentiate themselves. The co-belonging of Being and beings is now thought transitively as overwhelming and arrival: Being comes over beings and unconceals them; beings arrive and abide in sheltering the overcoming that unconceals them. Here, beings are not expropriated or abandoned by Being; rather they shelter the truth of Being.

When Nancy speaks of the annulment of the ontological difference, he seems to think something similar to the Heideggerian step back into the domain where Being and beings can be experienced from out of the difference in which they are held apart and toward each other. Nancy comes to think of the ontological difference, of the fact that Being is not a being, by looking back to the Latin etymology of the word '*rien*'. As Nancy points out, *rien* does not mean 'not a thing at all' but rather the thing itself, *res*, insofar as it is no thing, that is, insofar as it empties itself out of its essence or whatness.[39] Here Nancy differentiates between *le néant* (nothingness, *das Nichts*) and *le rien* (nothing, *rem*, the thing). Nothingness is what Being turns into as soon as it is posited in its difference from beings, as the universal and the highest. Nothing, on the other hand, is the thing taken in its existence rather than in its essence: 'Nothing is the thing tending toward its pure and simple being of a thing, consequently also toward the most common being of something and thus toward the vanishing, momentary quality of the smallest amount of beingness [*étantité*]' (CW, 103). In the *res* as *rien*, the ontological difference is cancelled as a difference between two realities, Being and being, the ground and the grounded, but also as the abandonment of beings by Being, the withdrawal and reserve of Being. There are only beings, nothing behind, beneath or beyond them. In other words, there is no difference between existence and the existent; the existent's 'reality' is nothing other than the putting into play of its own existence. Hence, the annulment of the ontological difference has nothing to do with the confusion between Being and beings or a forgetting of their difference. Rather, 'This step back [from the ontological difference into the dif-ference] is the *identity of being and beings*: existence. Or more precisely: freedom. Freedom: *the withdrawal of every positing of being, including its being posited as differing from beings*' (EF, 167).[40]

We started by saying that for Nancy, being means positioning: *that* a thing is rather than *what* it is. In speaking in this way, we seemed to repeat the *essentia/existentia* distinction that Heidegger diagnoses as the key feature of metaphysical thinking (*existentia* is the actual presence or givenness of some 'what'). Then, we saw that nothing (or being) is the thing tending toward the simple and most common being of a thing. This seemed again to reaffirm Being as *existentia* and remain within the metaphysical thinking of Being as essence and existence. Yet, as we have seen in our previous discussion of Nancy, 'positioning' is not for him a metaphysical notion: it is neither essentialist nor existentialist, neither the position of an essence, nor the pure position of an existent that would have to make its own essence. Rather, the positioning of essence is an offering, an exposition so that the essence is not posited in-itself, in pure self-presence, but handed over to itself, 'exposed to being *of* itself, *for* itself, and *unto* itself what it is *in* itself'.[41] The existent does not stand there within its essence but is fully engaged in existence, in an active relation with its Being.

Like Merleau-Ponty, then, but through a different route, Nancy undoes the metaphysical difference between *existentia* and *essentia* in favour of a thinking of presence that is not pure positivity but includes a moment of negativity that is not the other of presence but its opening. The central point of contention in both Merleau-Ponty's and Nancy's reappropriation of Heidegger's later thought is how to think the withdrawal of Being without falling into the dichotomy between presence and absence, positivism and negativism. According to Merleau-Ponty, Heidegger would not escape this alternative because he still tries to express Being directly. As a result Being turns into Nothing. For Nancy, on the contrary, Heidegger still holds on to a thinking of Being as what keeps itself in reserve. As such, Being would be withdrawn behind presence as a kind of super-presence, and hence Heidegger would not completely succeed in overcoming onto-theology.

In 'Proximity and Distance', Michel Haar argues that Merleau-Ponty's ontology lacks a thinking of the gift as excess and reserve. There would be in Merleau-Ponty's thinking a forgetting of negativity and nothingness so that despite all the talk of dehiscence, fold and non-coincidence, the flesh would lack a principle of conflictuality and be harmonious and reassuring.[42] One might also level a similar criticism against Nancy's ontology insofar as being is fully at play right at the beings themselves and nothing is held back. Yet both Nancy and Merleau-Ponty in their own ways attempt to rethink negativity with the help of but also against Hegelian dialectic and Heidegger's Being as refusal. They both argue against a certain understanding of negativity as reserve while also trying to think a certain kind of excess. It is this issue of negativity and its relation to non-coincidence and excess that we track in the last chapter of this study.

Notes

1. See Bernet, 'Perception et vie naturelle (Husserl et Merleau-Ponty)', in *La vérité du sujet*, 165.
2. Sartre, 'Merleau-Ponty Vivant', in Stewart (ed.), *The Debate between Sartre and Merleau-Ponty*, 617. See also VOI, 43, 102.
3. See Richir, 'Le sens de la phénoménologie dans *Le visible et l'invisible*', Esprit 66, no. 6 (1982): 142. For more references, see VOI, 101–3.
4. Richir, 'Le sens de la phénoménologie', 142.
5. See Dastur, 'La lecture merleau-pontienne de Heidegger dans les notes du *Visible et l'invisible* et les cours du Collège de France (1957–1958)', *Chiasmi International* 2 (2000): 373–87 and Haar, 'Proximity and Distance with Regard to Heidegger in the Late Merleau-Ponty', in Vallier, Froman and Flynn (eds), *Merleau-Ponty and the Possibilities of Philosophy*, esp. 168–73. An earlier version in a different translation was published in the *Journal of the British Society for Phenomenology* in 1999.
6. For a reading of the later Merleau-Ponty from the point of view of Heidegger that clearly shows all that Heidegger would reject in Merleau-Ponty's ontology, see Haar, 'Proximity and Distance', especially the last section, 177–82.
7. Bourgeois, 'Merleau-Ponty and Heidegger: The Intentionality of Transcendence, the Being of Intentionality', *JBSP* 25, no. 1 (1994): 31. Problematically, however, Bourgeois attributes the quote he uses to defend this point to the *Phenomenology* while it is in fact found in 'The Intertwining – the Chiasm' at VI, 151.
8. Schües, 'Heidegger and Merleau-Ponty: Being-in-the-World with Others?', in Macann (ed.), *Martin Heidegger: Critical Assessments, Volume II: History of Philosophy*, 357.
9. Haar, 'Proximity and Distance', 167. See PP, 451–2.
10. Nancy, 'The Being-With of Being-There', *Continental Philosophy Review* 41, no. 1 (2008): 8.
11. Nancy, 'The Being-With of Being-There', 11.
12. Nancy does find this understanding of authenticity present in Heidegger, especially in §37 of *Being and Time* on ambiguity. See 'The Decision of Existence' in BP.
13. See Schües, 'Heidegger and Merleau-Ponty', 365. The interlocutor here, however, is not Heidegger but more traditional idealists such as Pierre Lachièze-Rey and Léon Brunschvicg, whose book, *Le progrès de la conscience dans la philosophie occidentale*, Merleau-Ponty has just quoted a couple of lines earlier.

14. See Heidegger, *Metaphysical Foundations of Logic*, §10. Metaphysical neutrality is not ontic indifference to bodiliness, hence it is not guilty of the same 'abstraction' as Cartesian ontology and the sciences that are grounded upon it. It is, as Heidegger says, the necessity of the 'neutrality' of the origin, the 'authentic concreteness of the origin, the not-yet of factical dispersion [*Zerstreutheit*]' (137).
15. For a reading of the Zollikon seminars in the context of Merleau-Ponty's notion of flesh, see VOI, chapter 5.
16. See Taminiaux, 'Was Merleau-Ponty on the Way from Husserl to Heidegger?', *Chiasmi International* 11 (2009): 21–30 for more details.
17. Dastur, 'La lecture merleau-pontienne', 378.
18. The summary of the lecture course which is published in *Notes de cours 1959–1961* under the title 'La philosophie aujourd'hui' appears in the *Résumés de cours. Collège de France 1952–1960* under the title 'La possibilité de la philosophie' and is translated in *Themes from the Lectures* as 'Philosophy as Interrogation'.
19. For all the references regarding this anti-anthropological turn, see VOI, 36–43.
20. On interrogation, see Barbaras, *The Being of the Phenomenon*, chapter 9.
21. Taminiaux, 'Was Merleau-Ponty on the Way from Husserl to Heidegger?', 24.
22. The expression 'Das intentionale Ineinander' is found in the Beilage XXIII in the *Crisis*, which Merleau-Ponty translates and comments on in the 1958–9 lecture course (NC, 383–8). Husserl also speaks of an 'Ineinander der Erfüllungen' in Husserliana XV (Nr. 34) in a note on desire, especially sexual desire (or instinct) seen from a transcendental point of view. Husserl speaks of *Trieb* (desire, instinct) that in its originary mode (*Urmodus*) reaches into the other (*hineinreichen*) and of a *Triebintentionalität* that relates us to the other as other and to her correlative desire. The fulfillment (*Erfüllung*) of desire, Husserl continues, does not consist in two juxtaposed desires that would remain external to each other but rather in a unity (*Einheit*) of both primordialities that is established through '*das Ineinander der Erfüllungen*' (Husserliana XV, 593). What seems to interest Merleau-Ponty in this manuscript is the way in which Husserl questions the relation between 'Ichzentrierung' and universality of intentional implication. In the notes to *The Visible and the Invisible*, Merleau-Ponty speaks of 'the coupling of the bodies, that is, the adjustment of their intentions to *one sole Erfüllung*' (VI, 233). In the third sketch for the 1959–60 lecture course on Nature, Merleau-Ponty speaks of 'desire considered from the transcendental point of view as the common framework [*membrure*] of my world as carnal and of the world of the other. They all end up at one sole *Einfühlung* (cf. Husserl's unpublished texts)' (N, 225). There are good reasons to believe that it should read *Erfüllung* and not *Einfühlung* (*Einfühlung* being what allows that there be one sole *Erfüllung*). Indeed, later on, in the eighth sketch, speaking again about the libidinal body, Merleau-Ponty speaks of two desires 'linked into a unique *Erfüllung*' (N, 282).
23. Merleau-Ponty claims that this expression is used by Husserl in the *Cartesian Meditations* (see S, 169), but this is not quite accurate. Husserl does speak of an intentionality that constitutes, in my sphere of ownness, a new sense of being (*Seinsinn*) that goes beyond (*überschreitet*) my monadic ego in its own ownness (or own singularity, *Selbsteigenheit*) (see §44) but he does not use the active noun *Überschreitung* anywhere. At this point in the *Cartesian Meditations*, Husserl is looking for something that goes beyond or transcends my sphere of ownness but he does not speak of an intentional transgression as if my consciousness would reach into the other, at least not here. In §51 Husserl does speak of an *intentionales Übergreifen* (translated as overreaching) at work in *Paarung*.
24. Which does not mean that Merleau-Ponty wasn't already on the way to this new conception through his critiques of Cartesian-Sartrian ontology. If Heidegger's work resonates with him, it is because he finds in it something toward which he was, through a different path, already on the way. Yet this way through the sensible makes a difference in the non-metaphysical conception of Being each thinker ultimately develops.

25. Merleau-Ponty, *The Prose of the World*, 46.
26. Heidegger, *Basic Problems of Phenomenology*, 110, 117.
27. Richir, 'Le sens de la phénoménologie', 142. Haar, on the contrary, wonders whether Merleau-Ponty's ontology also doesn't end up being abstract: 'But are not the ideas of a universal "sensible in itself" and of an ahistorical surplus itself themselves abstract, precisely in being situated in the absolute concreteness of "being as the pure *il y a*" (*VI*, 139)?' (Haar, 'Proximity and Distance', 168).
28. Kant, *Critique of Pure Reason*, A592/B620–A603/B631; Heidegger, *Basic Problems*, §7.
29. Nancy, 'Of Being-in-Common', in *Community at Loose Ends*, 2.
30. For a reading of the abandonment of being as it relates to the imperative of being, see Raffoul, 'Abandonment and the Categorical Imperative of Being', in Hutchens (ed.), *Jean-Luc Nancy: Justice, Legality and World*, 65–81.
31. See Heidegger, 'Anaximander's Saying', in *Off the Beaten Track*, 254.
32. See also Roney, 'Evil and the Experience of Freedom: Nancy on Schelling and Heidegger', *Research in Phenomenology* 9, no. 3 (2009): 374–400.
33. Heidegger, *The Question Concerning Technology*, 28–34, here 32.
34. Heidegger, *The Question Concerning Technology*, 31, n. 24.
35. Heidegger, *Pathmarks*, 252, 260.
36. Nancy, *L'impératif catégorique*, 145. An abridged version of the chapter from which I am quoting is translated as 'Abandoned Being' in *The Birth to Presence*, but the paragraph I am referring to is omitted. See BP, 40.
37. See Derrida, *Given Time, I. Counterfeit Money*, 20–2. See also Derrida, *Margins*, 26, n. 26, where Derrida comments on a sentence from Heidegger's lecture 'On Time and Being', which reads: 'The gift of presence is the property of Appropriating (*Die Gabe von Anwesen ist Eigentum des Ereignens*).'
38. Heidegger, *Identity and Difference*, 65. See also the translator's introduction, 17, n. 3.
39. As Littré explains, the literal meaning of the word *rien*, which goes back to its etymological root in the Latin *rem* (accusative of *res*), is 'something'. Only when the negative particle *ne* or *ni* is added to form the locution *ne rien . . .* or *ni rien . . .* does it mean 'nothing'. In this way, the sentence '*il serait dangereux de rien entreprendre*' means 'it would be dangerous to undertake something', while the sentence '*il serait dangereux de ne rien entreprendre*' means the exact opposite, namely that it would be dangerous to undertake nothing or not to undertake something. As a noun, *un rien* means a very small thing, something that is almost nothing at all, as in the phrase '*pleurer pour un rien*', 'to burst into tears for a trifle'. To get a sense of the poetic possibilities afforded by French *rien*, let us suggest Serge Gainsbourg's 1964 song, *Ces petits riens*.
40. Here, Nancy seems to be thinking of existence more in terms of Heidegger's *Ereignis* and not as the human being's insertion (*Einrückung*) in the There. See Heidegger, *Contributions to Philosophy (Of the Event)*, §179.
41. Nancy, 'Of Being-in-Common', in *Community at Loose Ends*, 3.
42. Haar, 'Proximity and Distance', 181.

Chapter 8

Two Ontologies of Sense

Merleau-Ponty's move from phenomenology to ontology, which can also be interpreted as the fulfilment of phenomenology,[1] happens when Merleau-Ponty seeks to understand neither the subject nor the world, nor their relation as a third term, but the primordial in-between, that is, how the subject's being in the world and the world's existence for the subject are upheld by something that encompasses them, which he will call 'wild being', or 'vertical being'. Vertical being is the dimension of encroachment or of the union of incompossibles, the 'world where everything is simultaneous' (S, 179), the *totum simul* of every thing, of every profile (VI, 219).[2] From our discussion of the relation of Merleau-Ponty's later thinking to Heidegger's, we know we should be careful not to turn Being into a Big Object, a positivity, a congealed infinity or a hidden In-itself. Being is not elsewhere; rather, it is an internal possibility of this world. It is the element, the milieu of things that cannot be reduced to any one thing but only transpires in them. In the words of Gary Madison, replying to Theodore Geraets:

> 'Being' is here neither a supreme and necessary being (*ens causa sui, ens realissimum*) nor a transcendental logical principle (a 'that without which' nothing is thinkable). It has neither logical nor ontic reality; it is therefore not so much a *ground* as an abyss, an unfathomable and inexhaustible source of *transcendence*.[3]

If Being is the inexhaustible source of transcendence, then transcendence as the movement of sense is not something that is bestowed upon beings by the human. Transcendence is not a feature of human existence but a movement within Being as such.[4] The question is: what must Being be so that it is the inexhaustible source of transcendence?

It is in order to acquaint us with this new kind of Being that Merleau-Ponty will revisit the phenomenon of self-sensing, focusing on the chiasm at the heart of our carnal being. Our body as a sensible sentient is, as Merleau-Ponty claims, a 'remarkable variant' or a 'prototype' of Being so that its constitutive doubling, paradox or chiasm is not one of 'man' but one of Being itself (VI, 136). The question I want to raise in this final section is: to what degree does Merleau-Ponty's notion of the flesh and its constitutive paradox introduce a difference – differance, spacing – at the heart of sense, which would bring Merleau-Ponty's later thought in closer proximity to Nancy's ontology? In what sense is flesh a differential principle? Or is flesh, not just as it is experienced in my own body but also as a prototype of Being, still a monological principle that guarantees from the start the fittedness of sensing and sensed? How should we understand this common ontological fabric (*étoffe*) (VI, 200, 262) Merleau-Ponty sometimes speaks of in reference to the flesh? Is it an undifferentiated glob, or a principle of differentiation?

In what follows, I do not intend to argue that Merleau-Ponty is a precursor of Derrida or Nancy. Neither do I intend to argue that Merleau-Ponty remained unable to accomplish a real break with the metaphysics of subjectivity either because of his untimely death or because of some deeper desire for integrity, unity, wholeness, and hence for a certain form of presence. Proving either claim would require that we sift through Merleau-Ponty's work to find the seeds of a deconstructive thinking that only took root later on. As will become clear in what follows, it is indeed possible to find such seeds. But as will also become clear, we also find in Merleau-Ponty's lecture courses, posthumous texts and unpublished notes much that goes against such a view. If I choose to follow Merleau-Ponty's later reflections on the flesh and the chiasm, it is not so much to settle the issue of whether he was or was not a 'proto-deconstructionist'. This question has already given rise to an extensive literature.[5] And given the unfinished status of Merleau-Ponty's later work, it is probably impossible to settle this question once and for all.

Without settling this question, however, I still believe that bringing Nancy's thinking to bear on Merleau-Ponty's later texts can open up unexpected resonances that can guide our interpretation of some of the more difficult claims we find in Merleau-Ponty's unfinished work. Let us remind ourselves that when Nancy speaks positively of the phenomenology of the body, it is in relation to the figure of the chiasm, which points to the radical openness or exposure of the touching-touched body to the world. Here is the passage in full:

> My hands touch one another; my body recognizes itself coming to itself from an outside that it itself is, taking into itself again the world outside it.

> The chiasm of the flesh that is described so well by the most insightful phenomenology of the body . . . reminds us that our being entwined with the world has always, from the start, exposed us right down to our most intimate depths. The 'inside' is always between outside and outside, and this between – the between of its lair, its cave of myths and phantoms of interiority – is, in the end, nothing but another outside. (C II, 82)

The affinity between Nancy and Merleau-Ponty would be found in a torsion between inside and outside, one that teaches us that we are exposed 'right down to our most intimate depths'. The question then is whether the chiasm of the flesh allows us to think a radical breach or spacing at the heart of what exists or whether, as Nancy said of the phenomenologies of the body, 'everything always returns in interiority' (C, 128).

Whereas in the *Phenomenology of Perception* Merleau-Ponty used communion to characterise sensing, in the later works sense (and sensing) will explicitly be thought in terms of divergence or *écart*. When Merleau-Ponty first introduces the motif of the *écart* in his 1953 lecture course at the Collège de France, it is in order to conceptualise what is sensed in a diacritical way rather than as an essence or a given signification that could be possessed in isolation, in an 'I know that'.[6] The point is not, or not yet, to think of the *écart* as the basic principle of an ontology of sense. Here, rather, Merleau-Ponty is taking up the analyses of the Gestalt and of the *bougé* (shifting, haziness) found in the *Phenomenology* and investing them with a normative dimension: the background is a level, dimension or norm and the figure a certain style of divergence or modulation of this norm that is at the same time destabilising and motivating.[7]

What interests me is to follow the way in which the *écart* plays out in Merleau-Ponty's understanding of the flesh to ask about the role it plays in his understanding of the self as self-sensing, and – since carnal being is a prototype of Being – of being itself. If it turns out to play a central role, then this will make a rapprochement with Nancy easier. Before we proceed, it should be pointed out that the resonances between the two authors that guide the encounter I am staging here can easily be overlooked in the English translations because the word *écart* has multiple meanings and is variously translated. In Nancy *écart* is translated as separation, displacement, apartness, gap or swerve;[8] in Merleau-Ponty it is sometimes also translated as separation, but most often as divergence, deviation and spread.

1. Merleau-Ponty, *écart* and the flesh

The ambiguity of the concept of flesh has been outlined by many commentators. Indeed, Merleau-Ponty not only uses the word 'flesh' to refer to the Husserlian *Leib*, but also speaks of the flesh of the visible, the flesh of things or the flesh of the world, so that flesh becomes what he calls 'an element of being' (VI, 139). Whether these different uses of the word 'flesh' are compatible is not my worry here.[9] My focus is rather on the role divergence plays in the flesh and the relation between the flesh and the structure of the chiasm in its imminent reversibility.

Merleau-Ponty does use the word 'flesh' to refer to my own body insofar as it is self-sensing, the body that was already the topic of the analysis of the *Phenomenology of Perception*. Here again, as in the *Phenomenology*, Merleau-Ponty emphasises the reversibility of sensing, and the fact that the sensing body is always of the world, but he now draws the ontological consequences of that discovery: the structure of my own self-sensing flesh will teach me something about Being as such. The important thing to notice here is that the visible/tangible is first in the order of explanation. Rather than explaining visibility starting from vision, we need to explain vision starting from visibility. The reversibility of the flesh leads Merleau-Ponty to posit the priority of the sensible over the sensing in the order of Being. Undoing the dichotomy between noumenon and phenomenon, Merleau-Ponty starts from a visibility without vision, or a sensibility without sensation.[10] The world is sensible in itself: the world is not only sensible *for* a sensing being that would be the ground of its (the world's) sensibility; rather the world is already pregnant with all possible (and incompossible) sensibilities, so that vision or touch happens as a fold in the midst of a world that is already visible/tangible without being constituted as such by a conscious subject. As Merleau-Ponty writes:

> because my eyes which see, my hands which touch, can also be seen and touched, because, therefore, in this sense they see and touch the visible, the tangible, from within, because our flesh lines and even envelops all the visible and tangible things with which nevertheless it is surrounded, the world and I are within one another, and there is no anteriority of the *percipere* to the *percipi*, there is simultaneity or even retardation. . . . When I find again the actual world such as it is, under my hands, under my eyes, up against my body, I find much more than an object: a Being of which my vision is a part, a visibility older than my operations or my acts. (VI, 123)

Merleau-Ponty's position is somewhat counter-intuitive. It seems obvious that both visible and tangible can only be what they are by being correlated to a seeing or touching power, a consciousness or a body that would be responsible for its visibility or its tangibility. But this is exactly what Merleau-Ponty is denying. 'The flesh of the world', Merleau-Ponty writes,

> is of the Being-seen, i.e. is a Being that is *eminently percipi*, and it is by it that we can understand the *percipere* . . . [which] is finally possible and means something only because *there is* Being, not Being in itself, identical to itself, in the night, but the Being that also contains its negation, its *percipi*. (VI, 250–1)

Let's pause here and try to make sense of what Merleau-Ponty is saying. Something appears, there are phenomena. The question is: does that necessarily mean that there has to be a constituting consciousness? Must phenomenality necessarily be linked to a consciousness? If Being is Being-in-itself then phenomenality can only be explained by means of something other than Being, for example, Sartre's For-Itself. But this is not the case if Being and appearing – Being and meaning or sense – essentially belong together. Of course, for phenomenology too being and appearing belong together, but for the later Merleau-Ponty the relation is more complicated. Something remains 'outside' of the appearing, but as the outside of the inside, as the Being *of* meaning: something resists the appearing – what Merleau-Ponty calls vertical, brute or wild being – and guarantees that appearing is never finished or complete.[11]

We must understand the event of phenomenality or vision, then, as taking place in the midst of a world that is already visible insofar as it contains latencies, incompossibilities and fissures to which my body as seer-seen (*voyant-vu*) or visible seer (*voyant visible*) will respond: 'vision happens among, or is caught in, things – in that place where something visible undertakes to see, becomes visible for itself by virtue of the vision of all things' (PoP, 163, trans. mod.). We will come back to this enigmatic 'vision of all things' below. For now, we only want to point out that understanding the event of vision as the folding or coiling over of a visible segment of the world complicates the relation between interiority and exteriority. The coiling over does not create an inside or a private ego but rather opens the 'coiled body' to an intercorporeity.

Because the folding of the flesh is dehiscence, a separation in the midst of the flesh without being a full distinction or rupture, this folding leads to a contortion of the inside/outside divide, or as Merleau-Ponty writes, to the inside and the outside 'turning about one another' (VI, 264). Vision does not happen inside the body (within consciousness) and outside the world, but as a fold within the world. Vision is the outside of the world (and hence inside), but this outside is inside the world (and hence outside itself). In other words, consciousness envelops the world since the world is *for* consciousness, but consciousness is also enveloped by the world, since it is *within* the world that consciousness takes place. This is what Merleau-Ponty means when he says that the world is inserted between the two leaves of my body because my body is inserted between the two leaves of the world:

> The body unites us directly with the things through its own ontogenesis, by welding to one another the two outlines of which it is made, its two lips: the sensible mass it is and the mass of the sensible wherein it is born by segregation and upon which, as seer, it remains open. (VI, 136)

My flesh, then, as a being of two leaves is what it is thanks to a visibility or a sensibility that is older than all of my intentional acts and that I can never fully recuperate within myself. It is this originary delay between the mass of the sensible and the sensible mass that lights up the spark that will make the self and make it sense.

In a note from May 1960, Merleau-Ponty speaks more specifically of the primordial divergence at the heart of the two-dimensional being that is the self:

> The *touching itself, seeing itself* of the body is itself to be understood in terms of what we said of the seeing and the visible, the touching and the touchable. I.e. it is not an act, it is a being at (*être à*). To touch *oneself*, to see *oneself*, accordingly, is not to apprehend oneself as an ob-ject, it is to be open to oneself, destined to oneself (narcissism) – Nor, therefore, is it to reach *oneself*, it is on the contrary to escape *oneself*, to be ignorant of *oneself*, the self in question is by divergence (*d'écart*). (VI, 249)

At this stage of our study, what is fascinating is how this note, with its mention of *être à* and of *écart*, resonates with Nancy's own thinking.[12] Let us read this working note with Nancy in mind.

By now, we are familiar with Nancy's understanding of the 'self' or *soi* as differance, which structure is not limited to the human being or even to sentient life but also characterises the mineral existence of the stone. Derrida coins the neologism 'differance' to underline both the spatial meaning of the French verb *différer* (to differ, to be distinct, discernible, separate) and its temporal meaning (to defer, postpone, relay through a detour). Differance names both spacing and temporisation: it names the dynamic division of an interval that allows for meaning, for presence. What is 'first' then is the gap or spacing that divides and relates: a spacing that allows for identity (or 'self-identification') but only as an effect of the spacing that has always split any present into two, leaving each haunted by the trace of another. For Nancy, differance means that there is an irreducible spacing or gap, *écart*, at the heart of the self thanks to which something like a self can exist, that is, be present *to*, *être* à, itself and others. Since the spacing or diaresis of the self is 'originary', there is, properly speaking, no self-presence prior to any differentiating: the self is an effect of the *écart* so that the self has always already started by altering itself and can never catch up with what would be a pure origin to coincide with itself. Self-identification, then, the relation of the self to self, does not take the form of a subject or an ipseity. It is not the Hegelian 'self-restoring sameness' or 'reflection in otherness within itself',[13] a detour through an outside at the end of which the subject reappropriates this exteriority and comes back to itself. Rather, selfhood consists in a movement of being-to or being-toward, in which the '*to* of the to-itself [à *de l'à-soi*] . . . is first and foremost the fissure, the gap [*l'écart*], the spacing [*l'espacement*] of an opening' (FT, 7).

If this gap or spacing from self to self were ever to be bridged or closed, then there would be no self and no sense or sensing. In Nancy's words again:

> To have sense, or to make sense, to be sensed, is to be to oneself insofar as the other affects this ipseity in such a way that this affection is neither reduced *to* nor retained in the *ipse* itself. On the contrary, if the affection of sense is reabsorbed, sense itself also disappears. (FT, 6)

In Merleau-Ponty's words: to be destined to oneself is not to reach oneself but to escape oneself. If the self were to reach itself in (self-)sensing, if the otherness that affects the self and makes it sensing were reducible to the self, then there would be no sense. For both Nancy and Merleau-Ponty, the self that is reached or touched in the movement of being-to or being-toward is not identical to the point of departure of this movement. In fact, sense only happens in the divergence or gap between the two so that no points of departure or arrival can properly be said to exist independently of each other. What is is only by divergence.

So far, Merleau-Ponty's note seems to lend itself to a Nancean reading. Yet we intentionally glossed over Merleau-Ponty's appeal to narcissism. Does the appeal not reinforce Nancy's worry that even though the sensing body is an *être-à*, even though it is essentially opened to (itself), it remains in the end thought of on the model of the circle of self-presence closing in upon itself? The sensing body would be like Narcissus, who never experiences anything but his own reflection. If this is how we should understand Merleau-Ponty's use of the term 'narcissism', then it would undermine the role of the *écart* by subordinating it to a prior unity.

2. Narcissism and the reversibility of the chiasm

We must start by recalling that earlier in *The Visible and the Invisible*, when Merleau-Ponty used the term 'narcissism', it was to speak of a narcissism of all vision, or a narcissism of the flesh. Since vision doesn't happen in an ego, narcissism here doesn't mean that I am stuck within my ego and its representations. Rather, vision is narcissistic because it happens by dehiscence or folding of the flesh, of this common fabric to which seer and visible belong like warp and weft. Vision should be understood as the visible's quest for itself as visible in which a visible (a body) turns back upon itself in an attempt to catch or gather this visibility.

At the same time, insofar as the narcissism of all vision constitutes me as seer, there is also a certain narcissism of *my* vision, a desire to 'reach myself' as seer. I desire a doubling of vision: seeing myself see. Insofar as the one who sees is always also seen and the one who touches is always also touched, touching the other ('escaping *oneself*') is the way I have of coming back to myself or of being destined to myself, yet always through an *écart*. Insofar as it is as a visible thing among other visible things that I see, my vision in act always implicates my visibility, a visibility that is older than what my vision can actually grasp as its own object. In seeing (the other) I find myself as visible by virtue of the 'vision of all things'. The doubling of vision – seeing myself see – happens in and through the other, a visible that has the power to catch or gather my visibility, which is always the other side of my vision.

The key issue at this point is whether we should understand this doubling of sensing, this chiasm or reversibility of the seer and the seen, as a kind of specular or symmetrical reciprocity. The flesh would then be the element or milieu in which this reciprocal relation takes place, their means of communication which would be responsible for their adherence, cohesion or presence to each other. There are two different questions then: the question of symmetrical reciprocity within reversibility and the question of the cohesion of the two strands of the chiasm. The emphasis on divergence or *écart* allows us to answer the first question in the negative but it leaves the second question open. Let us first focus on the kind of reversibility at play in the chiasm before we tackle the second question.

The best image to think of the chiasm between visible and vision is that of incongruent counterparts.[14] Take a right-hand glove. It is always already lined with an invisible left-hand glove, but it cannot be this left-hand glove without the now visible right-hand glove becoming the invisible lining of a left-hand glove. A glove is always both a right-hand and a left-hand glove but in different senses of being: passive/active, actual/virtual. At the same time, we cannot say that both the right-hand and the left-hand gloves are mere appearances of a non-handed 'idea' of glove. The idea 'glove' could never be differentiated into right-handed and left-handed without descending into the world, in this case, into three-dimensional space. What we have is ontological complicity between right-handed and left-handed, each being the necessary doubling or lining of the other, without any identity between the two.[15] There is a necessary gap or divergence between the two that makes any congruence or superposition impossible.[16]

The relation of right-handed and left-handed within one glove exemplifies the relation between sensing and sensed within my body, and by complication between my body and the other *visibilia*. Think of the visible as a left-hand glove already lined with a virtual vision. The seer-seen that is my body is a convulsion of this *visibile*, one that reverses the glove so that it is actual vision lined with visibility, rather than a visible lined with a virtual vision. Sensing is then a kind of handshake between my body (right-hand glove) and a *visibile* (left-hand glove).[17] It is because both vision and the visible have another side or an inner lining, because there is more to the seer than just vision (the seer is a visible body) and there is more to the seen thing than its being-perceived here and now (the visible is lined with visibility or virtual vision), because both habour a certain opacity or depth, that they cannot be juxtaposed or posited side by side. This, again, is the meaning of 'verticality' in Merleau-Ponty's later work.

The chiral understanding of reversibility also helps us make sense of Merleau-Ponty's use of the image of the mirror in *The Visible and the Invisible*.[18] Often his language seems to imply that seer and visible bounce off each other in perfect symmetrical reciprocity. For example, speaking of the narcissism of all vision, Merleau-Ponty writes:

> the vision [the seer] exercises, he also undergoes from the things, such that, as many painters have said, I feel myself looked at by the things, my activity is equally passivity – which is the second and more profound sense of the narcissism: not to see in the outside, as the others see it, the contour of a body one inhabits, but especially to be seen by the outside, to exist within it, to emigrate into it, to be seduced, captivated, alienated by the phantom, so that the seer and the visible *reciprocate one another and we no longer know which sees and which is seen*. It is this Visibility, this generality of the Sensible in itself, this anonymity innate to Myself that we have previously called flesh, and one knows there is no name in traditional philosophy to designate it. (VI, 139, my emphasis)

In this passage, the chiasm seer-seen is presented as a reciprocation and the emphasis is put on the flesh, Visibility itself, as the element in which this reciprocal relation takes place. Since Merleau-Ponty also says that the flesh '*is a mirror phenomenon* [phénomène de miroir]' (VI, 255), it seems only natural to interpret the chiasm as straightforwardly reflective. The mirror (or your eyes) would give me access to a part of myself as through a ricochet. Here we would have a detour through an exteriority (reflection in the mirror) that would allow the self to come back to itself with a more complete, but ultimately undisturbed, understanding of itself. Such an interpretation of mirroring as the reflection-into-self of otherness seems to be supported if we recall that Merleau-Ponty borrows the figure of the chiasm from Valéry, who writes:

> As soon as gazes meet [intertwine, are caught in one another, *les regards se prennent*], we are no longer wholly two, and it is hard to remain alone. . . . You capture my image, my appearance; I capture yours. You are not me, since you see me and I do not see myself. What I lack is this me that you see. And what you lack is the you I see. (Valéry cited in S, 231–2)

Again, our question is whether we are supposed to understand this meeting of the gazes, where each holds the secret of the other, on the reflective model. Is it that the encounter with the other allows me to receive from them the part of me that I could not constitute myself?

What speaks against such an understanding is the last sentence of the quotation above: 'And no matter how far we advance in our mutual understanding, as much as we reflect, so much will we be different' (S, 232). In his notes for his lecture course on the literary use of language in 1953, Merleau-Ponty paraphrases Valéry in this way:

> a part of me is in the other. But if in this way there is not any juxtaposition anymore, there is also no identity since the other has of me what I do not have. Thus we are neither alone, nor two, but oneself in the other and the other in oneself.[19]

The 'mirroring' in the chiasm of the gazes, rather than allowing me to complete my own body-image by integrating what the other sees of me, opens the body more radically to the outside.

While the Hegelian model allows for a reflection-into-self of otherness, that is, for the identification of the mirror image as myself, there is no such moment of recuperation in Merleau-Ponty, no more than in Nancy. Indeed, taking mirroring literally means taking seriously the fact that the image in the mirror is reversed and cannot be superposed on to my body as it is in the world. The image is not merely me as if I were there, but is my other side (*mon envers*). So understood, mirroring does not allow the seer to catch her visibility and complete herself by integrating her external image into herself. Rather than leading to a more complete and unified sense of self, it opens a gap or split within herself. The key text here is a passage from Schilder's *Image and Appearance* in which he describes how the person who smokes his pipe in front of a mirror feels the contact of his fingers with the pipe in the mirror.[20] My body is able to feel its inside out there in the ghostlike fingers. The mirror 'carries the secrets of my own flesh away from it' so that my body schema lives out there at a distance from itself.[21] This is the true meaning of narcissism, again: 'to be seen by the outside, to exist within it, to emigrate into it, to be seduced, captivated, alienated by the phantom' (VI, 139). Here we can understand why, when describing the relation between seer and visible a couple of lines before this passage, Merleau-Ponty uses the strange image of two mirrors facing each other. Rather than a simple ricochet movement that would end where it begins, closing the circle, what this image implies is an open series of reflections where beginning and end indefinitely escape. In the discussion of the chiasm of the gazes, the detour through the outside is not at the service of an inside any more; rather the passage of the inside in the outside and vice versa, their circulation, must remain spaced out, *écarté* or open.

3. *Écart* as encroachment or separation

By emphasising the chirality of reversibility, I have tried to provide an interpretation of narcissism and mirroring that accounts for the irreducibility of the gap or divergence between the two sides of the chiasm. Such an interpretation allows for a rapprochement between Merleau-Ponty and Nancy. For both, as we have shown, there is always a divergence or *écart* between touching and touched, or seer and seen, so that no coincidence or superposition is possible. Here I agree with interpreters such as Lawrence Hass who emphasise the role of *écart* in reversibility and show that the Levinasian critique of Merleau-Ponty 'fails to do justice to the radical, differential account of *sens*'.[22] Our next question is, when juxtaposed with Nancy's notion of sense, just how radical is Merleau-Ponty's differential account? In other words, we want to ask whether the reversibility, which Merleau-Ponty thinks in terms of chiasm, mirroring and coupling (*Paarung*), succeeds in giving spacing, exteriority and alterity its due or whether it does not end up reinstating a massive unity at a higher level.

In order to specify our question, let us recall Derrida's claim in *On Touching* that in *succeeding* in interrupting itself, touch would still presuppose the propriety and integrity of a self-contained body or flesh. Jacob Rogozinski uses this claim to spell out the difference between the Merleau-Pontian chiasm and Derrida's.[23] While Husserl assumes that the chiasm has already happened and posits a constituting consciousness that is responsible for the success of the synthesis, Derrida assumes that the chiasm is impossible, that it always only interrupts itself. In refusing the Husserlian solution, Merleau-Ponty, like Derrida, emphasises interruption, non-coincidence, and hence a certain untouchable, that is, a blind spot that is the hinge or knot of the chiasm (VI, 254). Yet, always following Rogozinski, the difference would be that the originary difference or exteriority at the heart of the chiasm makes coincidence impossible for Derrida whereas for Merleau-Ponty it is the non-place where the chiasm occurs, that is, where interruption succeeds. It is this success that according to Derrida renders the intangible or untouchable – what Rogozinski will call the 'remainder' (*le restant*) – accessible, undermining its heterogeneity.[24]

This helps orient our question. What is at stake is what happens between the two strands of the chiasm. As with the glove, the chiasm that exists between vision and visible, touch and touchable, is not straightforwardly reversible. Between the two, there is a gap or blur that prevents coincidence, a zone of indeterminacy or undecidability that 'I' never occupy, since I am always either touching or touched, but that is experienced as a kind of blur, shift (*bougé*) or overhang (*porte-à-faux*) between the two (VI, 148, 256, 260). Yet Merleau-Ponty considers this gap to be always already spanned (*enjambé*).[25] It is worth quoting the passage in full:

> But this incessant escaping, this impotency . . . is not a failure. For if these experiences never exactly overlap, if they slip away at the very moment they are about to rejoin, if there is always a 'shift' [*du bougé*], a 'spread' [*un écart*], between them, this is precisely *because my two hands are part of the same body, because it moves itself in the world*, because I hear myself both from within and from without. I experience – and as often as I wish – the transition and the metamorphosis of the one experience into the other, and it is only as though the hinge between them, solid, unshakeable, remained irremediably hidden from me. But this hiatus between my right hand touched and my right hand touching, between my voice heard and my voice uttered, between one moment of my tactile life and the following one, *is not an ontological void, a non-being: it is spanned by the total being of my body, and by that of the world*; it is the zero of pressure between two solids that makes them adhere to one another. (VI, 148, my emphases)

What is clear in this passage is that the *écart*, the divergence that renders the coincidence or superposition of the two sides of the chiasm impossible, is not an 'ontological void' because the two sides are always already two sides *of* one body, one world, one flesh. Between the seer and the seen there is a 'between' that is more primordial than both. Of course, one could retort that the flesh is 'one' in the sense that it is an 'element' or a 'general thing', an '*incarnate* principle' (VI, 139, my emphasis) that exists only transspatially, as spread out differentially across individuals.[26] The flesh is not an all-pervasive substance, but the principle of doubling. To which we could retort that the role of this element, despite its differentiation, is to ensure the adherence of the two sides to one another, their communication or, dare we say, communion.[27] It is as if at the moment where he thinks the *écart* as principle – this would ultimately be what flesh is: the primordiality of *écart*, or of incarnate differance – Merleau-Ponty could not help but to posit the flesh as a grounding principle behind the *écart*.

For Nancy, the limit that exposes bodies to themselves and each other is exactly such an ontological void. The limit, the *extra* between the *partes*, is nothing but the sharing of the parts: their separation or spacing and their mutual exposition. The limit 'is therefore the interval, at once parted [*écarté*] and without depth or thickness, which spaces the plurality of singulars; it is their mutual exteriority and the circulation between them'.[28] If sense circulates between the singulars, it is not because something always already spans the two edges, or because one thing passes into the other, but rather because they remain separated and exposed on their edges. Merleau-Ponty's emphasis on promiscuity and encroachment (*empiétement*, *Überschreiten*) remains foreign to Nancy. For Merleau-Ponty, encroachment is the universal structure of world (VI, 234) and applies to all the chiasms or intertwinings (*entrelacs*, *Verflechtungen*) described in the fourth section of *The Visible and the Invisible* as well as in the working notes, for example that between perceiving and perceived, body and things, perception and movement, sensation and language. Speaking of what happens between singularities, Nancy also uses the image of the intertwining or the knot, but insists on the absolute separation of the different strands being knotted:

> This 'between' . . . does not lead from one to the other; it constitutes no connective tissue, no cement, no bridge. Perhaps it is not even fair to speak of a 'connection' [*lien*] about it: it is neither connected nor unconnected, but falls short of both. Or rather, it is what lies at the heart of the connection: the *inter*lacing [*l'*entre*croisement*] of strands whose extremities remain separate even at the very center of the knot [*nouage*]. The 'between' is the stretching out [*distension*] and the distance opened by the singular as such, as its spacing of sense. That which does not remain within the distance of the 'between' is only immanence collapsed in on itself and deprived of sense. (BSP, 5, trans. mod.)

For Nancy, even though everything is always in contact with everything, the 'law of touching' always remains 'separation' and 'heterogeneity' (BSP, 5). Without this separation that allows for the 'with' of being, there is nothing but the black hole of immanence: nothing comes to presence because nothing distinguishes itself from anything else. As Nancy writes in a different context: 'Nothing *gets through*, which is why it touches' (C, 11). This is why when speaking of the entanglement of singularities Nancy will prefer to speak of *mêlée* rather than mixture: a mixture is the confusion of two things in a new homogeneous thing, whereas a mêlée is the event of a knot, of an entanglement that is also a disentanglement.[29]

As I have tried to show, Merleau-Ponty does insist on the fact that there is no coincidence between one side of the chiasm and the other, and hence that each remains heterogeneous to the other. At the same time, the fact that one encroaches on the other also means that there is a minimal zone of transgression or overlapping (VI, 123, 218, 248), where the two are confused or blurred.[30] This is why Merleau-Ponty would never say, as Nancy did in the quotation above, that the zone of contact is 'without depth or thickness'. On the contrary, depth is for him the dimension of encroachment and latency. As we know, for the Cartesian ontology, there is no enigma of depth, depth being merely height or width seen from a different angle. This means that 'the encroachment or latency of things does not enter into their definition. . . . I know that at this very moment another man, situated elsewhere – or better, God, who is everywhere – could penetrate their "hiding place" and see them openly deployed' (PoP, 173, trans. mod.). Against this Cartesian ontology, Merleau-Ponty asserts depth as the relief and structure of the world. Depth is 'this invisible link that "holds together all things", and that holds us with them within it' (EC, 300).[31] Depth signals the co-belonging of the perceiving and the perceived, the fact that vision happens within the perceived world. As Saint Aubert puts it:

> Depth is rather a way of being of the world, which solicits in us a way of being to espouse its style. A way for the world to give itself to us and to call us in return to open ourselves to it, a way for it to wait for us and desire us, to invite us to abandon ourselves to its depth in order to perceive it. (EC, 392)

The dimension of depth then is also that of desire: vision – and sensing more generally – is desire because it responds to the visible world in which everything encroaches upon everything. Depth is not visible, but it is also not the opposite or the negation of visibility; rather it is the invisible dimension that makes possible what Merleau-Ponty calls the vertical world, the world that assembles incompossibles (VI, 228). Again, Merleau-Ponty calls this world vertical because it is not spread out horizontally in front of me. In this world, *visibilia* (including that *visibile* that is my body) encroach upon one another.

It would be wrong to think that because of the absence of encroachment this dimension of desire is absent from Nancy's work. The body, insofar as it is ex-posed, is always for Nancy also a body of pleasure, a pleasure that is not linked to desire-satisfaction but rather to *jouissance*, to that kind of pleasure which is always *a reaching* (C II, 17).[32] Indeed, in a recent book, Nancy explicitly links his notion of existence as being-outside-of-itself to the pulsion, push or drive of a passage to the limit that is called 'sex': existence is a sexistence.[33] Yet, even in *jouissance*, the limit is never breached. As Nancy writes, the body 'reaches its limit, passes to the limit, makes itself limitless' but even here there is no confusion and no blurring. As we mentioned in Chapter 2, the passage to the limit does not cross the limit; it approaches indefinitely, always remaining on the threshold. It 'does not cross [*ne franchit pas*] but brushes [*frôle*], touches, and in touching lets itself be touched by the outside' (C II, 98, trans. mod.).

For both Merleau-Ponty and Nancy, *écart* as divergence, spread or spacing is essential for sense. Yet, in the end, Merleau-Ponty and Nancy have different ways of conceiving this *écart*: as encroachment and promiscuity, or as unpassable limit. Without suggesting that this difference can or should be overcome, reading Merleau-Ponty and Nancy together allows each to raise a critical worry about the other's understanding of sense.

On behalf of Merleau-Ponty, one might worry that Nancy's insistence on the uncrossability and unpassability of limits operates a flattening out of the encroachments, overlaps and envelopments, of the depths and shadows that give the world and others their presence in the flesh. This worry is voiced by Christopher Watkin in his *Phenomenology or Deconstruction?*. Nancy would, according to Watkin, transpose Merleau-Ponty's characterisation of the intertwining of the visible and the invisible into 'a "flattened" understanding of the relation between world and sense in which sense is patent and exposed in the spacing of the world'.[34] Reading Nancy with Merleau-Ponty would allow us to bring to the fore the dimension of desire that is present in Nancy.

On behalf of Nancy, however, one might worry that Merleau-Ponty's insistence on encroachment and promiscuity against the Cartesian (and Sartrian) *partes extra partes* leads to the opposite excess: excess of proximity in a general regime of confusion where separation is lost. Saint Aubert, at the end of his long study *Être et chair*, raises this worry: 'Here, as elsewhere, the vertigo of the enveloping-enveloped, of a regime of *Ineinander* comes close to blur all differentiations. . . . [T]he "logic of promiscuity" . . . has the tendency to evacuate, in the end, the fundamental existential virtue of space that is *separation*' (EC, 380). Reading Merleau-Ponty with Nancy would allow us to recall the importance of the distinction or separation – the birth to presence – that the dehiscence of the flesh also evokes.

Rather than casting the differences between Merleau-Ponty and Nancy as substantive, I have proposed to cast them as differences in emphasis, each providing an important corrective to a *tendency* in the work of the other. As Carbone states:

> It would be as bad to think of a reversibility without *écart*, that is available to be *realized* as peaceful confusion of the related elements, as it would be to think of *écart* as a fracture, which, instead of opening together the different – and divergent – possibilities of those elements, would set their absolute distinction and therefore their reciprocal *extrusion*.[35]

Reading Nancy and Merleau-Ponty together can help us avoid both pitfalls, I have argued. Merleau-Ponty can help us emphasise the dimension of desire against a certain flattening out of relations we might be tempted to find in Nancy, whereas Nancy can help us work against the overabundance of proximity and promiscuity in Merleau-Ponty that risks erasing all separation in a general confusion.

4. Conclusion: Two ontologies of sense for our time

The main purpose of the preceding study was to stage a productive dialogue between Merleau-Ponty and Nancy, reading one through the lens of the other. Ultimately, the aim was not to argue that their positions are equivalent or even compatible, but rather to help focus our attention on what each – and what we as interpreters of one *or* the other – might be on the verge of forgetting. In the end, I hope to have proposed a more complete and more subtle interpretation of the two ontologies of sense proposed by Merleau-Ponty and Nancy. If for both sense is made 'within' or 'right at' Being itself through a process of diaresis or divergence, the way in which this diaresis or divergence is conceptualised in both ontologies also serves to evince the hypothesis behind this study, namely that there remains, in Merleau-Ponty's later work, a desire for some regime of indivision or confusion that is from the start foreign to Nancy's ontology.

The overarching goal of this study, however, was to respond to the new realist critique of post-Kantian philosophy, according to which all post-Kantian thinkers in the phenomenological tradition would remain unable to think an outside worthy of the name. They would all reduce being to sense and sense-making to a subjective process that would be the privilege of the human, however conceived. That this is not the case with either Merleau-Ponty or Nancy has become clear. Indeed, the very terms of the realist critique – subject/object, inside/outside, mind/body, thought/thing – are challenged within each philosophy. Rather than collapsing being into sense, or reinstating a strong divide between being and sense that it would be our duty to transgress, both Merleau-Ponty and Nancy displace and reassess the role of the limit in sense-making as the place of separation and exposure.

In the Introduction, I mentioned how the call for a new realist turn in Continental philosophy resonated because of the perceived inability of post-Kantian philosophy to confront the challenges of our time. Our time demands a decentring of the human and an attentiveness to the inhuman outside. What I have shown is that Merleau-Ponty and Nancy have something important to contribute if we are looking to develop a philosophy for our time. What I have not emphasised, however, is how what they are proposing is not just a new philosophy, or a new set of concepts, but a new way of being in the world. Emblematic here is the role they both reserve for art or artistic practice, an area I have not explored in any detail and which would deserve more attention. Indeed, rather than merely 'copying' the real or 'making up' imaginary things, both Merleau-Ponty and Nancy see art as an emblematic way of encountering the 'real' with all its mysteries. Art, or rather, artistic practice, is a way of being in the world that opens us to the inhuman within our anthropological worlds. Contrasting their engagement with artistic practice with the emphasis on science and on mathematics we find in speculative realism, especially in Badiou and Meillassoux, would be a natural extension of this study, one that could also lead to productive encounters with all the new speculative aesthetics that have developed on the heels of speculative realism and object-oriented ontology.

Another area worth exploring would be Merleau-Ponty's and Nancy's political philosophies. While they were faced with different historical situations – the aftermath of World War II for Merleau-Ponty and the collapse of the Soviet Union and the Eastern bloc for Nancy – the questions they came up against were not so radically different: the future of Marxism and communism, the critique of liberal capitalism, the question of violence and revolution. At the same time, as with art, Merleau-Ponty and Nancy are not content merely to reflect on the essence of the political and propose a new political philosophy. They are also actively involved in thinking the political events of their time as they unfold.

Here again, we are reminded that for both Merleau-Ponty and Nancy thinking is always embodied, situated and engaged. While this study has been focused on their respective conceptual understanding of the body, of things and of Being, the hope is that it leads to a transformation not only of our concepts and our ontologies, but also, and more importantly, of our way of being in the world, our praxis of sense. It is in light of this latter transformation that one will ultimately be able to judge the extent to which Merleau-Ponty and Nancy – one with the other or one against the other – offer us a philosophy for our time.

Notes

1. See Barbaras, *The Being of the Phenomenon*, 77.
2. Another way of describing the openness of Being is to say that it is polymorphous. On polymorphism, see EC, chapter 5.
3. Madison, *The Phenomenology of Merleau-Ponty*, 288.
4. The most thorough study to date of Merleau-Ponty's ontology as an ontology of sense, where sense is 'made' within Being itself, is David Morris's *Merleau-Ponty's Developmental Ontology*. Morris actually does the work of showing how sense is a movement in and of Being not only through a careful interpretation of Merleau-Ponty's texts but also by putting Merleau-Ponty in dialogue with scientific knowledge in the fields of immunology, genetics and embryology.
5. Gary Madison does argue that Merleau-Ponty anticipates Derrida's deconstruction of logocentrism and his concept of differance. Furthermore, rather than showing that Merleau-Ponty falls short of Derrida, he goes on to argue that Merleau-Ponty's philosophical humanism is a 'decided "advance" over Derrida's' and other poststructuralists' anti-humanism. See Madison, 'Did Merleau-Ponty Have a Theory of Perception?', in Busch and Gallagher (eds), *Merleau-Ponty, Hermeneutics, and Postmodernism*, 98. On the relation between Merleau-Ponty and Derrida, see also Jack Reynolds's excellent study, *Merleau-Ponty and Derrida: Intertwining Embodiment and Alterity*. Contrary to the essays found in M. C. Dillon's edited volume *Écart and Différance: Merleau-Ponty and Derrida on Seeing and Writing*, which all seem to assume that the thinkers are 'highly different, and even paradigmatically opposed' (Reynolds, *Merleau-Ponty and Derrida*, xiv), Reynolds seeks to bring the two into dialogue by undermining some of the assumptions behind the essays in Dillon, particularly the one according to which Derrida would be a semantic reductionist. See also Alloa, 'Merleau-Ponty and Derrida on *The Origin of Geometry*', *Philosophy Today* 58, no. 2 (2014): 219–39. Alloa traces the context of Merleau-Ponty's lecture course and Derrida's translation of Husserl's fragment and argues that Derrida's difference is already anticipated by Merleau-Ponty.
6. See Merleau-Ponty, *The Sensible World and the World of Expression: Course Notes from the Collège de France*, 13, 20–1. The *écart* is also a recurring theme of the 1954–5 lecture courses on institution and passivity. See Merleau-Ponty, *Institution and Passivity: Course Notes from the Collège de France (1954–1955)*, 7, 11, 131, 133, 136–7, 206.
7. See Morris, *Merleau-Ponty's Developmental Ontology*, chapter 1. See also Kaushik, *Merleau-Ponty between Philosophy and Symbolism: The Matrixed Ontology*, chapter 1, where Kaushik develops Merleau-Ponty's diacritical conception of *écart* by relating it to the Greek term διαίρεσις in Homer, Plato and Heraclitus.
8. In Nancy's corpus, we also find a series of words related to *écart*. Aside from the verb *écarter* (to displace, to disperse or to separate) and *s'écarter* (to sway from, to diverge, to move aside), and the noun *écartement* (displacement, disjunction, swerve, separation and sometimes also spacing), Nancy often uses terms such as *espacement* (spacing), *béance* (gaping), dehiscence, distinction or distension. Morris proposes to translate *écart* as disparity to emphasise the normative or comparative dimension of the notion. See Morris, *Merleau-Ponty's Developmental Ontology*, 38.
9. Barbaras thinks they aren't; see 'The Ambiguity of the Flesh', *Chiasmi International* 4 (2002): 19–26. Barbaras argues that 'The ontological transfer from my flesh (as body) to the world (as Flesh) would require an ontological shift much more radical than that which Merleau-Ponty makes in *The Visible and the Invisible*. It would require a characterization of inert matter through life, as it is grasped in our life; in short, it would require an ontology of life' (23). Barbaras develops this thought further in 'The Three Senses of Flesh', in Alloa, Chouraqui and Kaushik (eds), *Merleau-Ponty and Contemporary Philosophy*, 17–34. Lawrence Hass provides a helpful summary of the

multiple meanings of the word 'flesh' in Merleau-Ponty's later works in the Appendix to his *Merleau-Ponty's Philosophy*, 121–3.
10. To clarify this suspension of the subjective dimension in Merleau-Ponty's description of the being-perceived, it would be necessary to retrace his path through the Nature lectures. On the importance of these lectures for Merleau-Ponty's ontology, see again Barbaras, 'Merleau-Ponty and Nature', *Research in Phenomenology* 31, no. 1 (2001): 22–38. Len Lawlor, for his part, argues that Merleau-Ponty's ontology 'does not correct phenomenology's subjectivistic failures'. This would be because, unlike Deleuze, Merleau-Ponty starts with Being, which makes negation primary (Being is not-beings), and negation is always a 'subjective, even humanistic, practice'. See Lawlor, *Thinking through French Philosophy: The Being of the Question*, 96–7. For an alternative reading, see Toadvine, *Merleau-Ponty's Philosophy of Nature*, chapter 5.
11. The intertwining between Being and appearing/meaning/sense, between ontology and phenomenology, is also the conclusion of Derrida's long introduction to Husserl's 'Origin of Geometry', a fragment on which Merleau-Ponty lectured in 1959–60. The impossibility of deciding which is first, Being or appearing, leads Derrida to conclude that what is first and what remains irreducible is the opening between the two, the necessary passage of each into its other. See Derrida, *Husserl's 'Origin'*, 149–53.
12. In Nancy, *être-à* is most often translated as being-to or being-towards. See for example the section 'The End of the World' in SW.
13. See Hegel, *The Phenomenology of Spirit*, §18.
14. My explanation of chiral reversibility is strongly indebted to two excellent articles by David Morris: 'The Chirality of Being: Exploring a Merleau-Pontyan Ontology of Sense', *Chiasmi International* 12 (2010): 165–82 and 'The Enigma of Reversibility and the Genesis of Sense in Merleau-Ponty', *Continental Philosophy Review* 43 (2010): 141–65.
15. That is, in the space in which they are found. If we move to a higher dimensional space then we can superpose the two gloves but they also lose their chiral sense as incongruent counterparts. For example, paper cut-outs of our two hands can be superposed by turning one over, but three-dimensional sculpted hands can't.
16. For an explanation of this point, see Morris, 'The Chirality of Being', 166–7 and 'The Enigma of Reversibility', 145–7. See also VI, 263 for the passage on which Morris's interpretation is based. More generally, see also Hass, *Merleau-Ponty's Philosophy*, chapter 5. In the end, Hass will argue for the abandonment of the 'hegemony of reversibility' in our understanding of the flesh.
17. While we can agree with Jennifer McWeeny that all flesh is 'sentient-sensible in nature' so that there is no ontological difference between my body and other bodies, not all flesh is self-sensing. For McWeeny, asymmetry or non-coincidence presupposes symmetrical capacities for sentience (hence her argument in favour of a panpsychic reading of Merleau-Ponty's ontology). As she writes: 'the thing needs me in order to feel itself just as I need the thing to feel myself, the thing's sensibility calls forth my sentience and my body's sensibility solicits the sentience and sensitivity of the thing' (McWeeny, 'The Panpsychism Question in Merleau-Ponty's Ontology', in Alloa, Chouraqui and Kaushik (eds), *Merleau-Ponty and Contemporary Philosophy*, 128). But while she insists on indivision and on the thing's ability to *feel itself*, she does not underline the fact that Merleau-Ponty explicitly says that 'all the rest' 'feels itself (*se sent*) in me' (VI, 255, my emphasis) and not in itself like I do.
18. On the relation between the mirror and narcissism in Merleau-Ponty as well as the influence of Wallon and Lacan, see EC, chapter 3, §1. See also CPP, 87, where Merleau-Ponty discusses Lacan's interpretation of the myth of Narcissus. On the role of Lacan in Merleau-Ponty's Sorbonne lectures, see Welsh, *The Child as Natural Phenomenologist*, especially chapter 3, 'Syncretic Sociability and the Birth of the Self'.
19. Merleau-Ponty, *Les Recherches sur l'usage littéraire du langage*, 103. See also SC, 171.
20. The passage is found in Schilder, *The Image and Appearance of the Human Body*, 223–4

and is mentioned in 'Eye and Mind', PoP, 168. For a discussion of the role of Schilder and of this passage in particular in Merleau-Ponty, see EC, chapter 3, §3, 183–93.
21. Working note from 'Eye and Mind', cited in EC, 192.
22. See Hass, 'Sense and Alterity: Rereading Merleau-Ponty's Reversibility Thesis', in Olkowski and Morley (eds), *Merleau-Ponty, Interiority and Exteriority, Psychic Life and the World*, 102. See also Johnson and Smith (eds), *Ontology and Alterity in Merleau-Ponty*, which takes up the question of whether the *écart* is enough to account for a true experience of transcendence and otherness. I am obviously more sympathetic to Dillon's reading than to Lefort but I take Madison's reading – for whom flesh is *différance*: 'the trace of the other, the inscription of the other, in the subject's own selfhood' (*Ontology and Alterity*, 31) – as going too far.
23. See Rogozinski, 'The Chiasm and the Remainder (How Does Touching Touch Itself?)', in Raffoul and Nelson (eds), *Rethinking Facticity*, 229–52, esp. 229–38.
24. According to Rogozinski, Merleau-Ponty would think this 'heterogeneous element', this 'residue of non-flesh' that is 'both foreign to the flesh and yet within the flesh', only as temporal lag. See Rogozinski, 'The Chiasm', 238.
25. On coincidence and non-coincidence in *The Visible and the Invisible*, see OT, §9, Tangent III, esp. 211–15.
26. On trans-spatiality, see Barbaras, 'Merleau-Ponty and Nature', 35. Aside from the unpublished note mentioned by Barbaras, Merleau-Ponty also mentions the idea of trans-spatiality in his Nature lectures, for example in his discussions of Whitehead and von Uexküll (N, 113–22, 173–8).
27. In 'La chair comme diacritique incarnée', Emmanuel Alloa distances himself from Saint Aubert's emphasis on the psychoanalytic provenance of Merleau-Ponty's notion of flesh because it would overemphasise inherence and indivision at the expense of the diacritical process of dehiscence. See Alloa, 'La chair comme diacritique incarnée', *Chiasmi International* 11 (2009): 249–62. The question is whether differential processes compromise the 'unitary fabric' of sense or not. Renaud Barbaras shows how Merleau-Ponty seeks to maintain both the phenomenological requirement of duality and the ontological requirement of unity. He cites an unpublished note (which he does not date), where Merleau-Ponty states: 'I am looking for an ontological milieu, a field [*champ*] that unites both object and consciousness. And this is necessary if one wants to leave idealistic philosophy behind. But this field, brute being ... should not be conceived as a fabric [*étoffe*] in which object and consciousness are cut.' See Barbaras, 'Merleau-Ponty aux limites de la phénoménologie', *Chiasmi International* 1 (1999): 199–210.
28. Nancy, 'Rives, bords, limites (de la singularité)/Banks, Edges, Limits (of Singularity)', *Angelaki: Journal of the Theoretical Humanities* 9, no. 2 (2004): 46.
29. Already in the *Phenomenology*, *être-au-monde* meant *être mélangé aux choses*, 'intermingled with things' (PP, 466), and Merleau-Ponty could write: 'we are mixed up with the world [*mêlés au monde*] and with others in an inextricable confusion' (PP, 481). In *The Visible and the Invisible*, Merleau-Ponty also uses the word 'confusion' as synonymous with encroachment (see VI, 47) and also the word *mélange* ('compound': VI, 102; 'blending': VI, 35).
30. In 'The Philosopher and His Shadow', speaking of the 'ontological rehabilitation of the sensible' effected by Husserl's description of the touching-touched, Merleau-Ponty writes that 'the distinction between subject and object is blurred in my body' as well as 'in the things' (S, 167).
31. Saint Aubert is quoting a note by Merleau-Ponty from *La nature et le monde du silence*, dating probably from autumn 1957.
32. On *jouissance*, see also Nancy and Van Reeth, *Coming*.
33. See Nancy, *Sexistence*, 125, n. 20. It is worth pointing out that Nancy includes as an epigraph to the main section of the book a long passage from the *Phenomenology of Perception* about sexuality.

34. Watkin, *Phenomenology or Deconstruction?*, 147. See also 171, 206.
35. Carbone, 'Flesh: Towards the History of a Misunderstanding', *Chiasmi International* 4 (2002): 57.

Bibliography

Abram, David, *Becoming Animal: An Earthly Cosmology* (New York: Vintage Books, 2011).
——, *The Spell of the Sensuous: Perception and Language in the More-Than-Human World* (New York: Vintage Books, 1997).
Alaimo, Stacy, *Bodily Natures: Science, Environment, and the Material Self* (Bloomington and Indianapolis: Indiana University Press, 2010).
Alloa, Emmanuel, 'La chair comme diacritique incarnée', *Chiasmi International* 11 (2009): 249–62.
——, 'Merleau-Ponty and Derrida on *The Origin of Geometry*', *Philosophy Today* 58, no. 2 (2014): 219–39.
——, Frank Chouraqui and Rajiv Kaushik (eds), *Merleau-Ponty and Contemporary Philosophy* (Albany: SUNY Press, 2020).
Alquié, Ferdinand, *Descartes, l'homme et l'œuvre* (Paris: Hatier-Boivin, 1956).
——, 'Notes sur l'interprétation de Descartes par l'ordre des raisons', *Revue de Métaphysique et de Morale* 61, nos 3/4 (1956): 403–18.
Bannan, John F., *The Philosophy of Merleau-Ponty* (New York: Harcourt, Brace & World, 1967).
Barbaras, Renaud, 'The Ambiguity of the Flesh', *Chiasmi International* 4 (2002): 19–26.
——, *The Being of the Phenomenon: Merleau-Ponty's Ontology*, trans. Ted Toadvine and Leonard Lawlor (Bloomington and Indianapolis: Indiana University Press, 2004).
——, 'Merleau-Ponty aux limites de la phénoménologie', *Chiasmi International* 1 (1999): 199–210.
——, 'Merleau-Ponty and Nature', *Research in Phenomenology* 31, no. 1 (2001): 22–38.
Bennett, Jane, *Vibrant Matter: A Political Ecology of Things* (Durham, NC: Duke University Press, 2010).
Bernet, Rudolf, *La vérité du sujet: Recherches sur l'interprétation de Husserl dans la phénoménologie* (Paris: PUF, 1994).
Bourgeois, Patrick, 'Merleau-Ponty and Heidegger: The Intentionality of Transcendence, the Being of Intentionality', *Journal of the British Society for Phenomenology* 25, no. 1 (1994): 27–33.
Braver, Lee, 'A Brief History of Continental Realism', *Continental Philosophy Review* 45, no. 2 (2012): 261–89.
——, *A Thing of This World: A History of Continental Anti-Realism* (Evanston, IL: Northwestern University Press, 2007).
Bryant, Levi, Nick Srnicek and Graham Harman (eds), *The Speculative Turn: Continental Realism and Materialism* (Melbourne: re.press, 2011).

Calvino, Italo, *Cosmicomics*, trans. William Weaver (San Diego: Harcourt, Brace & World, 1976).
Canguilhem, Georges, *La formation du concept de réflexe aux XVIIe et XVIIIe siècles* (Paris: PUF, 1955).
———, *The Knowledge of Life*, trans. Stefanos Geroulanos and Daniela Ginsburg (New York: Fordham University Press, 2008).
———, *The Normal and the Pathological*, trans. Carolyn R. Fawcett (New York: Zone Books, 1991).
Carbone, Mauro, 'Flesh: Towards the History of a Misunderstanding', *Chiasmi International* 4 (2002): 49–62.
Cariolato, Alfonso, *Le geste de Dieu. Sur un lieu de l'Éthique de Spinoza* (Chatou: Transparence, 2011).
Carman, Taylor, *Maurice Merleau-Ponty* (Abingdon: Routledge, 2008).
Carman, Taylor and Mark B. N. Hansen (eds), *The Cambridge Companion to Merleau-Ponty* (Cambridge: Cambridge University Press, 2005).
Cohen, Jeffrey, *Stone: An Ecology of the Inhuman* (Minneapolis: University of Minnesota Press, 2015).
Dastur, Françoise, 'La lecture merleau-pontienne de Heidegger dans les notes du *Visible et l'invisible* et les cours du Collège de France (1957–1958)', *Chiasmi International* 2 (2000): 373–87.
Davidson, David, *Inquiries into Truth and Interpretation* (Oxford: Clarendon Press, 2001).
Derrida, Jacques, 'Declarations of Independence', *New Political Science* 7, no. 1 (1986): 7–15.
———, *Edmund Husserl's 'Origin of Geometry': An Introduction*, trans. John P. Leavey, Jr (Lincoln: University of Nebraska Press, 1989).
———, 'Force of Law', in Drucilla Cornell, Michel Rosenfeld and David Gray Carlson (eds), *Deconstruction and the Possibility of Justice* (New York: Routledge, 1993), 3–67.
———, *For Strasbourg: Conversations of Friendship and Philosophy*, trans. Pascale-Anne Brault and Michael Naas (New York: Fordham University Press, 2014).
———, *Given Time, I. Counterfeit Money*, trans. Peggy Kamuf (Chicago: University of Chicago Press, 1994).
———, 'Le toucher: Touch/To Touch Him', trans. Peggy Kamuf, *Paragraph* 16, no. 2 (1993): 122–57.
———, *Limited Inc*, trans. Samuel Weber (Evanston, IL: Northwestern University Press, 1988).
———, *Margins*, trans. Alan Bass (Chicago: University of Chicago Press, 1982).
———, *On Touching – Jean-Luc Nancy*, trans. Christine Irizarry (Stanford: Stanford University Press, 2005).
———, *The Politics of Friendship*, trans. George Collins (London: Verso, 2005).
———, *Writing and Difference*, trans. Alan Bass (London: Routledge, 2001).
Descartes, René, *The Philosophical Writings of Descartes*, trans. John Cottingham, Robert Stoothoff and Dugald Murdoch (Cambridge: Cambridge University Press, 1984).
Dillon, M. C., *Merleau-Ponty's Ontology*, 2nd edn (Bloomington and Indianapolis: Indiana University Press, 1988).
——— (ed.), *Écart and Différance: Merleau-Ponty and Derrida on Seeing and Writing* (Atlantic Highlands, NJ: Humanities Press, 1997).
Evans, Fred and Leonard Lawlor (eds), *Chiasms: Merleau-Ponty's Notion of Flesh* (Albany: SUNY Press, 2000).
Fóti, Véronique, *Vision's Invisibles: Philosophical Explorations* (Albany: SUNY Press, 2003).
Freud, Sigmund, *The Standard Edition of the Complete Psychological Works*, vol. 23, trans. James Strachey (London: Hogarth Press, 1961).
Gueroult, Martial, *Descartes' Philosophy Interpreted According to the Order of Reasons, Vol. 1: The Soul and God*, trans. Roger Ariew (Minneapolis: University of Minnesota Press, 1984).

——, *Descartes' Philosophy Interpreted According to the Order of Reasons, Vol. 2: The Soul and the Body*, trans. Roger Ariew (Minneapolis: University of Minnesota Press, 1985).
Haar, Michel, 'Proximity and Distance with Regard to Heidegger in the Late Merleau-Ponty', in Robert Vallier, Wayne Froman and Bernard Flynn (eds), *Merleau-Ponty and the Possibilities of Philosophy: Transforming the Tradition* (Albany: SUNY Press, 2009), 165–82.
Harman, Graham, 'I Am Also of the Opinion that Materialism Must Be Destroyed', *Environment and Planning D: Society and Space* 28, no. 5 (2010): 772–90.
——, 'On Interface: Nancy's Weights and Masses', in Peter Gratton and Marie-Eve Morin (eds), *Jean-Luc Nancy and Plural Thinking* (Albany: SUNY Press, 2012), 95–107.
——, 'Road to Objects', *Continent* 1, no. 3 (2011): 171–9.
Hass, Lawrence, *Merleau-Ponty's Philosophy* (Bloomington and Indianapolis: Indiana University Press, 2008).
——, 'Sense and Alterity: Rereading Merleau-Ponty's Reversibility Thesis', in Dorothea Olkowski and James Morley (eds), *Merleau-Ponty, Interiority and Exteriority, Psychic Life and the World* (Albany: SUNY Press, 1999), 91–105.
Hegel, G. W. F., *The Phenomenology of Spirit*, trans. A. V. Miller (Oxford: Oxford University Press, 1979).
Heidegger, Martin, *Basic Problems of Phenomenology*, trans. A. Hofstadter, rev. edn (Bloomington: Indiana University Press, 1988).
——, *Being and Time*, trans. John Macquarrie and Edward Robinson (New York: Harper & Row, 1962).
——, *Contributions to Philosophy (Of the Event)*, trans. R. Rojcewicz and D. Vallega-Neu (Bloomington: Indiana University Press, 2012).
——, *The End of Philosophy*, ed. Joan Stambaugh (Chicago: University of Chicago Press, 2003).
——, *Fundamental Concepts of Metaphysics: World, Finitude, Solitude*, trans. William McNeill and Nicholas Walker (Bloomington and Indianapolis: Indiana University Press, 1995).
——, *Identity and Difference*, trans. Joan Stambaugh (Chicago: University of Chicago Press, 2002).
——, *Metaphysical Foundations of Logic*, trans. Michael Heim (Bloomington and Indianapolis: Indiana University Press, 1984).
——, *Off the Beaten Track*, trans. Julian Young and Kenneth Haynes (Cambridge: Cambridge University Press, 2002).
——, *Pathmarks*, trans. William McNeil (Cambridge: Cambridge University Press, 1998).
——, *The Question Concerning Technology and Other Essays*, trans. William Lovitt (New York: HarperCollins, 1977).
Husserl, Edmund, *Cartesian Meditations: An Introduction to Phenomenology*, trans. Dorion Cairns (Dordrecht: Kluwer, 1999).
——, *Ideas Pertaining to a Pure Phenomenology and to a Phenomenological Philosophy – Second Book: Studies in the Phenomenology of Constitution*, trans. Richard Rojcewicz and André Schuwer (Dordrecht: Kluwer, 1989).
Ingold, Tim, *Being Alive: Essays on Movement, Knowledge and Description* (London: Routledge, 2011).
James, Ian, *The Fragmentary Demand: An Introduction to the Philosophy of Jean-Luc Nancy* (Stanford: Stanford University Press, 2005).
——, 'Lucidity and Tact', in Ian James and Emma Wilson (eds), *Lucidity: Essays in Honour of Alison Finch* (Cambridge: Legenda, 2016), 9–19.
——, *The Technique of Thought: Nancy, Laruelle, Malabou, and Stiegler after Naturalism* (Minneapolis: University of Minnesota Press, 2019).
——, 'The Touch of Things: A Review of *The Universe of Things: On Speculative Realism* by Steven Shaviro', *Cultural Critique* 97 (2017): 203–27.

James, Simon P., 'Merleau-Ponty, Metaphysical Realism and the Natural World', *International Journal of Philosophical Studies* 15, no. 4 (2007): 501–19.

Johnson, Galen A., 'Merleau-Ponty, Ponge, and Valéry on Speaking Things: Phenomenology and Poetry', in Ranjan Ghosh (ed.), *Philosophy and Poetry: Continental Perspectives* (New York: Columbia University Press, 2019), 175–94.

—— and Michael B. Smith (eds), *Ontology and Alterity in Merleau-Ponty* (Evanston, IL: Northwestern University Press, 1990).

Kant, Immanuel, *Critique of Pure Reason*, trans. P. Guyer and A. W. Wood (Cambridge: Cambridge University Press, 1998).

Kaushik, Rajiv, *Merleau-Ponty between Philosophy and Symbolism: The Matrixed Ontology* (Albany: SUNY Press, 2019).

Kwant, Remy C., *The Phenomenological Philosophy of Merleau-Ponty* (Pittsburgh: Duquesne University Press, 1963).

Lacoue-Labarthe, Philippe and Jean-Luc Nancy, *The Title of the Letter: A Reading of Lacan*, trans. François Raffoul and David Pettigrew (Albany: SUNY Press, 1992).

Landes, Donald, *Merleau-Ponty and the Paradoxes of Expression* (London: Bloomsbury, 2013).

——, 'Le sujet de la sensation et le sujet résonant. Communion et renvoi chez Merleau-Ponty et Nancy', *Chiasmi International* 19 (2017): 143–62.

Laporte, Jean, *Le rationalisme de Descartes* (Paris: PUF, 1945).

Latour, Bruno, 'Biography of an Inquiry: On a Book about Modes of Existence', *Social Studies of Science* 43, no. 2 (2013): 287–301.

Lawlor, Leonard, *Husserl and Derrida: The Basic Problem of Phenomenology* (Bloomington and Indianapolis: Indiana University Press, 2002).

——, *Thinking through French Philosophy: The Being of the Question* (Bloomington and Indianapolis: Indiana University Press, 2003).

McDowell, John, *Mind and World* (Cambridge, MA: Harvard University Press, 1996).

Madison, Gary, 'Did Merleau-Ponty Have a Theory of Perception?', in Thomas W. Busch and Shaun Gallagher (eds), *Merleau-Ponty, Hermeneutics, and Postmodernism* (Albany: SUNY Press, 1992), 83–106.

——, *The Phenomenology of Merleau-Ponty: A Search for the Limits of Consciousness* (Athens: Ohio University Press, 1981).

Meillassoux, Quentin, *After Finitude: An Essay on the Necessity of Contingency*, trans. Ray Brassier (London: Continuum, 2008).

——, 'Time without Becoming', lecture given at Middlesex University, London, 8 May 2008.

Merleau-Ponty, Maurice, *Child Psychology and Pedagogy: The Sorbonne Lectures 1949–1952*, trans. Talia Welsh (Evanston, IL: Northwestern University Press, 2010).

——, *The Incarnate Subject: Malebranche, Biran, and Bergson on the Union of Body and Soul*, trans. Paul B. Milan (Amherst, NY: Humanity Books, 2002).

——, *Institution and Passivity: Course Notes from the Collège de France (1954–1955)*, trans. Leonard Lawlor and Heath Massey (Evanston, IL: Northwestern University Press, 2010).

——, 'Man and Object', *Chiasmi International* 20 (2019): 93–5.

——, *Nature: Course Notes from the Collège de France*, trans. Robert Vallier (Evanston, IL: Northwestern University Press, 2003).

——, *Notes de cours 1959–1961* (Paris: Gallimard, 1996).

——, *Phenomenology of Perception*, trans. Donald Landes (New York: Routledge, 2012).

——, *The Primacy of Perception*, trans. J. M. Edie (Evanston, IL: Northwestern University Press, 1964).

——, *The Prose of the World*, trans. John O'Neill (Evanston, IL: Northwestern University Press, 1973).

——, *Les Recherches sur l'usage littéraire du langage. Cours au Collège de France, Notes, 1953*, ed. Emmanuel de Saint Aubert and Benedetta Zaccarello (Geneva: Métispresses, 2013).

——, *The Sensible World and the World of Expression: Course Notes from the Collège de France*, trans. Bryan Smyth (Evanston, IL: Northwestern University Press, 2020).
——, *Signs*, trans. R. McCleary (Evanston, IL: Northwestern University Press, 1964).
——, *The Structure of Behavior*, trans. Alden L. Fischer (Boston: Beacon Press, 1967).
——, *Themes from the Lectures at the Collège de France, 1952–1960*, trans. John O'Neill (Evanston, IL: Northwestern University Press, 1970).
——, *The Visible and the Invisible*, trans. Alphonso Lingis (Evanston, IL: Northwestern University Press, 1968).
——, *The World of Perception*, trans. Oliver Davis (London: Routledge, 2008).
Mickey, Sam, 'Touching without Touching: Objects of Post-Deconstructive Realism and Object-Oriented Ontology', *Open Philosophy* 1 (2018): 290–8.
Moran, Dermot, *Introduction to Phenomenology* (London: Routledge, 2000).
Morin, Marie-Eve, 'Worlds Apart: Conversations between Jacques Derrida and Jean-Luc Nancy', *Derrida Today* 9, no. 2 (2016): 157–76.
Morris, David, 'The Chirality of Being: Exploring a Merleau-Pontyan Ontology of Sense', *Chiasmi International* 12 (2010): 165–82.
——, 'The Enigma of Reversibility and the Genesis of Sense in Merleau-Ponty', *Continental Philosophy Review* 43 (2010): 141–65.
——, *Merleau-Ponty's Developmental Ontology* (Evanston, IL: Northwestern University Press, 2018).
Nancy, Jean-Luc, *Adoration: The Deconstruction of Christianity II*, trans. John McKeane (New York: Fordham University Press, 2013).
——, *Being Singular Plural*, trans. Robert D. Richardson and Anne E. O'Byrne (Stanford: Stanford University Press, 2000).
——, 'The Being-With of Being-There', trans. Marie-Eve Morin, *Continental Philosophy Review* 41, no. 1 (2008): 1–15.
——, *The Birth to Presence*, trans. Brian Holmes et al. (Stanford: Stanford University Press, 1993).
——, 'Le corps: dehors ou dedans. Cinquante-huit indices sur le corps', *Siniy divan* 9 (2006): 106–21.
——, *Corpus*, trans. Richard A. Rand (New York: Fordham University Press, 2008).
——, *Corpus II: Writings on Sexuality*, trans. Anne E. O'Byrne (New York: Fordham University Press, 2013).
——, *The Creation of the World or Globalization*, trans. François Raffoul and David Pettigrew (Albany: SUNY Press, 2007).
——, *Dis-Enclosure: The Deconstruction of Christianity I*, trans. Bettina Bergo, Gabriel Malenfant and Michael B. Smith (New York: Fordham University Press, 2008).
——, *Ego Sum: Corpus, Anima, Fabula*, trans. Marie-Eve Morin (New York: Fordham University Press, 2016).
——, 'Everything Finds Itself', *Oxford Literary Review* 39, no. 1 (2017): 1–6.
——, *The Experience of Freedom*, trans. Bridget McDonald (Stanford: Stanford University Press, 1993).
——, 'Extraordinary Sense', *The Senses and Society* 8, no. 1 (2013): 10–13.
——, 'Fantastic Phenomenon', *Research in Phenomenology* 41 (2011): 228–37.
——, *A Finite Thinking*, ed. Simon Sparks (Stanford: Stanford University Press, 2003).
——, *The Gravity of Thought*, trans. François Raffoul and Gregory Recco (New York: Humanities Press, 1997).
——, *L'impératif catégorique* (Paris: Flammarion, 1983).
——, *The Inoperative Community*, ed. Peter Connor (Minneapolis: University of Minnesota Press, 1991).
——, *Marquage manquant (et autres dires de la peau). Entretien avec Nicolas Dutent* (Paris: Les Venterniers, 2017).
——, 'Merleau-Ponty: An Attempt at a Response', in Emmanuel Alloa, Frank Chouraqui

and Rajiv Kaushik (eds), *Merleau-Ponty and Contemporary Philosophy* (Albany: SUNY Press, 2020), 297–302.

———, *The Muses*, trans. Peggy Kamuf (Stanford: Stanford University Press, 1996).

———, *Noli me tangere: On the Raising of the Body*, trans. Sarah Clift, Pascale-Anne Brault and Michael Naas (New York: Fordham University Press, 2008).

———, 'Of Being-in-Common', in the Miami Theory Collective (ed.), *Community at Loose Ends* (Minneapolis: University of Minnesota Press, 1991), 1–12.

———, 'Of Struction', trans. Travis Holloway and Flor Méchain, *Parrhesia* 17 (2013): 1–10.

———, 'On Derrida: A Conversation with Sergio Benvenuto', trans. Marcel Lieberman, *Journal of European Psychoanalysis* 19, no. 2 (2004): <www.psychomedia.it/jep/number 19/benvenuto.htm> (last accessed 14 October 2021).

———, *On Listening*, trans. Charlotte Mandell (New York: Fordham University Press, 2007).

———, *La peau fragile du monde* (Paris: Galilée, 2020).

———, *Une pensée finie* (Paris: Galilée, 1990).

———, *Le poids d'une pensée, l'approche* (Strasbourg: La Phocide, 2008).

———, 'Rethinking Corpus', in Richard Kearney and Brian Treanor (eds), *Carnal Hermeneutics* (New York: Fordham University Press, 2015), 77–91.

———, 'Rives, bords, limites (de la singularité)/Banks, Edges, Limits (of Singularity)', *Angelaki: Journal of the Theoretical Humanities* 9, no. 2 (2004): 41–53.

———, *The Sense of the World*, trans. Jeffrey S. Librett (Minneapolis: University of Minnesota Press, 1997).

———, *Sexistence*, trans. Steven Miller (New York: Fordham University Press, 2021).

——— and Adèle Van Reeth, *Coming*, trans. Charlotte Mandell (New York: Fordham University Press, 2016).

Norris, Christopher, 'Speculative Realism: Interim Report with Just a Few Caveats', *Speculations: A Journal of Speculative Realism* IV (2013): 38–47.

Peeters, Benoît, *Derrida: A Biography*, trans. Andrew Brown (Cambridge: Polity, 2013).

Perpich, Diane, '*Corpus Meum*: Disintegrating Bodies and the Ideal of Integrity', *Hypatia* 20, no. 3 (2005): 75–91.

Putnam, Hilary, *Reason, Truth and History* (Cambridge: Cambridge University Press, 1981).

Raffoul, François, 'Abandonment and the Categorical Imperative of Being', in B. C. Hutchens (ed.), *Jean-Luc Nancy: Justice, Legality and World* (London: Continuum, 2012), 65–81.

Reynolds, Jack, *Merleau-Ponty and Derrida: Intertwining Embodiment and Alterity* (Athens: Ohio University Press, 2004).

Richir, Marc, 'Le sens de la phénoménologie dans *Le visible et l'invisible*', *Esprit* 66, no. 6 (1982): 124–45.

Ricoeur, Paul, *Husserl: An Analysis of His Phenomenology* (Evanston, IL: Northwestern University Press, 1967).

Roffe, Jon, 'The Future of an Illusion', *Speculations: A Journal of Speculative Realism* IV (2013): 48–52.

Rogozinski, Jacob, 'The Chiasm and the Remainder (How Does Touching Touch Itself?)', in François Raffoul and Eric Sean Nelson (eds), *Rethinking Facticity* (Albany: SUNY Press, 2008), 229–52.

Roney, Patrick, 'Evil and the Experience of Freedom: Nancy on Schelling and Heidegger', *Research in Phenomenology* 9, no. 3 (2009): 374–400.

Rorty, Richard, *Objectivity, Relativism, and Truth: Philosophical Papers Volume 1* (Cambridge: Cambridge University Press, 1991).

———, *Truth and Progress: Philosophical Papers Volume 3* (Cambridge: Cambridge University Press, 1998).

Rugo, Daniele, *Jean-Luc Nancy and the Thinking of Otherness: Philosophy and Powers of Existence* (London: Bloomsbury, 2013).
Saint Aubert, Emmanuel de, 'Au croisement du réel et de l'imaginaire: les « ultra-choses » chez Merleau-Ponty', in Annabelle Dufourcq (ed.), *Est-ce réel? Phénoménologies de l'imaginaire* (Leiden: Brill, 2016), 240–58.
——, *Du lien des êtres aux éléments de l'être. Merleau-Ponty au tournant des années 1945–1951* (Paris: Vrin, 2004).
——, *Être et chair 1. Du corps au désir. L'habilitation ontologique de la chair* (Paris: Vrin, 2013).
——, *Le scénario cartésien. Recherches sur la formation et la cohérence de l'intention philosophique de Merleau-Ponty* (Paris: Vrin, 2005).
——, *Vers une ontologie indirecte. Sources et enjeux critiques de l'appel à l'ontologie chez Merleau-Ponty* (Paris: Vrin, 2006).
Sartre, Jean-Paul, *Being and Nothingness*, trans. Hazel A. Barnes (New York: Washington Square Press, 1993).
——, 'Man and Things', in *Critical Essays (Situations I)*, trans. Chris Turner (Chicago: University of Chicago Press, 2010), 383–465.
——, 'Merleau-Ponty Vivant', in J. Stewart (ed.), *The Debate between Sartre and Merleau-Ponty* (Evanston, IL: Northwestern University Press, 1998), 565–625.
——, *Nausea*, trans. Lloyd Alexander (New York: New Directions, 1969).
Schilder, Paul, *The Image and Appearance of the Human Body: Studies in the Constructive Energies of the Psyche* (London: Routledge, 1999).
Schües, Christina, 'Heidegger and Merleau-Ponty: Being-in-the-World with Others?', in Christopher Macann (ed.), *Martin Heidegger: Critical Assessments, Volume II: History of Philosophy* (London: Routledge, 1992), 345–72.
Shaviro, Steven, *The Universe of Things: On Speculative Realism* (Minneapolis: University of Minnesota Press, 2014).
——, *Without Criteria: Kant, Whitehead, Deleuze, and Aesthetics* (Cambridge, MA: MIT Press, 2012).
Sparrow, Tom, *The End of Phenomenology: Metaphysics and the New Realism* (Edinburgh: Edinburgh University Press, 2014).
Taminiaux, Jacques, 'Was Merleau-Ponty on the Way from Husserl to Heidegger?', *Chiasmi International* 11 (2009): 21–30.
Thomas-Fogiel, Isabelle, 'Merleau-Ponty: De la perspective au chiasme, la rigueur épistémique d'une analogie', *Chiasmi International* 13 (2011): 381–406.
Toadvine, Ted, 'Chiasm and Chiaroscuro', *Chiasmi International* 3 (2001): 225–40.
——, 'Limits of the Flesh: The Role of Reflection in David Abram's Ecophenomenology', *Environmental Ethics* 27, no. 2 (2005): 155–70.
——, *Merleau-Ponty's Philosophy of Nature* (Evanston, IL: Northwestern University Press, 2009).
——, 'Naturalism, Estrangement, and Resistance: On the Lived Sense of Nature', in Gerard Kuperus and Marjolein Oele (eds), *Ontologies of Nature: Continental Perspectives and Environmental Reorientations* (Cham: Springer, 2017), 181–98.
—— and Lester Embree (eds), *Merleau-Ponty's Reading of Husserl* (Dordrecht: Kluwer, 2002).
Vallega-Neu, Daniella, *Heidegger's 'Contributions to Philosophy': An Introduction* (Indianapolis and Bloomington: Indiana University Press, 2003).
Vanzago, Luca, 'Nature, Negativity, Event', *Chiasmi International* 11 (2009): 171–83.
Waelhens, Alphonse de, *Une philosophie de l'ambiguïté. L'existentialisme de Maurice Merleau-Ponty* (Louvain: Publications Universitaires de Louvain, 1951).
Watkin, Christopher, *Phenomenology or Deconstruction? The Question of Ontology in Maurice Merleau-Ponty, Paul Ricoeur and Jean-Luc Nancy* (Edinburgh: Edinburgh University Press, 2009).

Welsh, Talia, *The Child as Natural Phenomenologist: Primal and Primary Experience in Merleau-Ponty's Psychology* (Evanston, IL: Northwestern University Press, 2013).
Whitehead, Alfred North, *The Concept of Nature* (New York: Cosimo, 2007).
Wolfendale, Peter, *Object-Oriented Philosophy: The Noumenon's New Clothes* (Falmouth: Urbanomic, 2014).
Wright, Crispin, *Realism, Meaning and Truth* (Oxford: Blackwell, 1993).
Zahavi, Dan, 'The End of What? Phenomenology vs. Speculative Realism', *International Journal of Philosophical Studies* 24, no. 3 (2016): 289–309.
——, Sara Heinämaa and Hans Ruin (eds), *Metaphysics, Facticity, Interpretation: Phenomenology in the Nordic Countries* (Dordrecht: Kluwer, 2003).

Index

abandonment, 160–2, 164
Abram, D., 117n, 118n, 141n
absence, 19, 101, 122, 145, 154, 159, 164
Absolute, 2–4, 66, 100, 103n
absurdity, 9–10
activity, 36, 38, 43, 118n, 176; *see also* passivity
adversity, 105, 108–13, 117
agency, 105, 111, 113–15, 131
aggressivity *see* adversity
Alaimo, S., 125
alienation, 26, 70, 75; *see also* integration, narcissism, reappropriation, separation
Alquié, F., 48n, 49n
alter ego, 8, 155
ambiguity, 35–6, 38, 40, 42–5, 49n, 53, 66, 70, 91, 107, 116, 138, 156–7, 171
ancestrality, 9–10, 95–6; *see also* arche-fossil
animism, 18, 117n, 123, 131; *see also* materialism, panpsychism, vitalism
anosognosia, 72
anthropocentrism, 3–4, 17–18, 114, 138; *see also* human exceptionalism
anthropology, 52, 94–5, 97–9, 104, 153, 184
    anti-anthropologica turn, 147, 153, 166n
anthropomorphism, 17–18, 87–8, 102, 104–5, 107, 110, 113–16, 118n, 119, 123, 139

anti-realism, 2–3, 6–7, 117n; *see also* realism
anxiety, 149
apeiron, 12
arche-fossil, 9–10, 49n; *see also* ancestrality
Arendt, H., 151
Aristotle, 62
art, 39, 184
Ascension, 67
assemblage, 39, 63, 72
assimilation, 106, 115–16, 125–6

Bachelard, G., 109
Barbaras, R., 102n, 103n, 138, 185n, 187n
Beaufret, J., 42
being-in-the-world, 10, 15, 48n, 68, 102n, 121, 124, 148, 150; *see also* Dasein
Bennett, J., 118n, 140n
Birnbaum, A., 55, 60
birth, 11
    of reason, 138
    of self-consciousness, 38
    of sense, 17
    of the object, 90
Blondel, M., 29
body *see* embodiment, *Körper*, *Leib*, union
    body-object, 52
    body proper, 15, 57, 74, 81–2, 89
    body-subject, 81–2, 83n
    habitual, 39, 97
    lived, 15–18, 25, 27–8, 35–9, 42, 53, 61, 70–1, 73–4, 78–9, 81, 83n, 87, 100, 123–4

body schema, 38–9, 48n, 74, 81–6, 99, 178; *see also* disintegration, integration
Bourgeois, P., 148
Bréhier, É., 42
Breton, A., 109–11, 117n; *see also* surrealism

Calvino, I., 69n
Canguilhem, G., 14
carnal being, 19, 151, 156, 169–70; *see also* ontology, carnal
carnation *see* Incarnation
Cartesianism, 6, 16, 19, 25, 27–8, 30, 40, 46, 51–3, 71, 79, 101, 136, 151, 158, 182
  Cartesian circle, 47n
  see also Descartes, dualism, ontology, Cartesian, *partes extra partes*
chiasm, 15, 18–19, 145–6, 157, 169–71, 175–81, 187n; *see also* doubling, flesh, intertwinement, reversibility
chirality, 176, 178, 186n; *see also* counterparts, incongruent
Christianity, 66–8, 121–2
cogito, 17, 28, 31–3, 47n, 49n, 51, 53, 56, 138
  operative, 26, 41, 46, 50
  tacit, 26, 38, 41, 43–6, 100, 102n, 123
Cohen, J., 105, 113–16, 118n, 119
commensurability, 115–16, 124
communication, 74, 76–7, 82n, 128, 152, 175, 180; *see also* communion
communion, 39, 74, 82n, 180; *see also* communication
companionship, 115
conatus, 127–8, 140n; *see also* Spinoza, B.
corps propre see body proper
correlationism, 2–4, 10–11, 20n, 25, 87, 93–6, 100, 103n, 141n; *see also* Meillassoux, Q.
cosmos, 79, 121; *see also mundus*
counterparts,
  incongruent, 19, 175, 186n
creation, 45, 101
  ex nihilo, 121–2, 160
  of the world, 119, 122, 132, 160
  self-creation, 53
creativity, 43, 115; *see also* receptivity

Dasein, 10–11, 15–16, 21n, 121–2, 124–5, 148, 150, 152–3, 159–60; *see also* being-in-the-world

death, 11, 20n, 67, 106, 141n, 149
deconstruction, 1, 63, 121, 163, 169
  of logocentrism, 185n
  of the Subject, 51, 81
dehiscence, 165, 172, 182, 185n, 187n; *see also* diaresis, spacing
Deleuze, G., 76, 186n
depth, 15, 19, 29, 37, 55, 63, 68, 79, 90, 93, 97, 101, 102n, 111–13, 118n, 132, 142n, 146, 156–8, 170, 176, 180–2; *see also écart*, thickness
Derrida, J., 5, 12, 14, 49n, 54, 62, 64–7, 68n, 69n, 77, 103n, 129, 140n, 163, 167n, 173, 178–9, 185n, 186n
Descartes, R., 6, 16–17, 25–32, 34, 40, 43, 45–6, 47n, 48n, 50–6, 58–60, 66, 72, 81–2, 108, 151, 154; *see also* Cartesianism, dualism
desire, 14, 44, 51, 59, 65–6, 105–7, 110–13, 117, 118n, 126–7, 166n, 175, 181–3; *see also* sexuality
dialectics, 38, 43, 99–100, 112, 124, 157, 165
diaresis, 61, 63–4, 123, 134, 173, 183; *see also* dehiscence, spacing
dichotomy, 19, 49n, 128, 135, 145, 159, 164, 171; *see also* dualism
differance, 17–18, 26, 50, 57, 62, 77–8, 123, 126, 140n, 145–6, 169, 173, 180, 185n, 187n; *see also* Derrida, spacing
disentanglement, 30, 58, 80, 181; *see also* entanglement
disintegration, 41, 71–2, 131; *see also* body schema, integration
dislocation, 17, 26, 58, 70, 75, 77, 80–1, 83n, 114
divergence *see écart*
doubling, 19, 36–7, 65, 77–8, 169, 175–6, 179; *see also* chiasm, reversibility
doubt, 26, 32, 40, 46, 53–5, 91–3, 99, 154–5; *see also* perceptual faith
dualism, 7, 16–17, 27, 40–1, 44, 46, 52, 61, 70, 113, 131, 138; *see also* Cartesianism, Descartes, R. dichotomy, union

écart, 19, 64, 76, 83n, 170–1, 173–5, 178–80, 182–3, 185n, 187n; *see also* encroachment, flesh, separation, spacing
ego sum, 26, 45–6, 50–4, 56–7; *see also* mouth

INDEX | 199

element, 107, 114–15, 117, 118n, 131, 141n, 156, 168, 171, 175–6, 179, 187n
embodied existence, 16–17, 25–6, 38; *see also* body, embodiment
embodied life, 25, 28, 40, 45–6, 71; *see also* body, embodiment
embodiment, 102; *see also* body, embodied existence, embodied life
empiricism, 35, 42–3, 61, 68,
encroachment, 19, 47n, 118n, 155, 178, 180–1; *see also écart*, flesh, promiscuity
énonciation see utterance
entanglement, 58, 74, 80, 180–1; *see also* disentanglement, knot
envelopment, 39–40, 63, 71–2, 74–5, 78–9, 111, 155, 171–2, 182
envelop-phenomenon *see* envelopment
epoché see reduction
Ereignis, 15, 151, 162–3
es gibt, 147, 159–60, 162–3; *see also il y a*
essence, 18, 28, 33, 45–6, 47n, 58, 94, 100, 122–3, 127, 128, 130, 134, 137–8, 139n, 140n, 146, 151–5, 159, 163–4, 170; *see also* Wesen, Wesenchau
essentia see essence
Eucharist, 66
existentia, 18, 146, 164
existential philosophy, 34
exposition, 15, 17, 26, 50, 57–8, 60–4, 77, 80, 120–5, 128, 131, 133–5, 138, 149, 160, 164, 169–70, 180–3; *see also* limit
exposure *see* exposition
expression, 41–3, 44–5, 49n, 53, 58, 67, 73, 94, 96, 102n, 112, 138, 157–8
extension, 17, 27–8, 40, 46, 55–61, 63, 67–8, 71, 77–8, 82, 123, 125, 156; *see also res extensa*
exteriority, 26, 37, 55–62, 65–6, 70–1, 73, 75, 77–9, 101, 102n, 120, 123, 125, 127, 134, 172, 174, 177–80; *see also* interiority; outside, absolute

facticity, 3, 10–11, 31, 33, 93, 121, 149, 152
fideism, 3
finitude, 2, 10–11, 90, 93, 99, 120, 149; *see also* infinity
flesh, 15, 18, 19, 66–7, 73, 101, 104–5, 110, 112–13, 116–17, 118n, 125–6, 140n, 145–6, 150, 153, 155, 159, 165, 169–73, 175–6, 178–80, 182, 185n, 187n; *see also* chiasm
fold, 57, 62, 77, 101, 156, 165, 171–2, 175
folding *see* fold
for-itself, 105–7, 116, 135, 139, 172; *see also* in-itself
fragmentation, 71, 78, 83n
freedom, 87–8, 109, 116, 119–22, 133, 139n, 140n, 160, 162, 164
    of the world, 119, 122
Freud, S., 14–16, 50, 59, 63, 69n, 110, 112; *see also* psychoanalysis, sexuality

Gestalt, 27, 34, 94, 101, 170
givenness, 2, 7–10, 68, 96, 113, 119, 123, 164; *see also* intelligibility
Gueroult, M., 29–31, 45, 47n, 49n

Haar, M., 165, 167n
habitual life *see* body, habitual
hardness, 75, 123, 125, 137; *see also* stone
Harman, G., 114, 116, 132–3, 139, 141n
Hegel, G. W. F., 11, 73, 165, 174, 177
Heidegger, M., 3, 5, 10–14, 16, 18–19, 20n, 21n, 42, 51–3, 87–8, 119, 121–4, 128–9, 136, 139n, 140n, 145–65, 166n, 167n, 168
Heinämaa, S., 27, 40
hiatus, 127–8, 179
honey, 105–6, 109–10; *see also* pebble, stone
horizontal-mundane, 68; *see also* vertical-divine
human exceptionalism, 18, 114–15, 138; *see also* anthropocentrism
humanism, 29, 52, 119, 139n, 185n, 186n
Husserl, E., 4–5, 7–14, 19, 20n, 25, 32, 34–7, 42–5, 69n, 77–8, 94–5, 97, 100, 123, 146, 148, 150–3, 155–6, 166n, 178–9, 186n, 187n; *see also* phenomenology
Hyppolite, J., 42

idealism, 2, 21n, 32–4, 42–3, 45, 48n, 93, 103n, 138–9, 165n, 187n
    transcendental, 1, 4
    see also realism
il y a, 137, 141n, 147, 159–60, 162, 167n; *see also es gibt*
illusion, 32, 91
immanence, 8, 43, 91–2, 130, 138, 155, 189; *see also* transcendence

impenetrability, 70, 106, 124–5, 129, 134–5; *see also* penetration
in-itself, 5–6, 10, 21n, 25, 35, 45–6, 96, 105–8, 116, 122, 126, 128, 132–5, 139, 164, 168, 172
  In-Itself-For-Itself, 107, 117n
  in-itself-for-us, 89, 96, 100
  see also for-itself
Incarnation, 60, 66
Ineinander, 19, 48n, 74, 117, 118n, 146, 150, 152, 155–6, 166n, 182
infinity, 120–1, 168; *see also* finitude
Ingold, T., 129–31, 134, 141n
inhumanity, 17, 97, 102, 105, 107, 117; *see also* strangeness
inside *see also* interiority
  absolute, 55–6
  of the outside, 79, 112–3; *see also* depth
inside/outside divide, 6–7, 170, 172; *see also* limit
integration, 17, 26, 39, 48n, 63, 66, 70, 73–7, 81, 149, 169, 177–8; *see also* body schema, disintegration
intellectualism *see* idealism
intelligibility, 10, 99, 121–2; *see also* givenness
intentional act, 8, 173
intentionality, 7, 32, 71, 73, 97, 98, 100, 102n, 114, 119, 123, 124, 127, 136, 148, 155–6, 166n, 174
  operative, 148
intercorporeity, 48n, 172
interiority, 15, 26, 35, 55–6, 58–9, 61, 62, 67, 68, 69n, 70, 74, 77–8, 81, 94, 102n, 123, 131–3, 170, 172; *see also* exteriority, intimacy
interruption, 65–6, 77, 134, 178–9
intersensoriality, 39; *see also* object, intersensorial
intertwinement, 75, 118n, 151–2, 157–8, 177, 180, 182, 186; *see also* chiasm
intimacy, 55–7, 59, 69n, 97, 115; *see also* inside, absolute; interiority
intruder, 72–3, 126
irredentism, 65

James, I., 83n, 140n, 141n
Johnson, G., 108
jouissance, 181–2; *see also* desire, sexuality

Klein, M., 112
Körper, 17, 37, 81, 87; *see also* body, *Leib*
knot, 40, 179–81; *see also* entanglement

Lacan, J., 51, 109, 128, 186n
Lacoue-Labarthe, P., 51, 68n
Laplace, P.-S., 156
  Laplacian nebula, 95–6
Laporte, J., 49n
latency, 5, 33, 49n, 79, 98, 101, 156, 172, 181; *see also* depth, encroachment
Latour, B., 126–8, 140n
Leib, 17, 35, 37, 48n, 78, 81, 87, 150–1, 171; *see also* body, *Körper*
limit, 6, 11–3, 57, 61–2, 64, 120, 131, 180, 182
  of sense, 5–6, 8
  see also exposition, finitude, touching
linguistic turn, 6
logos, 44, 101

Madison, G., 100–1, 168, 185n, 187n
Marcel, G., 73
mass, 26, 45, 59–60, 72, 106, 125–6, 133, 173
materialism, 1, 16–18, 25, 88, 107–9, 119, 121–2, 125–6, 129–30, 134–5, 137, 140n, 141n
  eliminative, 18, 138; *see also* panpsychism, vitalism
  new, 87, 113, 126, 138, 141n
  see also realism
materials, 129–31, 134, 141n
matter, 25, 40–1, 66, 70, 105, 118n, 129, 131–5, 138, 140n, 141n, 185n,
mediation, 6–7, 42, 95, 138, 157
Meillassoux, Q., 1–3, 6, 9–13, 20n, 25, 95–6, 100, 103n, 114–15, 184
mêlée, 80, 180–1
melody, 40, 48n
metaphysics, 1, 4, 15–16, 40, 51, 53, 81, 117n, 145–6, 151, 156, 160–4, 166n, 169,
  of presence, 15, 66–7
mirroring, 19, 35, 37, 158, 176–8, 186n; *see also* narcissism
monism, 132
Morris, D., 185n, 186n
mouth, 46, 50, 52–4, 56, 58–9, 61–2, 68, 76, *see also* ego sum
mundus, 52, 79, 121; *see also* cosmos
mystery, 66, 157, 161–2; *see also* secret

narcissism, 19, 110, 116, 173–6, 178, 186n; *see also* mirroring
Nash, D., 130–1
natural inclination, 28–31
natural light, 28, 31, 47n

natural world, 4, 17, 87, 97–9, 101, 138; see also nature
nature, 25, 28–9, 34, 48n, 95, 97–101, 102n, 113, 126–7, 140n; see also natural world
nausea, 106, 108, 110, 116
néant see nothingness
negativism, 18–19, 29, 101, 146, 153–5, 164–5; see also positivism
negativity *see* negativism
non-coincidence, 19, 51, 165, 179, 186n
non-human entities, 5, 115, 125
non-sense, 8, 91, 100
nothingness, 44, 46, 106, 153–4, 159, 163, 165; see also rien

object, 115–16, 132
  absolute, 90
  and things, 108–13, 177n
  as *Gegenstand*, 8
  intersensorial, 76, 93–4
  perceptual or perceived, 76, 93
  see also body-object, ontology of the object, subject
objective thought, 45, 89–90, 96, 151, *see also pensée de survol*
objectivism *see* objectivity
objectivity, 1, 9, 48n, 61, 78
ontology
  carnal, 18, 145
  Cartesian, 35, 45, 96, 104–5, 108–9, 111, 113, 156, 166n, 181
  direct, 19, 146, 151, 154, 157–8
  indirect, 19, 147, 157
  object-oriented, 87, 114, 116, 141n, 184
  of the existent, 29, 47n
  of the object, 27, 29, 40, 47n, 104–5, 108–9, 111, 113–14
  Sartrian *see* ontology, Cartesian
organism, 34–5, 40, 48n, 63, 78, 129
outdoors
  the great, 6, 25; see outside, absolute
outside *see* exteriority
  absolute, 6, 12–13; see also outdoors, the great

painting, 42, 97, 111, 157–8
  classical and modern 111–12
panpsychism, 18, 117n, 118n, 123, 138, 140n, 186n; see also animism; materialism, eliminative; vitalism
partes extra partes, 17, 40, 59, 71–2, 78–9, 123, 129, 180, 182; see also Cartesianism
passivity, 15, 36, 38, 43, 108, 118n, 176; see also activity
pebble, 105, 109–10, 126, 142n; see also honey, stone
penetration, 59, 66, 76, 98, 123–4, 129; see also impenetrability
pensée de survol, 33, 138–9; see also objective thought
perceptual faith, 92; see also doubt
performative, 17, 53
phantom limb, 48n
phenomenology, 4, 91, 92, 100
  and Nancy, 83n, 134, 136, 169–70
  and ontology, 103n, 014, 148, 150–1, 168, 172, 186n
  Husserlian, 4, 7–10, 20n, 34, 42, 44
  limits of, 10, 12–13, 99, 101
  of phenomenology, 43
  transcendental, 32, 34, 153
  see also Husserl, E., Heidegger, M., reduction
philosophy of existence *see* natural inclination
philosophy of the understanding *see* natural light
plurality, 76, 78, 80–1, 83n, 101, 129, 132, 134–5, 149, 180; see also singularity, singular plural
Ponge, F., 104–5, 107–10, 115, 138
positivism, 18, 29, 146, 153–6, 164, 168; see also negativism
positivity *see* positivism
post-deconstruction, 65–6
post-Kantian philosophy, 1–2, 49n, 183–4
promiscuity, 19, 48n, 118n, 180, 182–3; see also encroachment
psychoanalysis, 51, 74, 105
  of things, 105–7, 109; see also Bachelard, G., Sartre, J.-P.
  see also Freud, S., Lacan, J.
psychologism, 7, 9, 42
psychology, 27, 32, 34–6, 42, 74

rapport, 128
realism, 12, 16–18, 21n, 25, 65–6, 93, 103n, 141n, 183
  metaphysical, 4, 12, 117n
  new, 18, 100–1, 113, 126, 138, 183–4
  speculative, 1–7, 9, 20n, 87, 91, 96, 184
  transcendental, 7, 35
  see also idealism, materialism

reappropriation, 10, 26, 57, 70, 78, 82, 174; *see also* alienation, integration, separation
receptivity, 43; *see also* creativity
reduction, 9, 20n, 43, 61
   phenomenological, 7, 32–4
   transcendental, 7, 10, 32–4
reductionism, 14, 132, 185n
reflection
   and the unreflected, 12, 16, 25, 28–9, 31–3, 46, 138
   into self, 177
   radical, 32–4, 43, 100
relation *see* rapport
res cogitans, 25, 46, 49, 57
res extensa, 25, 79, 123; *see also* extension
resistance, 31, 41, 81, 97, 99–100, 103n, 105, 109–10, 112–13, 125, 129, 134, 136; *see also* adversity, impenetrability, thickness
resurrection, 67
retranchement see withdrawal
reversibility, 19, 36–7, 171, 175–6, 178, 183, 186n; *see also* doubling, chiasm
Richir, M., 147, 159
rien, 122, 128, 154, 160, 163, 167n; *see also* nothingness
rock *see* stone
Rogozinski, J., 178–9, 187n
Rorty, R., 6

Saint Aubert, E. de, 18, 27, 42, 107, 113, 117n, 118n, 147–8, 150, 181–2, 187n
Sartre, J.-P., 14, 104–10, 113–16, 117n, 118n, 120, 136, 147, 151, 153–4, 172
scepticism, 2, 21n
Schilder, P., 48n, 74, 82n, 177n
Schües, C., 148–9
secret, 97–8, 107, 111, 157, 177–8; *see also* mystery
Seinsverlassenheit see abandonment
self-experience, 44
self-reflection, 37
self-sensing, 15–17, 19, 25–6, 34, 46, 65–6, 74–5, 78, 101, 169–71, 186n; *see also* touching
selfhood, 133, 174; *see also* diaresis, difference
sensibility, 38–9, 57, 59, 76, 118, 151, 155–7, 169, 171, 173, 186n
separation, 6, 25–6, 58, 67, 70, 118n, 125, 130–1, 141n, 156, 170, 172,
178, 180, 182–3, 185n; *see also écart*, encroachment, flesh, spacing
sexuality, 63, 105, 110, 112, 128, 166n; *see also* desire, Freud, S.
Shaviro, S., 4, 105, 113–14, 119
singular plural, 76, 80, 129, 132, 145, 149, 180
singularity, 12–13, 58, 60, 80, 121–2, 125, 129, 131–5, 166n, 180
skin, 60, 62–3, 65; *see also* surface
solipsism, 128, 149
soul *see* union
spacing, 17–19, 45, 50, 58, 60–2, 64, 67, 72, 76–7, 79, 123–4, 126–9, 131, 133, 141n, 145–6, 162, 169–70, 173–4, 178, 180, 182, 185n; *see also* dehiscence, diaresis, difference
speculation, 4
speculative turn *see* realism, speculative
speech, 43, 158
Spinoza, B., 127, 140n; *see also conatus*
Stoics, 128
stone, 18, 73–4, 82, 87–8, 93, 97, 106–7, 109, 111, 113–16, 117n, 118n, 119, 121–35, 137, 139, 140n, 142n, 161, 173; *see also* hardness, pebble
strangeness, 5, 58, 73, 97, 115; *see also* inhumanity
structuralist turn *see* linguistic turn
style, 39–40, 80, 94, 109, 152, 170, 181
subject, 51–4, 72
   subject-object divide, 6, 15, 25, 126, 138
   subject-object relation, 25, 124
   transcendental, 121
   see also body-subject, deconstruction, object, transcendental consciousness, transcendental ego
substance *see res cogitans, res extensa*
surface, 38, 63, 123–7, 130–1, 141n; *see also* skin
surrealism, 104–5, 109, 111; *see also* Breton, A.
synaesthesia, 75

table, 9, 36, 78, 152
Taminiaux, J., 151
Taylor, C., 7
teleology, 40, 99
thickness, 63, 92, 98–9, 102n, 112, 123, 180–1; *see also* depth, resistance
thrownness, 10–11, 160; *see also* death

Toadvine, T., 100, 118n, 140n
touching
    and the stone, 124–5, 128, 130–2
    and the untouchable, 69n, 179
    and touched 169, 173–5, 178–80, 187n; *see also* self-touching
    and vision, 37, 171
    Derrida's critique of, 64–6
    interdiction of, 67–8
    self-touching 15, 35–7, 65–6, 69n, 71, 75, 77–8
    see also body, doubling, flesh, reversibility, self-sensing
trans-corporeality, 125
transcendence, 8, 15, 43, 87, 91–3, 97, 102n, 139, 148, 151, 153, 168, 187n; *see also* immanence
transcendental consciousness, 8–10, 12, 34, 124
transcendental ego, 8, 33, 37–8, 43, 78
transhumanism, 117n

union
    of the soul and the body, 16–17, 25–31, 41, 46, 50, 52, 60, 66, 70–1
    see also body, lived
Unsinn see non-sense
unum quid, 50, 52, 54, 56–7, 70
utterance, 26, 51–4, 56; *see also ego sum*

Valéry, P., 177
vertical being *see* wild being
vertical-divine, 68; *see also* horizontal-mundane
vision, 16, 27–9, 37, 79, 89–90, 112, 125, 142, 156–7, 171–2, 175–6, 179, 181
    profane, 96, 131
vitalism, 14, 18, 40, 119, 138, 140n, 141n; *see also* animism; materialism, eliminative; panpsychism
void, 72, 79, 128, 179–80

Watkin, C., 182
weight, 123–6, 128, 134–6
Wesen, 19, 146, 150, 152, 159; *see also* essence, *Wesenschau*
Wesenschau, 150–2, 155; *see also* essence, *Wesen*
whateverness, 132–3, 141n
Whitehead, A. N., 127
Widersinn see absurdity
wild being, 131, 168, 172
wild things, 12–13, 17, 87, 100, 102, 104
withdrawal, 17, 26, 34, 50, 55–8, 99, 115, 153–5, 157
    of Being, 19, 146, 159–61, 164
Wright, C., 12, 21n

Zahavi, D., 4

EU representative:
Easy Access System Europe
Mustamäe tee 50, 10621 Tallinn, Estonia
Gpsr.requests@easproject.com

www.ingramcontent.com/pod-product-compliance
Lightning Source LLC
Chambersburg PA
CBHW070355240426
43671CB00013BA/2510